CW01635408

A DISAPPOINTING CHILD

A MEMOIR

DIANA HARDIE

USSONS

CHAPTER 1

According to my mother, I was a disappointing child.

She hadn't wanted a baby. She had been too young to endure such an ordeal, but if she was to be handicapped by a child, she had been confident it would be a son. Certainly not a girl with plain hair and a stubborn little frown.

I was born in 1918 during an air raid in the East End of London, and as a child, I often felt guilty I had upset my mother so much just by being born.

My grandfather tried to explain to me when I was old enough to understand. He told me about the war and said Mother had been afraid, because until then, death had been reserved for soldiers and sailors. It hadn't come raining down out of the sky on defenceless civilians.

It didn't help that her relatives were all extremely self-centred. On the night she went into labour, there were twelve family members living in the crowded terrace house my grandmother rented, but when whistles sounded in the street to warn of an air raid, her mother, sisters and brothers, ran out of the house to seek shelter. My father, a special constable, had been out on duty and only my grandfather stayed with her as she struggled to give birth to me.

At the end of our street, a new Sessions House was being built, and the basement had yet to be fitted out as cells. It was as good an air raid shelter as anyone could find in those days, and whenever the warning whistles blew, people snatched up their children and ran.

But it was not easy to reach the shelter of the unfinished basement. Women were lowered down sheer walls, crying children were handed down in the darkness to mothers straining on tiptoe to reach them. Often, fear kept them there all night, crowded together in darkness on the cold stone floor.

Looking back, the experience must have been hell for my grandmother. She was, in her own opinion, a reduced gentlewoman. Normally, she did not mix with her neighbours, all of whom she considered coarse and common.

Now and then, one of them would knock on her front door and ask for help. Many could neither read nor write and they would bring official forms to be filled in or letters they needed written. Then she would pen, in her own flourishing hand and her own cryptic words, whatever message was needed.

But neighbours were only allowed inside by appointment. There were formalities to be observed. The parlour on the ground floor had to be unlocked, dusted, and the window opened to freshen the stale air. The brass fender would be polished, and the carpet cleaned, a long process with damp tea leaves scattered across it, then carefully brushed off on hands and knees.

Of course, Grandmother never undertook any of these menial tasks herself. In better days, she would have had a maid, but in my memory, times had changed. She had slipped a long way down the social scale, although she never acknowledged it, but she had plenty of daughters. There was always one she could keep at her beck and call.

I rarely went into the parlour. From my earliest days, I would not have ventured in unless invited. The parlour was for visitors. Now and then, on a Sunday evening, it would be opened for a brief family gathering and Uncle Eric or Uncle Ernie would play the latest music-hall songs on the candle-stick fronted piano while the rest of the family sang at the top of their voices, much to the irritation of the neighbours.

I loved watching Uncle Ernie play. He couldn't read music and had never had a lesson in his life, but he played the piano with his whole body. His fingers hammered the keys while his elbows flapped up and down at his sides in time with the music. His head wagged, his feet tapped, and his skinny body shivered with the effort until he burst into such a fit of coughing, he was forced to retire and let Uncle Eric take over.

I felt sorry for Uncle Eric. Most people did. The youngest boy in the family, shy and weak-chested, my grandmother dominated him completely. While my grandfather looked on drink as an evil, she liked a glass or two of stout and enjoyed going to the pub at the corner of the street. Anything, she said, was better than sitting opposite my grandfather every evening as he read the bible.

She never demeaned herself by going into the public bar where the language was ripe and men spat freely on the sawdust-covered floor.

No, she was a lady. She went to the private bar, but even there, a woman was looked down upon if she was not accompanied by a male. So, from the day Eric could be passed off as fourteen, he went to the pub with his mother. He was an alcoholic long before he was an adult.

No one entered the parlour without my grandmother's permission. It was not possible, as she wore the key on a string around her neck. The parlour was a shrine, cut off from the rest of the house, sacred to the style of life she felt befitted her social status.

Her own grandmother had been a rich woman who owned the Blackmore Estates near Bristol. When her daughter bore an illegitimate child, the old lady tossed her out but kept the child. In her judgement, the baby was an innocent victim and should not be made to suffer.

She christened the baby Annie and brought her up in a life of luxury. The big house and the surrounding estates with their farms and tenants were her home. She was educated at the famous Red Maid School in Bristol and she wanted for nothing. In return, she was expected to behave as a well-bred young lady of her day.

But Annie had other ideas, the main one being to escape from the strict control of her grandmother, and do as she pleased. At seventeen, she ran away to London, planning to find her mother. She succeeded, but her mother was living in squalor with a sailor and had a brood of other illegitimate children. She turned Annie away, no doubt influenced by the fact that, now and then, her mother sent money to ensure her other children didn't starve. There would be no more handouts if she was found to be harbouring Annie.

Annie shortly before she left her grandmother's house.

And so my grandmother found herself alone in a strange city. Too proud to go back to Bristol, she found work serving in a pie shop near the London docks. At that time, dockers queued daily, hoping to be offered work. They were a rough lot and groups of them crowded into the pie shop to buy food and ogle the new girl with her expensive clothes and la-de-da accent.

Among them, one stood out from the rest.

He wore the same work-stained clothes as his companions, but his shoulders were broad and his manner confident. Ernest Leopard was a natural leader, and if anyone disputed the fact, a swift fight always ended in his favour. He might have had blonde curls, bright blue eyes and a helping of French blood, a combination that attracted every female eye, but at heart he was a cockney. Life had not been kind to him, but he had learned to seize the few opportunities it presented.

Annie fell for his charms at once. Within weeks, she was pregnant. They married quickly and moved into a cramped backroom near the docks. Annie had been adamant. One day, she was sure, her grandmother would find her, and when she did, she was determined not to admit to the same plight as her mother. Marriage, at least, was respectable.

The baby was barely a week old and Annie was alone with it when one of Ernest's friends came looking for him. The young fellow was drunk and ridiculed Annie when she tried to send him away. What the hell was she so cocky about? Had Ernest told her how much he had won by getting his leg over her? His mates had clubbed together and bet him five pounds he couldn't get Miss High-and-Mighty into bed.

Poor Ernest. He won his five pounds, but he paid for the rest of his life. From that moment on, my grandmother hated my grandfather.

Ernest was an honest man and when Annie questioned him, he admitted the bet but told her he had married her, not because she had forced him, but because he loved her.

It made no difference. She never forgave him.

Months later, a letter did arrive for Annie, after her grandmother's solicitor had managed to trace her, but by then, she was pregnant again.

The letter said her grandmother was gravely ill and asked Annie to return to Bristol as quickly as possible. Before

Annie could scrape together enough money for the fare to Bristol, she received another letter. Her grandmother was dead.

Pregnant, and with a sickly child, Annie did not make it back to Bristol in time for the funeral, but she was certain her grandmother had wanted them to be reconciled. Perhaps she had mentioned her in her will? Perhaps the old lady had even named her as her heir?

A few days later, sitting in the drawing room of the magnificent house that had been her childhood home, Annie faced her grandmother's solicitor. When she questioned him, the old man shook his head. He had searched the house from top to bottom but had found no trace of a will.

Annie knew her grandmother kept important papers in a secret drawer in the back of an old clock in her study, but when she looked, the back of the clock had been prized off and the drawer was empty.

If my great-great grandmother did make a will, it was never found.

The solicitor warned Annie she would need to prove her identity if she was to make a claim on the estate. If she could not not, and no other claimant came forward, the property and all her grandmother's money would go into Chancery and be passed to the government.

Annie had no birth certificate. She had nothing to prove her existence, or even to prove her mother's existence. When her grandmother had tossed her daughter out in disgust, she had burned every paper relating to her.

There was nothing my grandmother could do but return to the mean little room near the docks, but she never forgot the life she felt should have been hers. Her instincts told her that her grandmother had forgiven her and had left a will that would have given her back the life of a lady, but she had no proof and no money to hire solicitors to search for it.

Annie and Ernest had twenty-three children, twelve of

whom she buried at birth, yet she never forgave him and she never stopped hating him.

CHAPTER 2

I was always a believer. From childhood, I believed in fairies, elves and Father Christmas, in God, the baby Jesus, and beautiful winged angels who kept watch over us, and even though I had never witnessed one, I believed in miracles.

Yes, I was a believer, but I learned early in life not to talk about the things that really mattered to me. They were best kept hidden away, unsullied by the ignorance and ridicule of others.

My parents were married in a church. I was christened there, as was my brother, four years later. That, to my knowledge, was the limit of my family's connection with religion. What spiritual education I received was thanks to the various schools I attended.

I learned to sing carols at Christmas for baby Jesus, born in a stable. Then I shed tears at Easter when he was nailed to the Cross. It was confusing because it seemed only weeks since I had rejoiced at his birth. However, I soon realised questioning anything concerned with religion was frowned upon at school and pointless at home.

As I grew older, I learned there were many questions that it was better not to ask.

My mother was not a gossip, even though she lived in a neighbourhood where a juicy scrap of scandal was a rare chance to brighten a drab existence, but it was impossible to live on the same street as the gloomy building known as the Sessions House without believing it held dark and sinister secrets.

Sometimes, when I was out with Mother, black vans drew up outside it and policemen bustled people inside.

I longed to know what it was all about, but if I slowed down to look, Mother's hand grasped me firmly by the wrist and dragged me past.

Soon, the square black outline of the building began appearing in my dreams and my imagination transformed it into the home of ogres and demons.

The building next to the Sessions House was equally mysterious. It must have had a name, possibly a grandiose one, but I never knew it. Our neighbours simply referred to it as the Fleapit.

I have no idea how big it was inside. Wild horses would not have dragged any member of my family through its dingy portals and past the grubby red velvet curtain that dropped back into position behind each customer. Not even my father, although I think, secretly, he would have loved to have gone.

Every week a small, hand-painted poster appeared on the wall outside, promising thrills and excitement. There were clumsy pictures of cowboys riding across deserts and voluptuous women beckoning invitingly.

It all seemed exotic and mysterious to me. I longed to know what went on inside, but I knew better than to ask.

If I showed the slightest hesitation as I passed the entrance to the Fleapit, I was in trouble. It was a disgusting place, Mother told me. I didn't understand, but I was sure it was more than the fleas that bothered her.

Until I was five and went to school, the street was my view of the world. To other children, it was a playground, but I was never allowed down to play with the rest. Other people's children carried diseases and head lice and their speech was common. I was not to mix with them. Instead, from my upstairs window, I sat and watched.

Sometimes, when the older children were at school, I would stare at the endless vista of chimney pots stretching away on the other side of the street. Now and then, sparrows hopped among them, or a cat prowled.

The chimney pots were all individual, some curved, some straight, some squat, some tall, and where they crowded together in groups, I imagined they were families and wove little stories around them.

But it was the street that held my interest. Chalked hopscotch squares decorated the pavements until the rain washed them away. Ropes hung from the gas light standards, where youngsters took it in turns to swing on them. Sometimes the lamplighters tore them down when they came to light the gas lamps at dusk, but mostly they were left dangling invitingly.

Boys played alley-gob with stones or flicked cigarette cards against house walls, hoping to win more, while girls played Mothers and Fathers, setting up house on a doorstep, anyone's doorstep. They would undress their dolls, put them to bed in a twist of old blanket, sing them to sleep, then sit together to chat and sip imaginary tea from cracked cups.

If the house door was open, the play would encroach a little further, then further still, into the passage as more children joined the make-believe tea party.

Most women were tolerant. Their own children were usually among the players, and many of the front doors were permanently open. Children and neighbours ran in and out at will. In winter, when self-preservation demanded the doors were closed, a length of string was tied to the door knocker with a key on the end. This would be tucked into the letterbox so that all and sundry could let themselves in. There was no fear of theft. No-one had anything worth stealing.

The game I loved to watch most, the game every child in the street joined in, was French and English. Not Germans and English, although we had just fought a long, bloody war with the Germans, but the old enemies, French and English.

It was exciting. Half the children lined up on one side of the road, the other half facing them on the opposite pavement. From my window I could sense the mounting excitement, the jostling for positions, the shouts of the chosen generals striving to hold back their troops until the order was given to attack. Then both armies would charge head-on at each other, meeting in the middle of the road in a shouting, squealing melee with the smallest bowled over and trampled underfoot. The object was to take the pavement on the other side.

It was always a good battle, hard fought, no holds barred, with a few girls standing by as nurses to tend the wounded. Cuts and grazes were wrapped in strips of newspaper filched from the pile Mrs Meade kept on her doorstep to wrap up her vegetables. More serious injuries, such as the occasional tooth knocked out, were escorted back home to Mother.

There was a glorious freedom and a wonderful, exciting abandon about the battles. If they happened. Often, they just fizzled out. The East End children were fiercely patriotic, and many had lost fathers or brothers in defence of their country. No-one wanted to be French. Sometimes so many minor scuffles broke out preparing for the battle, the generals lost interest and went back to tossing their cigarette cards.

CHAPTER 3

I was three when I realised Father was bald.

He hadn't always been. I know that because there was a photograph on the mantelshelf of him and Mother on their wedding day.

My Father on his wedding day.

The morning I found out, I was awake early. Being the first one into the big brass bed every evening, my place was against the wall. Next came Mother, then, on the outside, my father. Sometimes there was an element of claustrophobia, being sandwiched between the wall and two sleeping adults, and I was clambering over Mother when I caught sight of Father. He was sound asleep with his mouth wide open and he had no hair.

Mother was awake instantly. She snatched me back against the wall and her hissing whisper was frightening. "George! Cover yourself up!"

Father's bare head disappeared beneath the bedclothes.

The moment it was out of sight, she whipped me out of bed and tossed me into my clothes.

"You need to go to the lavvy."

There was a perfectly good rose-decorated po under the bed, but I understood. The lavatory was three floors down and across the yard. It took a long time for small legs to get there and back, so I was always in need of the lavvy when my presence was not wanted.

When I got back, Father was dressed and sitting at the table... with hair.

The most natural thing would have been for me to question my mother about such an amazing happening, but even at that age I knew there were things you asked about and things you didn't, things that fanned some latent spark within her to a raging fury.

However, Mother must have realised an explanation was necessary.

"Daddy is different from other gentlemen," she said. "He takes his hair off every night and puts it in a little box under the bed. That way, he keeps it nice and tidy, but he doesn't want you to tell anyone else about it. It's a secret."

That is all she told me, and it seemed rather exciting. I was sure few other children had a father who took his hair off to go to bed.

What Mother didn't tell me was that, when I was a year old, my father had caught the virulent Spanish flu that swept the country in the wake of the First World War. Unlike many, he recovered, but a year later, he had a serious relapse and was rushed to Guy's Hospital.

Once there, he had a nervous breakdown, and within weeks, all his hair fell out.

He was a young man, and the doctors assured him his hair would grow back, but how long it would take they did not know.

Mother, horrified at the thought of being seen with a bald

man, insisted he must have a wig. The doctors tried to dissuade her, warning that a fine regrowth of hair was unlikely to survive the constant rub of a wig, but Mother was adamant.

In those days, wigs were made by hand from real hair, and the cost was exorbitant. Despite all my mother's tears and tantrums, neither she nor any of her family could raise such a sum.

It was Edie, Father's sister, who came to the rescue. She worked hard and lived frugally. Her savings bought the wig that lived in the box under our bed.

Strangely, although it would have seemed natural for Mother to feel grateful to Edie, she never did. Perhaps she felt guilty that she had been selfish. I don't know. I only know that Edie was never invited to our home and her name was never mentioned, despite the fact an envelope always arrived for me on my birthday. The money it contained bought a hair ribbon for me and the rest went into the family purse.

Then, at Christmas, Edie would arrive with an expensive present from Hamley's, the toyshop in Regent Street. She stayed for a quarter of an hour, drank a cup of tea, then left.

And no hair ever grew on my father's head again.

Auntie Edie

I have thought about it a lot, but there was really only one aspect of life on which my parents agreed. They both loved animals. Neither of them had any great feeling for human beings. My father looked down on anyone he considered of a lower class than himself and hated anyone who had more money than he had. My mother hated women, all women, including her sisters, her brothers' wives, her neighbours, the music-hall performers, even the female members of the royal family. She saw them all as a personal challenge to her, although I didn't realise that until I grew older.

Animals were different. Not that there was not much space for four-legged friends when we lived two floors up in a single room.

We did have a canary. One of the workmen at the coal depot where my father worked as a clerk had been loading his cart when he spotted the cage. It had been tossed over the wall. The bars were bent, and the door smashed, but the little yellow bird huddled inside was still alive.

Father wrapped the whole thing up in newspaper and brought it home on a crowded tram. That was one of the few nights I remember him staying up late.

He owned no tools, not even a hammer, because he never did odd jobs or repairs, but that night he sat for hours straightening the bent bars of the cage by hand while the canary rested in a cloth-lined saucepan near the fire. Next morning, the cage hung beside the window and the canary sang.

But it was the dogs I remember most. Now and then, a stray dog would find its way into the coal depot. Large, small, timid, aggressive, hungry, sick, they came in all shapes and sizes. The only things they had in common was that they were all filthy with coal dust and unwanted. No-one ever enquired about any of them.

The coalmen would feed the latest stray from their lunch packs then, when it was time to lock up the depot for the night, rather than toss it out into the street, they would take it to the office.

Father brought them all home on the tram in rush hour, trailing behind him on a piece of old rope. He couldn't resist them.

Knowing how Grandmother would react at the sight of

yet another stray, if the dog was small enough, he would stuff it up the front of the suit he wore to the office.

If the dog was too big, he would have no choice but to run the gauntlet of Grandmother's anger as it left dirty paw-prints along the passage and up the stairs.

I don't know how many times it happened, but the routine was always the same. Mother would settle the newcomer on sacks in a corner of the room while Father went down to the scullery to get a fire going under the copper.

Old copies of The News of the World, the only newspaper my family ever bought, were spread over the floor and the tin bath brought up from the scullery, followed by buckets of hot and cold water. A good helping of Lysol and some carbolic soap and the dog, large or small, would be bathed and brushed.

Once the creature had been rubbed dry on an old towel, Father tied the rope back around its neck and set out for the police station.

Mother's family thought he was insane. So did many of the neighbours, but in his own eyes, he was simply doing a kind deed. No-one was going to be attracted to a tatty, dust covered stray, but washed and brushed, the dog might stand a chance.

He was right. At the local police station, he made friends with two old, dog-loving sergeants. One or other of them was always on duty when he arrived with another freshly groomed dog and they made it their hobby to find homes for Father's canine orphans. Very few of them were ever passed on to the Dog's Home.

One night, there was a stray that differed from the rest. She was gingery-brown, short-haired, medium-sized and bandy in the front legs, a mongrel with no obvious breed lines. She was dirty and thin, her pads caked in blood from walking, but she had soft brown eyes and her tail jerked at a kind word.

And she was heavily pregnant.

They bathed her like the rest, but Father couldn't bring himself to walk her all the way to the police station. Instead, he settled her on an old piece of blanket near the fire, and during the night, she produced one small ginger-brown pup.

They called the old dog Nell, and she never did make the long walk to the police station. Instead, a blanket under the bed became her domain. Her paws healed and every evening, Father walked her around the block.

As for the puppy, my grandfather took it. To Grandmother's annoyance, he called it Flossie, after a music-hall performer he had admired as a young man. Flossie was playful and appealing, but unfortunately, she was also very timid. For her temperament, she had come to the wrong home. The moment an argument broke out in the house, or voices were raised in anger, she scampered upstairs and burrowed down between the sheets of the first bed she found.

Once hostilities were over, the search for Flossie would begin and the poor, shivering little heap would be found between the sheets in a puddle of pee.

She often chose the bed in which my three aunts slept, so it is not surprising it was one of them who found her a new home. She went to an elderly couple who fell in love with her at first sight and I'm sure she never wet anyone's bed again.

~

Many things made me feel guilty as a child.

Sometimes it was the disappointed look Mother gave me. She never said anything directly, but I knew I was lacking. My hair was too straight and my face too round. And I should have been a boy.

At other times, it was because one of my aunts criticised the way Mother cared for me and the remark flared into a family quarrel.

Mostly, though, I felt guilty about my grandmother. I knew I should love her, but I couldn't.

I remember her as an enormous woman, fat and grey-faced with pudgy hands that fidgeted impatiently.

She spent most of her time in an armchair beside the fire in the basement kitchen. Once the domain of some unfortunate skivvy, the room was dark even on the brightest day. The only light came from an underground window beneath a grating in the pavement outside.

The shadows, the musty smell of dampness, the tramp of feet passing over the grating outside, everything about that basement kitchen frightened me, but the most frightening thing of all was my grandmother.

I was terrified of her, yet it was a fear I cannot explain even now. The very sight of her, slumped in a dark heap in that dark room, filled me with apprehension.

I never went into the basement kitchen unless sent with a message from my mother. Then I stood, stiff-backed and tense, as far from Grandmother's chair as possible.

It was an unnatural, inexplicable fear. She was an old woman. I should have felt sorry for her, but I did not.

She was not ill or crippled, but she never lifted a finger to cook or clean or do anything about the house. Instead, she complained constantly. Whenever one of my aunts, spurred by her moans, offered to take her to the music-hall to cheer her up, she would be dressed in minutes in her big fur coat, a bunch of violets pinned to the lapel and her bird-of-paradise hat skewered firmly to her lank grey hair.

I didn't want to hate her. I knew it was wrong to hate, but I didn't want to be near her. More than anything, I didn't want her to kiss me.

At least in that, I was lucky. She made no attempt to come

near me, but the sound of her harsh voice demanding attention made me race for the safety of my parents' room in case I was expected to answer the summons.

To me, the whole house seemed dark and menacing, especially the staircase and the landings. Narrow windows hung with thick lace curtains shut out inquisitive neighbours and most of the light, and the dark wallpaper, covered with even darker varnish, was lit by a gas light turned to its lowest setting.

Grandmother was not a woman to spend if she could avoid it. The gas meter under the basement stairs only worked when a shilling was inserted and cut off the supply the moment the shilling ran out.

There was always an argument going on in the house. Many petered out, but some led to violent fights, and most of them began with sudden darkness. Whose turn it was to produce the next shilling was always fiercely argued.

It was the rule of the house that my parents put their weekly contribution of shillings on the shelf over the meter each time they paid their rent. For the rest of the family, it was a continual contest.

Everyone claimed they had put in the last shilling. They were stony broke, or were just going to bed and didn't need a light. While the arguments continued, Grandmother appeared to be fast asleep in her armchair, her handbag clasped on her lap, untroubled by the shouting, or the threats of violence that escalated in the darkness.

Often my parents, or even a visitor, would grope their way down to the basement and part with a shilling that had been saved for some other necessity. Strangely, the returning light always woke Grandmother. Then she would call for the newspaper and settle herself comfortably, while Grandfather was dispatched to make a cup of tea.

The only time I recall Grandmother producing a shilling was when she was waiting to go up to bed. She refused to sleep in the dark. A gaslight burned all night above her bed, and on the table beside it were laid out her favourite foods, grapes, fruitcake, even oysters, in case she was peckish in the night.

No-one ever commented on her little luxuries, and no-one ever knew how much money she kept in the handbag that stayed by her side night and day.

My three aunts worked in a cigarette factory owned by Carreras, where they made Black Cat cigarettes. They were leaf strippers. It was hard, dirty piece work, paying well if you could keep up the pace. Most of the money they brought home on a Friday night went straight into Grandmother's outstretched hand, yet she never looked either grateful or happy.

I was always afraid of fire.

Living upstairs as we did, the staircase was the only escape route from the house. My grandfather had an old cat called Minnie that he treasured. Every night before bed, he searched for Minnie to make sure she was safely inside before the doors and windows were locked.

Unfortunately, he searched with a lighted candle. The wallpaper on the staircase was varnished to resist dirty marks, and the varnish was highly flammable. Also, the little tables on the landings were draped with cloths edged with bobbles. When Grandfather peeped under a table in his eagerness to find Minnie, he had only to touch one bobble with the flame, and within moments, the whole landing would be ablaze.

How many times I was wrapped in a blanket, then carried downstairs by my father, I do not know, but the clanging bell of a fire engine racing into the street, the smell of smoke, the panic and arguments that raged after the firemen had gone, leaving the staircase and landings saturated and blackened, are a vivid part of my early life.

I learned later that the fire brigade was never called to any other house in Swan Street while my mother's family lived there, yet they were a familiar sight.

~

Grandfather admitted his vicious temper had often led him into fights in his youth. He worked on the London docks and was known for his strength and fiery nature. However, as he grew older, he changed his way of life and turned to religion.

As with many converts, he loathed what he considered to be his earlier weakness and the endless arguing of his family upset him. His instincts told him he should step in and try to control them, but he was old and he was afraid. With hindsight, I think he was afraid that, one day, his own self-control would give way.

Whenever the family fights became too fierce, he retreated to the basement kitchen and stoked the fire, heaping on newspaper, kindling wood, cardboard, anything he could find, as though the fury of the fire could calm his anger.

Inevitably, the chimney caught fire. As soon as flames flared out of the chimney pots, the fire brigade would be called. Sometimes before, sometimes after, the neighbours tired of the rowdiness and foul language and called the police.

As I said, I was terrified of fire, yet my father loved the spectacle of someone else's house burning. If we were out and he heard the clang of a fire engine, he would immediately break into a run while I clung to his hand and scurried to keep up.

When we reached the fire, he would stand fascinated, as

the blaze spread and windows burst with the heat, sending vivid tongues of fire leaping out.

There was one fire I never forgot. I dreamed about it, night after night, waking in a terrified sweat until my mother made Father promise never to take me to a fire again.

But that didn't take away the memory. I can still see it now. I can still feel the sickness and the horror.

A blind couple had a little shop near Swan Street, where they sold baskets and all kinds of things made of cane. It was a tall, narrow building, and they made their baskets in the rooms above the shop. On the floors above, they kept their stock and high up on the top floor, they lived with their two children who were their eyes.

The fire broke out on the first floor while the shop was shut and the family was on the top floor. News spread quickly and Father dragged me all the way.

When we reached the scene, the two middle floors were ablaze. There was no way down, and the firemen had no ladders long enough to reach the top floor. Through the smoke, we watched the blind couple and their children helpless at the windows. No-one survived.

I felt sick. I wanted to go home, but Father was still watching when Mother came and took me away.

CHAPTER 4

I was four when an incident occurred which changed the pattern of my life.

A young curate from a nearby church knocked on our front door and asked if he could speak to the mother of the child at the window.

Mother went down after a few minutes, during which she had donned her best dress and pinned her hair up into a bun fronted by the usual row of flat curls.

The curate was polite. He hoped he wasn't intruding, but he often passed on his way to church and he had noticed the little girl who sat at the window.

Sometimes he waved to her, and she waved back. He wondered if she was ill or crippled? If so, he thought he might visit her, as she must be very lonely. Or better still, perhaps he could bring some children from his Sunday school class to play with her?

Poor young man. He could not have anticipated Mother's reaction. Her daughter was perfectly healthy, she screamed. And she didn't need strangers telling her how to bring up her own child. If he was looking for somewhere to poke his nose in, there were plenty of dirty, little urchins covered in sores and alive with lice. He had no right to pester decent people.

Normally, she didn't swear, but that day she let herself go. I could hear it all through the open window as he stood on the step. Others heard it too, and women came to their front doors, wiping their hands on their aprons or standing, arms folded, listening.

It was Grandfather who intervened and sent the shaken young curate away, but even when the front door had slammed shut, the tide of Mother's anger roared on, fuelled by comments from her sisters and even my grandmother.

"He's right! Poor little bitch! You can't keep her shut up in that room forever. She'll have to go to school soon, then you'll have to let her out."

I cried a lot.

However, once Mother's fury subsided, she had second thoughts. I was not going to play in the street. She was adamant about that, but there must be ways for me to mix with other children.

Her first idea was to take me to a park a few streets away.

I am sure she had never been there before because her face froze as we turned a corner and were faced by a small open area between the houses. To me, the word 'Park' conjured visions of mowed lawns, towering trees and colourful flower beds. Here, there were no trees, no flowers, and no grass. Iron benches stood at intervals around the perimeter, but the only concession to childhood was a row of swings and a maypole, all set solidly in asphalt, so any fall was bound to be a painful one. The chains hanging from the maypole ended in iron rings to which the children clung. The bigger, rougher boys, whose feet reached the ground, raced round and round non-stop until little ones squealed to them to stop or fell off.

I would have loved to have had a turn on a swing, but the

battle that erupted among the crowd the moment one became free was too much for my mother. She vowed we would never go back.

To give Mother her due, she did not concede defeat easily. She was determined I would grow up to be a lady, so I must play in a more suitable place.

She chose Green Park. It was the nearest of the Royal Parks. There, babies were pushed in their prams by uniformed nannies while children of my age walked demurely beside them. Sometimes, while the nannies chatted together on a bench, the older children played together with a ball or a top.

That was the atmosphere Mother wanted for me. She dressed me in my best, put a ball in her handbag and off we went.

It was a long walk, much longer than Mother had expected. By the time we got to Green Park, I was so tired I didn't want to play with any of the well-dressed children. All I wanted was to curl up on a bench and go to sleep.

Eventually, we went home by bus after waiting in a long queue behind tired office workers. Father was agitated because we were so late getting back and Grandmother was disgusted. "Ridiculous walking all that way. She ought to know better in her condition."

I didn't understand what that meant at the time and I was too tired to care.

Mother seemed subdued after that. She bought me a packet of crayons and some paper and moved the table closer to the window so I could draw when I was tired of looking out.

My aunts' comments were caustic. "Back at the bloody window! Poor little bitch! You've got to do something about her. Like a ruddy pet parrot in a cage, she is!"

This time, Mother didn't fight back. Instead, she cried. It

wasn't like her. I think even my aunts were taken aback because they came and asked if they could take me out as a treat.

I had never been out with my aunts before. They were a strange trio, always squabbling, always competing, yet all wanting the same things from life, lots of flashy clothes, plenty of flirting and men with money who could lavish presents on them and take them to shows in the West End.

Edith, the eldest, was highly strung and hated to be crossed in anything. She could be boisterously happy one minute yet plunged into black depression the next.

Violet, the middle one, was entirely different. Plump and plain with mouse-brown hair, she always struggled to compete with her two, more attractive, sisters.

Trixie, the youngest, was described by her siblings as "a spoiled little cow." The only one of the family to stay at school until she was fourteen, she saw herself as far more intelligent and attractive than the others.

The fact she did the same job as her sisters, stripping tobacco in a factory, meant nothing to her. One day, she would get herself a rich husband and show her sisters what she was really worth. In the meantime, she spent every penny of her wages she could keep from her mother on clothes and enjoying herself. She wore her hair in a Cleopatra cut, straight at the sides with a fringe across her forehead. Her hair was her greatest pride, and she put tremendous effort into keeping it black, shiny, and beautiful.

Cosmetics and ready-made beauty products were rare, and apart from powder, rouge and lipstick, most of the care my aunts lavished on themselves was simple and basic.

Edith rubbed carbonate of magnesium powder into her face to cleanse it and set her curls with a solution of gum Arabic. Violet rubbed castor oil into her hair to darken it and put a paste of cucumber and milk on her freckles. Once a week, Trixie spread beaten egg all over her hair. She was certain it kept it shiny and black. Beauty was very important and time-consuming for all of them.

I am sure Mother must have been surprised when her sisters offered to take me out. At any other time, she would have quizzed them about where they were going, but as I realised later, she had a lot on her mind just then.

My aunts didn't tell me much except that Grandmother was coming too, and we were going to have afternoon tea in a proper tearoom. For me, that sounded exciting enough.

We went to Lyons Corner House, a big restaurant on the Strand. My aunts and my grandmother wore their best finery, and I was dressed in the coat, hat, and matching ruff Mother had made for me. There were fancy cakes, the like of which I had never seen before, served by waitresses in black dresses with white aprons and head-dresses, and a string orchestra played in the background.

It was wonderful and when we stepped out into the street again, I would willingly have gone home and shared with my parents all the excitement I had experienced.

But the treat was not over. When I asked where we were going, my aunts laughed. My grandmother didn't.

"You wait. She'll have your guts when she finds out," she warned.

"Get away," Edith said. "It'll do the poor little devil good. Don't worry. She won't understand the jokes, but she'll love the singing and dancing."

They took me to a music-hall, and they were right. I loved every moment. I loved the crowds jostling in the queue outside, the breathless rush up the stairs holding Trixie's hand to grab a row of good seats, then the fierce defence of them while Grandmother toiled slowly up to take her place. I loved the bag of toffees we passed from one to the other, the cheer of excitement as the orchestra burst into life, and finally, the breath-taking moment when the curtain went up.

I sat entranced by everything, perched on a pile of coats to be sure I could see, revelling in the spectacle and the laughter of the audience, even though I had no idea what had amused them.

Mother was horrified when we got home. I had never known her turn the full force of her anger against her sisters before. Father hurried me upstairs and put me to bed, and for once, while angry voices raged downstairs, I dreamed of music and dancing and singing and laughter.

Soon after the trip to the music-hall, Mother made a decision. She still refused to allow me to play in the street, but she accepted I should not be cooped up in one room all the time. The yard at the back of the house was to be my playground.

The yard was a tiny patch of concrete filled with accumulated rubbish, surrounded by high walls that shut out the sun. Obediently, Father set about clearing the rubbish and painted whitewash over the flaky walls.

In one corner was the lavatory, in another stood the dustbin, and in the third corner was a makeshift shelter that housed a lonely cockerel.

Someone had named him Charlie, and he had been living in the yard since the previous December when Father had bought a ticket in a raffle.

The prize had been a chicken dinner for Christmas. Father was beside himself with excitement when he found he had won, but he had not expected to be presented with a large cockerel that was still very much alive.

Having managed to get it home on the bus, he found no-one in the family was willing to wring its neck.

Eventually, Uncle Eric nailed together a shelter to protect

the poor creature from the weather and the old lady next door had donated a rusting roll of wire netting.

I liked Charlie. He was my friend.

You may think, from my description, that my new playground was not very impressive, but to me it was Heaven. It was mine.

Grandfather found an old chair for me and Mother asked Mrs Picton at the corner shop for a cardboard box. In it, I kept all my special possessions, a cup with no handle, a square from a blanket, bits and pieces of ribbon and wool, tops of jam jars and sauce bottles, scraps of material, feathers from one of Grandmother's old hats and a host of other oddments. Rubbish, no doubt, but to me, they were treasures that fed my imagination. From them I could conjure up anything from a tea-party to a music-hall where I could sing and dance with ribbons and feathers in my hair.

I had always felt my parents' eyes on me in the room upstairs, but in the yard I was free, and I was never lonely. I had Charlie and my dolls to talk to, and if I tired of them, there was always God and the angels, and Jesus, and the fairies.

I told my Aunt Trixie one day that I talked to God and the angels. She thought it was hilarious. She told everyone in the house, as well as my aunt and uncle, who lived up the street from us.

Mother was defensive about it at first, but in the end she laughed too. I didn't like that. It made me feel silly, and I cried when I was alone in the yard.

I never told anyone about God and the angels after that. Except Grandfather. He didn't laugh. He just held my hand tight and said he thought it was a good idea to keep it as a secret between him and me.

Soon after that, I heard Grandmother shouting at him because he had taken too long going shopping.

Later, he came into the yard and brought out some little

books hidden under his waistcoat. He had limped all the way to the second-hand bookstall in the market and bought them for me.

I loved them. They were full of pictures of gnomes and fairies and all their adventures. I wanted to show them to everyone, but he insisted they were to be our secret, just his and mine, and he would look after them for me.

I didn't realise then that since the day of his accident, he had never had any money of his own. Grandmother held the purse and clung tightly to every penny that went into it. Once every fortnight, she grudgingly bought a tin of pipe tobacco for Grandfather. That was all. He never complained, but I realised much later that he cheated on the change he brought back from the shopping. A penny here and a penny there and he could keep a secret tin stocked with sweets and buy little books for his granddaughter.

Grandfather was an honest man, but circumstances can make cheats of us all. I loved him and I understood.

~

Looking back to childhood, some memories are little more than vague impressions, blurred by time, others are as vivid as the day they happened. I shall never forget the day Father took me to Kenley Common.

He rarely took me anywhere alone, except to the Old Tin Cow, a few streets away. I loved going there. To me, it was fascinating. A grimy old strip of wall down an alley, but in the middle of it was a tap and above that a hole. You put a penny in the hole, then held your jug under the tap and out came a stream of milk.

Sometimes milk spilled and went sour on the ground, attracting lots of flies. Mother didn't approve of the Old Tin Cow. We only went there in an emergency when the dairy was closed.

Our milk was usually delivered by the milk cart with its big churns and measures. Jugs were left outside every house overnight. Strangely, I don't remember covers being put on the jugs and sometimes there were rowdy quarrels when neighbours' cats or dogs helped themselves.

On the morning that he took me out, Father made his mind up very suddenly. Mother was usually first up, but that morning she was still in bed when we left and she didn't even bother to give him instructions on how I should be dressed or how to curl my hair round his fingers like she always did. He just pulled it back in a heap and tied it with a ribbon. Then he cut some bread, poured water into a bottle and put it all in a bag with some apples.

I didn't even have time to say goodbye to Mother. Father hurried me down the stairs and my grandmother stood at the bottom and watched us go.

I can remember a ride on the top of a bus, an open piece of land covered with bushes that seemed to go on forever, a stretch of rough grass where we sat and ate the bread and the apples, and waking up curled into my father's arms.

It was on the long walk back to the bus that I saw the daisies, a little white carpet of them beside the track. We picked a bunch, and he tied his handkerchief round them so my eager hands didn't make them wilt.

It was late afternoon when we got home, and by that time, I had a baby brother.

He was shown to me with great pride, but I wasn't impressed. He never stopped crying. I was much more interested in my daisies.

Disappointed with my reaction, Mother shooed me away, telling me to find Trixie and ask her to put them into a pot of water.

But Trixie had other ideas.

"Daisies!" She pounced on them. "Never had a daisy chain, have you? Well, I'll make you one."

I watched as she stabbed her thumbnail through each delicate stem, threaded them carelessly together, then hung them round my neck.

By the time I was allowed upstairs to my mother again, the tiny white flowers had wilted. I picked them apart and put them in a cup of water, but by morning they were all dead.

Sometimes, it is difficult for grown-ups to understand the simplicity of a child's mind. To me, Trixie had deliberately killed my beautiful little flowers, and it was a long time before I forgave her.

I always loved flowers, but Swan Street never boasted a blossom, not in a vase, a window or a window box.

However, Father did make one floral effort. After my brother's birth, Mother became depressed and when she was depressed, she became savagely critical of her surroundings, the district, the street, the house and the cramped room in which we lived.

Father was an impractical man, but sometimes he made a genuine effort. Those times were few and far between and nearly always ended in disaster.

With the best of intentions, Father decided a window box full of flowers would cheer up our room. He asked one of the coal-heavers at the yard to make him a box and the man came and fixed it to our windowsill.

Father brought home a bag of earth he gathered from the railway embankment and a packet of seeds.

Time passed.

I looked at the box of bare earth every day and at last a tiny green shoot appeared, then another, then another.

Father was a meticulous man, and he had planted the seeds in a straight row, sixteen of them. It is no feat of memory to recall that. I heard every detail of his effort over and over from my mother and always in a tone of disgust.

The plants grew swiftly, and each put up a single stem.

Up and up, they went, thickening and growing until the tips vanished out of sight. Eventually, a display of giant yellow sunflowers amused everyone in the street, and all that could be seen from inside our room was a row of sixteen upright stems, like evenly spaced prison bars.

CHAPTER 5

Occasionally, on a Saturday evening, my parents took me to the market and there, sandwiched between a second-hand bookstall and a stand that sold pieces of leather for mending boots, was a little table crammed with flowers. It belonged to an old lady in a black bonnet and shawl who was always busy making wreaths.

I didn't know the names of the flowers she sold, but the sight and perfume of them was sheer joy. I wanted to stand and stare and sniff, lost in a wonderland of delight, fiercely resisting my parents' efforts to drag me away.

One evening, when they were waiting their turn at a fruit stall, I slipped away and went back to the old lady. One bunch of flowers stood out from the rest. I couldn't take my eyes off them. I didn't know what they were then, but I do now. They were roses, beautiful apricot-coloured, long-stemmed roses.

"What yer staring at?" The old lady barely glanced up from her work. "Them there? Tuppence each, they are."

I was still staring when my parents found me. For once, I was not cowed by Mother's anger. I wanted tuppence. I wanted a rose, and I was prepared to cry, stamp my feet, or throw a tantrum to get my way.

Father was shocked by my determination. Left alone, I am sure he would have given me the tuppence, if only to escape the attention of the people watching us, but Mother was a different proposition. Tuppence was a lot of money. I had to learn that no amount of tantrums would get me my own way. Red-faced with embarrassment, she dragged me away from the stall.

At home, I went to bed hungry and in disgrace, but I never forgot those beautiful apricot-coloured roses.

Perhaps some good came from the incident in the market. Later, when she had calmed down, Mother admitted my love of flowers was genuine and some weeks later she announced that she and Father had been saving up to give me a special treat.

We were going to go into the country and see flowers growing wild in the fields. She showed me pictures in a newspaper of smiling crowds climbing off excursion buses, their arms full of bluebells and primroses.

It would be the most exciting day ever.

Back then, there was no thought of preserving the countryside. To townsfolk, it was a wonderful communal garden waiting to be ravished by anyone lucky enough to reach it.

In Spring, the train and bus companies ran Bluebell Excursions that were very cheap and allowed Londoners the chance to escape from the city and return with baskets full of wildflowers.

Mother made sandwiches, and we went by train. I had never been on a train before and this one was packed with laughing families.

I don't remember where we went, but when we followed the crowd out of the station, there was greenery all around us, trees, bushes, and fields full of grass. There were even bright flowers planted in neat rows outside the station.

It was a long walk from the station to the bluebell fields. My baby brother was carried first by one parent and then the other. Gradually, we dropped behind the rest of the passengers and as we walked, the sky clouded over.

We had gone a long way, through a village and past farmhouses, but the bluebells were not even in sight, when the rain began. Softly at first, and I begged for us to go on. We could shelter under trees, I pleaded. Soon the sun would come out again and everything would be lovely.

Then the heavens opened. In a few moments, we were drenched. The baby began to cry, then scream.

There was a barn near the road, and beyond that, a farmhouse where an elderly woman was feeding chickens. She signalled to us.

"I thought I heard a baby crying," she said and shepherded us into a barn. "You poor things."

We must have been a pitiful sight. The woman pulled out bales of straw for us to sit on, then brought us mugs of hot chocolate from the house.

I was happy at first, waiting for the rain to stop so we could press on to the bluebells. But the rain went on and on and eventually I realised it was all over. We would turn back. No bluebells, no primroses, just a long, wet walk back to the railway station.

That was when I cried. Hearing me, the woman came back and Mother explained why I was so upset.

"Bluebells?" The woman shook her head. "I'm afraid I can't help you there, my love, but I'll tell you what. As soon as the rain stops, we'll see what we can find."

She was as good as her word. Her hand in mine, she took me to the farmhouse and through into her garden. It was alive with bright flowers and from them she picked me a bunch so big I could barely carry it.

I never forgot that day or the fields of bluebells I never saw. Nor did I forget the beautiful flowers I was given or the kindness of the lady who gave them to me.

From then on, the countryside was real to me. It was not just a picture in a book. It was a wonderful place beyond the grime and the bustle of the city where flowers grew in profusion and people were kind and understanding.

My grandmother was one of the twelve people who formed The Royal Arsenal Co-operative Society, the first Co-op, and it was a family tradition for Mother to do her weekly shop at the local branch.

It had been hoped that if a group bought in bulk, it would bring savings to families in need of them, and it did. The idea spread and the membership grew. New branches of the Co-op were opened in other areas and one of them was within walking distance of Swan Street.

Mother became a member as soon as she married, but she still bought oddments during the week from the corner shop, a pennyworth of pickles, an Oxo cube, or two ounces of tea to tide us over until the weekend.

And eggs.

Eggs always came from the corner shop because it was easier to take them back if they were bad. As I grew older, I dreaded Mother breaking eggs and finding a bad one. Wrinkling her nose, she would plump it into a basin, shells and all, put a cloth put over the top to lessen the smell, then despatch me to confront Mrs Picton.

The shopkeeper would frown at the sight of the basin and twist her head away as the cloth was taken off. Sometimes she hinted they were old eggs, left in the cupboard for too long, but she always replaced them.

The main weekly shopping, however, came from the Co-op. As soon as Father arrived home on a Friday evening, even before he had had his tea, we would set off.

For me, it was the highlight of the week. I loved the mysterious dark streets and alleyways that led to the shop. I loved the glorious smells of tea and coffee and herbs and watched fascinated as every item, sugar, rice, pearl tapioca, biscuits, was carefully shovelled into dark blue paper bags and weighed on the scales.

Then, when the items were all listed and priced and the bill had been paid, the correct amount of metal tokens would be handed over to tally with the cost of the groceries. At home, the tokens were kept in a biscuit tin on the mantelshelf. Then, a couple of weeks before Christmas, they would all be counted.

At the Co-op, a big notice announced how much profit had been made in the year and therefore how much dividend would be paid to each member for their metal tokens.

As with many other families, that "divvy" was our Christmas spending money. It provided our share towards the family Christmas dinner, bought the ingredients for the big cake, which Mother always made, and ensured Santa Claus could manage a few treats for our stockings.

As I said before, I loved our Friday visits to the Co-op. Strangely, it was the one place I can remember being made to feel important. The manager was a middle-aged man with a shock of curly hair and a cheerful smile. He always greeted me and took a few minutes to talk to me. Years later, Grandfather told me the manager and his wife had a little daughter, but she had died at five years old.

One Friday, the manager greeted me as usual, then with a big smile, he presented me with a comic. He confided that his little girl had loved comics, and this one had been her favourite.

It was Tiger Tim's Weekly.

I had never seen a comic before. It was brightly coloured and wonderful. Pleased by my delight, the manager read me the front-page antics of Tiger Tim, and the other pupils at Mrs Bruin's boarding school.

"I knew she would like it," he said as we left. "I'll have next week's ready for her on Friday."

But Mother's mood had changed.

"Don't worry," she said coldly. "If she likes it, we'll get it for her."

I never went to do the Friday shop again. The family tradition of being a member of the Co-op was strong enough that my parents still shopped at the local branch and hoarded the metal checks for Christmas, but from then on, I was left behind with my grandparents.

My mother was a strange woman. Her pride was everything to her, and she could turn in a moment from friend to foe. Nothing antagonised her more than anyone becoming too friendly.

But she did keep her word. From that day on, she bought me Tiger Tim's Weekly every Friday. I loved it. I sat alone in my white-washed yard and revelled in the adventures, the mischief, the treats, the excitements and the secrets of the wonderful characters that peopled the pages.

At the time, I never questioned why I loved Tiger Tim's Weekly so much. Why I lived and relived each incident, imagining myself into every page. Looking back, I understand not only why I loved it then, but why I went on loving it. It was more than an escape from reality and loneliness. It was a standard of perfection.

In Tiger Tim's Weekly, Christmas and birthday parties were full of cheer and happiness. There was no fear, no anger, no drunken brawls. Picnics were an oasis of bright tablecloths, big cakes, bottles of pop and fun and games against a background of a cloudless blue sky, bright green grass and trees covered with flowers. A trip to the seaside meant endless golden sands, bright blue sea, and ice-cream stands with gaily striped awnings. No litter, no pollution, and no arguments.

I loved it and I was innocent enough to believe that, away from our house, away from our street, that was what the world was really like.

CHAPTER 6

It was about this time the attic room at the top of Grandmother's house was cleared of rubbish and white-washed. Then my Aunt Mabel came to live in it with her two children.

Grandmother had an obsession. She wanted to go to Australia. To her, Australia was the Golden Land, the great escape from the world she lived in and hated.

She was very good at hating. Sometimes, it seemed to me it was the only emotion she enjoyed. She hated foreigners, French, German and Italian in particular. Arabs were evil. Asians, Africans, or any other dark-skinned people were bearable only as servants. She despised Jews and Catholics and loathed the Scots, the Welsh, and the Irish. She couldn't stand North Country people or those from the Midlands, and to her, Londoners from north of the Thames were no better than foreigners. Added to that, she didn't trust anyone with brown eyes.

I never knew how she felt about Australians. I don't remember her ever mentioning them. It was as though they didn't exist and Australia was a huge, empty paradise, waiting with open arms to welcome those who could get there. And she was determined to get there. She had been planning it for years.

While two of her sons, Albert and Edmund, were still at school, she had contacted a charity that arranged for orphans and needy children to be given a fresh start in Australia.

When the boys cried, she told them that if they worked hard and earned a lot of money, she would come and live with them and bring all the family with her.

At first, Grandfather refused to sign the papers allowing the boys to go, but in the end, she had her way.

The next to be sent was a daughter, Annie. The charity took her willingly. She was strong and healthy, and they were short of girls.

But Aunt Mabel had upset her mother's plans by getting pregnant. She had married quickly and went on to produce another baby before her husband died of typhoid fever.

Grandmother saw the sad event as another opportunity.

She had written to Albert and Edmund, who were working in Australia by this time, and persuaded them to put up the money for Mabel and her family to be accepted as immigrants.

Another link was forged.

Strange, isn't it? The pattern of our lives is formed long before we are born. So much for imagining we are the masters of our own destiny.

I can clearly remember the morning Aunt Mabel thrust her ten-year-old son into a taxicab and left without a backward glance at the angry family and neighbours gathered on the pavement to watch her go.

Maybelle, her daughter, was only nine months older than me and had contracted typhoid fever, the disease that killed her father. She was in an isolation hospital.

Typhoid was taken seriously back then. It spread quickly and killed too many.

The authorities had sealed the rooms where the family

lived and sent in the contamination squad. With no possessions and nowhere to live, Aunt Mabel had been grateful to move into the tiny attic at the top of my grandmother's house.

At last, the immigration papers had come through and a date had been fixed for the family to leave for Australia. There were health checks, of course, but my aunt and her son passed them. Aunt Mabel never hesitated. She and my cousin, Ernie, were free to sail, and she had no intention of waiting. Maybelle, if she survived, could be cared for by the family until the authorities arranged for her to sail to Australia.

The decision caused an uproar. Even my grandmother, keen as she was to transplant the entire family to the Golden Land, could not stomach the thought of a five-year-old girl being left without her mother, then despatched to the other side of the world in the care of strangers.

For days, the battle raged. My parents tried to keep aloof, but our neighbours had no such inhibitions. In the East End of London, family was all important. Children might be poorly fed, housed and clothed, but no-one deliberately hurt them. No decent mother would desert her child.

But Aunt Mabel was adamant. She had a chance to escape, and she went.

Maybelle survived and came out of hospital a few weeks later. Grandmother had looked after too many children in her life and had no intention of caring for another. My aunts were out at work each day, so there was only one answer. Mother took her in. Maybelle slept in an armchair and cried every night.

I remember wishing someone would send her out to her mother. Now, I can understand how she felt, how any child would have felt, but at the time, I only knew that her misery and resentment were focused on me.

She smashed the head off my precious doll, tore up my

books, and worst of all, she bit me whenever we were alone. My arms, legs, and face were covered with bite marks and Mother refused to be seen out with me. So, when she went to the shops, it was Maybelle who went with her and I was left at home.

It was three months before Maybelle left, a small figure in a round straw hat, clutching a little doll Uncle Eric had bought for her and holding tight to the hand of a stern-faced woman.

It was another four months before a letter arrived saying Maybelle had reached her mother safely. There was no word of thanks and Mother was furious.

With Aunt Mabel gone, Grandmother let the attic room to lodgers, a young couple, the wife's elderly mother and a baby girl named Beatty.

They had one room with a sloping-ceiling and a little gas stove. That was all. There was no fireplace and no sink. The only water supply in the house was in the basement and all water for drinking, cooking or cleaning had to be carried upstairs in a bucket, then carried down again when used.

Washing clothes was a communal activity that was done in the basement. I can remember the shelf with two washing tubs standing on it, the huge mangle, and the built-in copper in the corner. Whenever hot water was needed, the fire beneath the copper was lit and at Christmas the boiler itself was scrubbed clean and puddings, all tied up in their white cloths, were boiled in it for the traditional eight hours.

Mother hated the lodgers living above us. To her, they were common beyond belief. She was especially disgusted that they put washing soda in the copper, boiled their clothes in it, then carried the same water upstairs to bathe Beatty. Perhaps that is why her baby cheeks always looked as red as a ripe cherry.

I, too, resented the lodgers. The yard had been my own special place where I could be alone with my make-believe, but in open defiance of Grandmother's orders, they strung washing lines from one side to the other. Lines that always had something dripping from them, including sheets, blankets, or even a mattress when a bed had been wetted.

I expected Grandmother to object, but she didn't. Perhaps she thought she had little hope of letting the attic room to anyone else.

Then Charlie died. Mother and I found him one morning when we crossed the yard to the lavvy. To this day, I don't know why my friend died. Perhaps it was because he had started crowing every time he recognised someone as a friend. It was the final straw. I never played in the yard again.

I don't know what happened to Charlie. Perhaps someone ate him. My grandfather told me not to think about it, but for days the sickly smell of hot feathers came from the oven in the basement and Grandmother had a new feather pillow for her bed.

CHAPTER 7

Of all the regular visitors who came to Swan Street, the most welcome was the Barrel Organ man. He came in the afternoon, parked his organ in the middle of the road and began winding the handle.

Fortunately, the milkman and the baker came in the morning so there was rarely anyone to disturb him. The brewery horses didn't come back till evening and cars were such a rarity that the sight of one brought the curious to every door to stare.

Watching from my window, I envied the children who gathered round the barrel organ. Little girls danced while boys mimicked them and others sang along with the noisy tunes that were belted out, all popular songs, and very patriotic.

Then, when his arm ached from winding, he stopped and there was a rush into the houses to beg a copper to put in his hat to encourage him to stay. Many children didn't bother. They knew there were no coppers to spare.

I liked the Barrel Organ man, but Grandmother didn't. He had shiny black hair and a big black moustache, and she swore he was Italian.

The Hokey-Pokey Man made no secret of the fact he was Italian. He regularly set his stand on the pavement halfway up the street and his voice echoed in either direction.

"Cumma buy de hokey-pokey." His bellow was always the same. "Aipenny de hokey-pokey. Luvverly hokey-pokey."

I never tasted hokey-pokey. I understand it was like ice cream and came in little biscuit cups, but it was much cheaper than ice cream, and that made it suspect, at least to my mother.

The Roundabout Man didn't come very often. His weary donkey pulled a little cart on which sat a round red seat. It could take four children or five if they were small. The moment enough eager customers were seated, the Roundabout Man started up a gramophone on the front seat of the cart and wound the big handle jutting from the side. Then, very slowly, the children went round and round.

He was an old man. His white hair was thin, and he sweated so much his shirt was wet and stained. Some mothers said he didn't do enough for the penny he charged, but he didn't look as though he could do any more. In between rides, he sat on the edge of the pavement and drank from a little bottle he kept in his back pocket.

Sunday tea was always a special meal. A procession of street vendors saw to that, their eager cries ringing out above the bells of the church in the next street.

I always watched for the Muffin Man. He carried his wares on a wooden tray balanced on his head, covered with a big white cloth. You had to take your own plate out to him and wait while he set his tray down on the pavement, sorted out your muffins, then meticulously spread the white cloth back into place. I loved muffins, and I loved being allowed to toast them in front of the fire.

The Watercress Man carried an enormous basket on his arm, and the watercress was tied up in neat little bundles, but the Winkle Man was my favourite. He pushed a coster's barrow and winkles and shrimps were piled on it in big heaps. He had no scales, just two iron measuring jugs, and he sold by the pot-full.

I loved winkles. I dreamed of having a big plate piled high with them. Sadly, I was only ever given four or five and a large plate of bread.

On the mantelshelf, a row of pins was kept stuck into the bobble-edged runner. On Winkle Sundays, they were brought down and handed round. They were the tools with which we would earn our tea.

It took me a long time to coax each winkle out of its shell, gently turning the pin so the poor winkle didn't break in half and leave its tail end to slip back into the shell where, despite all my efforts, I would never see it again. Once you were considered old enough to "pick a winkle" by yourself, no-one helped you.

The Provident Cheque Man called every Monday. I know because we had cold meat on a Monday. Every week was the same. A small joint on Sunday and cold meat on Monday, and sometimes Mother sent me to the corner shop to buy a pennyworth of mustard pickles as a treat.

The Provident Cheque man was round and cheerful and he would smile at me and say, "Pickles again? You are a lucky girl, aren't you?"

Mother always had Provident Cheques. They bought shoes, socks, material to make winter coats, even a suit for my father. You took out a one-pound cheque and paid it back one shilling a week for twenty-one weeks. They could only be used at certain shops, often with little choice, but when money was scarce, they gave a chance to buy now and pay later. The Provident Cheque man knocked on the door every week to make sure all debts were cleared on time or you ended up on a blacklist.

The only alternative to Provident cheques, if you urgently needed money, was a quick and secretive visit to the pawnbrokers in the High Street. You could pledge anything at Uncle's, the nickname for all pawnbrokers. Few people owned anything valuable, but when they were short of money for food, families pawned clothes, bed linen, clocks, even their meagre assortment of cutlery.

One woman in the street regularly pawned the black suit that had been handed down through her family and only redeemed it when it was needed for a funeral. My mother often pawned her wedding ring. The longer you left your possessions with Uncle, the more it cost you to get them back and there was a time limit when the item became Uncle's property. The last time Mother pawned her wedding ring, she never got it back.

The insurance man came on Tuesdays. He was a stern-looking man and carried a black book. As far as I could see, he called at every house in the street, even the poorest. Sometimes he collected a shilling or two, sometimes only a few coppers, sometimes nothing, just a promise that the next Tuesday would be better.

My mother always had insurance. She kept the book on the mantelshelf, and every Friday when Father brought his wages home, she put a sixpence beside it.

One day, I talked to Grandfather about it.

"Folk pay what they can afford," he said. "They like to feel that if somebody dies, they've got enough to put them down properly."

The caller who roused the most interest was the doctor. The moment he came into the street, bag in hand, women came to their doors and gathered in whispering groups. You didn't send for the doctor unless all the family remedies had failed and someone was very ill indeed.

Like most children, I had my share of health problems. I had sties on my eyes, red swellings, oozing puss that dried hard and made it difficult to see, and wicklows, painful, swollen poisons around my fingernails.

Such complaints were commonplace and no-one bothered a great deal. Sties were rubbed with gold, usually a mother's wedding ring, and eventually they went away. Wicklows were more troublesome. The fingernails had to be dipped into hot water, as hot as could be borne without screaming and bothering the neighbours. That drew the poison out and eventually they, too, went away.

If wicklows were too persistent, the last cure was to sacrifice the infected nail completely and pull it out. Mother frowned on that, not because of the pain involved, nor because she would have to pay a doctor's fee for one quick tug. She objected because after such crude treatment, the nail grew back ugly and misshapen. My nails, like my teeth, had to be perfect. They were a testament to her care.

There were those who insisted that sties, wicklows, chilblains, and a host of other miserable childhood complaints were the result of poor diet, but Mother ridiculed the idea.

The doctor had a shop in the High Street. There was a curtain across the window to hide the inside from public view and a row of wooden chairs formed the waiting room. The shop bell, still in position, rang every time a patient went in or out.

Behind the shop, a storeroom served as the surgery, and a corner,curtained off from the shop itself, was the pharmacy. The doctor saw two or three patients, then while they waited, he crossed to the pharmacy and made up the prescriptions. Medicine was included in the one-shilling fee.

Having the doctor visit was a completely different matter, in our house, at least. The tension and excitement it caused seemed to override any concern for the patient.

Suddenly cleanliness was all that mattered. The passage and stairs had to be swept and dusted, the best bedroom, Grandmother's, cleaned and aired. To my knowledge, those were the only times my grandmother ever allowed a bedroom window to be opened. The jug from the jug and basin set on the washstand was filled with fresh water and soap and a clean towel laid out beside it.

The bed was made up with the best white linen, kept solely for such an occasion, and if the weather was cold, a fire would be lit in the grate.

Once the room was ready, the patient had to be washed, changed into clean nightclothes, fingernails checked and hair brushed. Only then was the invalid transferred to the best bedroom and laid out in bed.

Afterwards, when the doctor had prescribed a remedy, snapped his bag shut, washed his hands and been escorted to the front door, the process went into reverse.

The sufferer returned to a shared bedroom. The best linen was folded and put back in the cupboard. Coal from the fire was picked out, piece by piece, and carried down to the stove in the basement. And often, despite the doctor's efforts, people died.

I stood in the High Street and watched many funerals pass. Father loved them, and, in my innocence, so did I. I loved the sleek, black horses with their waving plumes, the beautiful flower wreaths piled high in the hearse, and the way passers-by all stopped, the men taking off their hats and holding them against their chests.

But I can only remember two funerals in Swan Street itself. I watched the first from my window with Mother peering down over my shoulder. She seemed disappointed.

"Only two horses, no plumes and barely any mourners. Not an impressive a send-off." She sniffed.

But then, Mrs Bailey wasn't an impressive person. She was a thin, grey lady who wore baggy grey clothes. Her hair was grey, her face was grey, so grey that the lines and wrinkles etched into it looked almost black. I don't remember the colour of her eyes. She had a way of closing them when she spoke.

Not that many people spoke to her. Mainly, they avoided her. Mrs Bailey had bowel cancer. It was as though she had a curse upon her and no-one wanted to be touched by it.

I didn't know what cancer was, but from whispered conversations I overheard, bowels seemed to be very important to grownups, and if they stopped, something desperate had to be done.

It still amazes me, even now, that adults can whisper together in the presence of children and not realise how sharp little ears can be and what strange ideas and worries can take shape in little minds. Whispers mean secret things, and secrets are frightening because otherwise grown-ups would not need to whisper.

Of course, I knew people died. Old people who had lived a long time got tired, then went to Heaven.

It sounded rather nice. I wasn't sure whether the hearse took them all the way there and I never asked. It was easier to build my own pictures in my head. I imagined the Golden Gates opening and the beautiful black horses, plumes bobbing, trotting through them, to be welcomed by angels.

Never once did I imagine that children died.

I didn't really know Hettie. She lived two doors away, but I saw her sometimes as I looked down from my window. It was easy to recognise her mop of red curls. She was about the same age as me, and Grandfather told me we would start school at the same time.

Our house was one of a terrace, all built exactly the same. They each had a narrow window at the back that ran from the first floor right up to the second floor and gave light to the staircase.

That Sunday morning, our house was quiet. Grandmother and most of the family had been to a music-hall the evening before, ending up in the pub at the end of the street, and were sleeping soundly. Mother had made porridge for my father as a treat and she was angry because I wouldn't eat it.

Even from two doors away, we heard the crash of glass and Hettie's terrified scream. She had been playing about on the stairs and fell against the window, her weeping mother explained later.

Hettie died on the concrete in the yard. I can still see her coffin, small, white and covered with flowers. The whole street turned out to watch and men and women cried unashamedly.

From that moment onwards, I was terrified of going up the stairs in our house that led past the long window. As I crept up them, I cowered back against the banisters as though the panes of glass had a life of their own and could reach out and pull me through them.

CHAPTER 8

I started school a week after my fifth birthday. I know because the new hair ribbon, the long white socks and the checked dress my mother made from one of my aunt's old ones were all birthday presents ready for the great day.

Looking back, I had not the slightest idea what school would be like, and no-one tried to explain. It was just one big excitement. There would be hundreds of other children and I would learn lots of wonderful things. Beyond that, I had no idea.

I wasn't worried. Every week I read about Mrs Bruin's school in Tiger Tim's Weekly. I couldn't read myself, but I always pestered someone to read that page to me, and I was sure my school would be just as much fun. Nothing could dampen my excitement, neither the Lysol bath the night before my first day, nor the hours spent drying my hair in front of the fire, not even the last painful scrape through with a lice comb.

Before I went to bed, Mother announced she was going to curl my hair. She had cut two of Father's old collars in half and divided my hair into four sections.

To my dismay, she wound each section of hair tightly around a collar until it formed a solid ball against my scalp. Then each ball was tied in place with a ribbon.

Try as I might, I couldn't lay my head on my pillow. Whichever way I turned, the collars stuck into my head and pulled my hair.

"Don't make a fuss. By tomorrow, you will have beautiful ringlets," Mother said.

From that night on, I would always sleep on four great lumps of hair.

Next morning, I wrinkled my nose as a dollop of eucalyptus oil was smeared across my handkerchief. Then Mother hung a linen bag containing a block of camphor around my neck. She assured me it would ward off any diseases the other children carried.

It was my first day at school, and I was late.

I didn't realise it then, but I was destined always to be late. Mother had no sense of time. That particular morning, she fussed over the big pink bow in my hair. It had to be set right, just as my shoes had to be polished until I could see my face in them.

Nothing could have been further from my mental image of a school than the scene that greeted me as I walked through the forbidding black iron gates, holding tightly to Mother's hand.

Facing me was a grimy building, three floors high, with flights of stone steps leading up the outside to the upper floors. It sat squat and huge in a grey asphalt playground in which hundreds of children, boys and girls of all ages, had lined up in long parallel rows. Teachers walked slowly up and down to ensure there was silence, save for the tolling of the school bell.

When it stopped, there was only the scrape of little boots, as one by one, the rows of children disappeared into the grey building, the boys climbing the stone steps to the second floor, while the girls used a different set of steps to the first floor.

The infants were shepherded through a door at ground level, and suddenly the playground was empty.

"Now remember," Mother said, "ask where the lavatories are. Don't be shy. We don't want any accidents." It was the only advice she gave me.

We found the rest of the new pupils gathered in the Headmistress's office. Parents were told their children must arrive clean the following morning. The school doctor would examine them and the nurse would inspect their heads for lice and nits.

Mother was furious. Her child was always clean, and I certainly didn't have nits or lice.

She was the only mother who objected, and I my cheeks blazed with embarrassment.

All my life, she embarrassed me, yet something in my nature made me feel guilty, as though it was my fault she had drawn attention to herself. But at that moment, it was a fleeting guilt. There was too much else to think about.

For years, I had dreamed of going to school. It was the moment I would become a real person with a life of my own and a real name.

I had been christened Hilda, after my mother, but I had always been known as Little Hilda. No-one ever called me anything else, and I was the only person I knew who had the derogatory preface of Little before their name.

But at school I was Hilda, not a diminutive of someone else, but a real person on an equal footing with the other children.

I loved school. The classroom walls were painted dark green at the bottom and stone colour at the top. The windows were so high up that even if you climbed onto a bench and then up onto a desk, you could barely touch the bottom of the frame.

There was no chance of being distracted by the world outside, but it didn't matter.

I loved the big important-looking blackboard, the huge fire grate and the high cupboards on either side of it. I loved the other children, all of them, the ones who smiled at me and the ones who scowled. One day, I was sure, they would all be my friends.

And I loved the lessons. Our books and pencils were put out every morning and gathered up again every afternoon. Sometimes, we had lumps of grimy plasticine which we moulded into ornate shapes, then rolled back into a ball and put back in the cupboard, ready for the next lesson. And sometimes there were bundles of string, some white, some dark red, that were handed out with chunky wooden knitting needles.

Mother had already taught me to knit, so I used my string up quicker than anyone else and had to sit, hands folded quietly in my lap, until the order came to "pull out your needles, wind up your string and leave it in a nice neat ball ready for next time."

My favourite thing about school was the chanting. We chanted the alphabet, our tables, our prayers and any scrap of information the teacher wanted to impress upon us.

What I had not expected was the excitement of breaking the rules. Not me. I would never have dared to step out of line, but other children did.

In Swan Street there were no railings, but on the way to and from school we passed rows of houses with basements that were accessible from the street. Iron railings protected passers-by from falling down the steps.

Children, mostly boys, used to run along the railings with a stick. An old iron poker was even better. The noise was wonderful. It filled the street, hammering and reverberating in your ears, until people raced angrily out of the houses and the culprits sprinted away.

To me, it was wonderful, second-hand excitement. I could imagine the fun of the deed and the thrill of escape. It was a glimpse of freedom I had never experienced.

~

On my second day at school, I was examined by the doctor and nurse. The nurse marked me as free of vermin, but the doctor looked serious and announced I had enlarged tonsils. They must be dealt with.

Strangely, my mother did not object. She was responsible for my cleanliness and my manners, but tonsils were different. She could not be blamed for the size of my tonsils.

A week later, I was taken to Great Ormond Street Hospital. I can remember a sea of other children, all about my own age, seated with their mothers on rows of long wooden benches. Some were crying, and some looked as though they were about to be sick.

A nurse found us space on a bench beside a small boy and a woman in a black shawl.

"It'll be a couple of hours," she said. "Half the new kids in London must be having their tonsils done. Still, it doesn't take long. Just a snip and you'll be on your way home again."

We waited for hours and I spent the time huddled against my mother, watching the bed bugs circle the neck of the small boy beside me, seeing them disappear inside the greasy collar of his coat, then reappear and crawl up into his ears.

I can still see them now. Some things you never forget.

The nurse was right. The operation took only a few minutes. In those days, tonsils were not removed. They were just cut, and we went home on the tram.

It was that evening, when Father was home from work and the meal was being dished up, that I vomited blood all over the tablecloth.

Mother's screams brought everyone in the house

running. Even my grandmother. She took one look and shouted to Grandfather, "Get a taxi quick. I'll pay for it. I'm not having her die here!"

She must have been very worried. It was the only time I ever heard her offer to pay for anything.

~

I can recall very little of the next few weeks, only a vague impression of being alone in a white bed and Mother crying constantly. Later, Trixie filled me in on the details.

Trixie was like that. Most of her life was spent trimming her hair, bleaching the nicotine stains from her fingers and looking for a rich husband, but I think she felt that, as the youngest of my aunts, she had a special bond with me and when we talked, she never pulled her punches.

"Everybody thought you were going to die. The hospital couldn't stop the bleeding and your Gran nearly went barmy," she told me. "Uncle Tom, your granddad's brother, died all of a sudden, and when she heard, she had a fit. Everything happens in threes, she said, so if Uncle Tom died and you died, too, then she was scared stiff she'd be the third. Nearly killed your mother, she did. Said it was all her fault. Hadn't got sense enough to bring up a child properly. Bleeding to death wasn't natural."

When I came out of hospital, it was months before Mother allowed me to go back to school. She was sure that in my weakened state, I would be vulnerable to every disease known to man.

So, I found myself back at the window, staring down enviously at the children in the street once more. With his quiet understanding, Grandfather brought me three books from the second-hand stall in the market. One of them was Alice in Wonderland.

Mother pounced on it with genuine delight. She had

heard about it and had always wanted to read it, and now she would read it to me while I rested.

And she did. She read Alice in Wonderland to me, and when it was finished, she read it again. And again. She loved it.

But I didn't. I couldn't bear the thought of being trapped down a rabbit hole and I didn't like the strange creatures and people Alice met down there. I just wished Mother would read me Tiger Tim's Weekly.

~

Although I had been away for so long, Mother was reluctant to let me go back to school and perhaps she was right. Within weeks, I caught whooping cough. It was only a mild attack, but it was bad enough to take home and give to my baby brother, Cecil. He was not yet two, and he took it badly.

Hilda and Cecil.

Mother said she blamed herself. If she hadn't listened to me when I pestered her to go back to school, she would have kept me home longer. But I knew she really did blame me, and as the whooping cough wracked his tiny body, I was terrified Cecil would die and it would be my fault.

There seemed to be little the doctor could do.

“It will run its course,” he said, “but he needs plenty of fresh air.”

Every day, Mother walked the streets with him or Grandfather sat with him in the grounds of Trinity Church, which was nearby.

“He needs proper fresh air,” Grandmother said. “Not the sooty muck we breathe in round here. He needs to go to the seaside.”

I had never been to the seaside. I knew it cost a lot of money and we never had any. Some children in our street went on holiday in the summer. They went to the hop-fields and lived in tents. The grown-ups and older children worked, picking and packing the hops while the younger children played in the fields. Then, when the day’s work was done, once the hops were weighed, and the pay allocated, it was time to gather round a bonfire and play games or sing and dance to the music of mouth organs and concertinas.

It sounded like paradise to me, but I knew it was common and not the sort of thing my family would consider doing. I would not have dared to say so, but it seemed to me that the hop-picking families always looked cheerful, while mine never stopped arguing.

One day, however, Father came home from work looking very pleased with himself. That evening he told me we were going on holiday to the seaside for a whole week.

Perhaps I looked puzzled, or perhaps I asked awkward questions because I had been told we had no money for such a luxury. Father took me to one side and told me not to worry. The gee-gees were paying for it and I wasn’t to ask any more questions.

I didn’t understand. Not then.

All that mattered was that I was going to the seaside. Not to Southend, which was the nearest place, not to Margate at the mouth of the River Thames, but to Ramsgate, which really was beside the sea.

And we weren't going on a train. We were going on one of the pleasure steamers that left from London Bridge and made their way down the river, then out to sea and along the coast until they reached Ramsgate.

We went two days later, our clothes packed into an old suitcase and two shillings, a gift from Grandfather, tucked into the pocket in my knickers so I could buy a bucket and spade and perhaps some sweets.

At the last minute, Mother poured half a bottle of gripe water down the throat of my sleeping brother. Grandmother was horrified, but Mother was unrepentant. She wasn't going to have him wake up and do that awful whooping cough while we were on a crowded steamer.

She need not have worried. Cecil slept like an angel for the entire journey.

A crowd waited for the passengers as they streamed off the steamer. There were grown-ups among them, but mostly they were children. Some were neatly dressed, hair combed, faces scrubbed, but others were grubby and aggressive.

Their cries of "Good clean lodgings only two shillings a night. No fleas, no bedbugs," rang out louder than the rest and in their eagerness, they ran forward and caught at passengers' hand, urging them away from their competitors.

Mother chose a clean, cheerful girl. She led us through the back streets to a terrace house with crisp lace curtains at the windows. The woman who opened the door smiled too, and the burly man behind her offered to carry our suitcase upstairs.

He was halfway up when Cecil began to cough. Mother rocked him in her arms, but the wracking whoops echoed through the house.

Immediately, the woman shepherded us down the stairs and out the front door. The man deposited our suitcase beside us on the pavement.

"I'm sorry," the woman said. "I've got kids of my own and

I'm not having whooping cough in this house. You'll have to find somewhere else."

There were notices offering lodgings in the windows of several other houses along the street, but Cecil was still coughing and they all turned us away.

Street after street, we walked, Father carrying the suitcase, Mother struggling to pacify the baby. Then it began to rain. Dusk was already creeping in and nothing was as I dreamed it would be.

We stopped at a corner shop, and Father bought two newspapers. He held one over me, and Mother held one over Cecil as we turned into yet another street.

An elderly woman stood at an open door. She watched as we knocked and were turned away. Then, as we approached, she shouted, "What do you think you're doing with a baby out in weather like this?"

Father explained, and she eyed us up and down before nodding.

"We've got no kids, me and my old man. I charge half-a-crown a night. You all sleep in one bed. I'll bring a jug of clean water every morning for you to wash, and I'll give you tea and a boiled egg for breakfast. If you want, you can buy something and bring it in for your tea. I'll cook it and you can eat it on the table in your room. All right?"

She was as good as her word. She dried our clothes beside the grate in the kitchen and made us a cup of tea.

It was dark by the time she took us up to our room and sent Father round the corner to buy fish and chips. Later, when I was in bed and Cecil was still coughing, she knocked on the door and held out a pot and a spoon.

"My mother had seventeen kids. She made this and gave it to us when we were ill. Try to get a spoonful down him. Two if you can. He'll soon settle."

Mother was doubtful, but she was exhausted. Giving in, she dribbled a spoonful of the mixture into Cecil's mouth.

Gradually, he calmed, and as his breathing became easier, he fell asleep.

Next morning, I went down to the sea. It wasn't a bit like the seaside in Tiger Tim's Weekly, but it was wonderful. We bought a bucket and spade and Father knelt beside me and showed me how to pat the sand firmly, so when I turned the bucket upside down, I had the beginnings of a sand castle.

I had never seen him so happy. He was wearing the same suit he wore to work, but he had taken the detachable collar off his shirt and his feet were bare. Looking back, I don't think he had any other clothes, just the one worn suit.

I loved the sand and the way it trickled through my bare toes, but most of all, I loved the sea itself. My mother tucked my dress inside my knickers so I could paddle without it trailing in the water. At first, I objected, but then I saw every little girl had her dress tucked inside her lace-trimmed knickers, just as every father took off his shoes and socks and rolled up the legs of his trousers, and every mother surreptitiously unhooked her suspenders and rolled off her stockings. There were no special clothes for the beach and no such things as changing rooms. All modesty had to be hidden behind a towel.

At one end of the sand was a brightly striped tent. Twice a day, it was opened up to reveal a small stage with a piano. This was where the Pierrot show took place, and every morning and afternoon, I begged Father to take me along to it.

There were no seats. The audience crowded round to enjoy the singing, the dancing and the jokes. Then, when the show was over, a round little man in a bright costume and a red wig came out with a collecting box. That was when Father hurried me away.

By the end of the week, Cecil was a great deal better. He slept a lot and when he did cough, it sounded less frightening. Mother was relieved and grateful. When it was time to go home, she thanked the woman who had taken us in and asked if she could have the recipe for the medicine that had helped Cecil so much.

"Oh, it's mostly gin," the woman said cheerfully. "My mother was very fond of gin."

CHAPTER 9

Back at school, I was determined to catch up with the rest of the class and I asked my father if he would help me learn to read and do sums. He wasn't keen. Usually, he came home from the coal wharf so tired he went straight to bed after the evening meal.

There was no point in asking Mother, as she had been kept home from school to look after her little sisters. Grandmother made her hide in a cupboard every time the school inspector called to keep up the pretence she had gone to live with an aunt in the country.

But it was Mother who insisted Father help me with my schoolwork. She was determined I would have the chances she had been denied. In some way, she saw any success of mine as a vindication of her own worth. To her, I was a symbol of what she could have achieved had she been given the chance.

She wanted me to succeed, and she wanted me to be a lady. Inevitably, she disapproved of my choice of school friends. There were a few children whose speech and cleanliness met her standards, but to her disgust, I preferred to mix with those she called 'the common dregs'.

Maisie lived opposite us in Swan Street, but, as I was never allowed out to play, I only saw her at school.

Maisie's family was very poor. Her father was in prison, and so was her uncle. I often wondered if she had enough to eat. She was painfully thin and her milk teeth went black and fell out long before they should have done.

It didn't seem to worry her. She still beamed happily, showing a row of blackened stumps. But it did bother others in the street, the motherly souls with children of their own. Occasionally, as I looked down from my window, I saw Maisie called to an open door and presented with a slice of bread and dripping. And sometimes, when she ran an errand to Mrs Picton's corner shop, the old lady gave her an egg.

Maisie never took the egg home. She would borrow a safety pin from one of the other children and carefully make a hole in the shell, then she would sit down on the edge of the pavement and suck out the raw egg, smiling round at the children who gathered to watch.

Maybe she liked raw egg, or maybe it was some kind of party trick to draw attention to herself. There was little that was attractive about her, from her baggy, hand-me-down clothes to her straggling hair that she scratched continually.

Yet, for all her problems, Maisie was always happy. She had an instinctive compassion for small creatures and didn't care that this made her an object of ridicule to her classmates.

When a boy stamped on a big black spider, Maisie carried the crushed body home on a scrap of paper. Next day at school she told us her Mother had said a little prayer over its matchbox coffin before it was despatched on its way to Heaven by the flush of the lavvy in the yard.

There was one girl in my class who became my best friend. Her name was Mary. I don't remember her surname. I doubt if it ever mattered to me.

Mary didn't live in Swan Street. She lived around the corner where the houses huddled closer together. Two steps led straight off the pavement down into the living room and in some of the houses the floor was still bare earth.

Mary already had six brothers and sisters and she marvelled that I only had one baby brother. She seemed genuinely sorry for me.

Mary and I were like two little old ladies. We talked seriously of many things as we stood together at the school gate waiting for Mother to collect me. We discussed what we would like to do when we grew up. I had never forgotten the music-hall and wanted to sing and dance, but Mary wanted to be a nurse.

No-one ever collected Mary after school. She was six, the same age as me. Sometimes she walked home with her elder brother or sister, but mostly she negotiated the maze of side streets and the busy main road alone. She only lived around the corner from me, yet Mother never invited her to walk home with us.

"Best not to encourage children like that," she said, but she never explained why.

Life seemed to have many mysteries but few explanations.

Mary had been my friend for nearly a year when one day she didn't arrive at school. She was away the next day too, and I missed her. Then the teacher broke the news to the class. Mary had been crossing the main road on her way home from school when she had been knocked down by a lorry. She was in hospital, but both her legs had been amputated.

It was a long time before she came out of hospital and back to the little house round the corner. I think even

Mother was shocked, and when our neighbours started a fund to buy a wheelchair, she put some coins in the tin and allowed me to visit Mary.

My friend was propped up, white and still, in a chair beside the stove. To cheer her, I talked about the wheelchair the neighbours were hoping to buy for her and she smiled, but at the front door her father shook his head, pointing down at the two steep steps that led up to street level.

"Best not to build her hopes up," he whispered. "We ain't got no place here to keep a wheelchair."

In the tests to decide who should move up from the Infants into the Girl's School, I came top of the class. My prize was a copy of Alice in Wonderland. I wanted to give it to Mary, but Mother was outraged. A school prize, she insisted, was something to be treasured for a lifetime.

I made another special friend when I moved up to the Girl's School.

Amy was a left-over. In those days, children didn't move up through the school according to their age. At the end of the year, there were tests and if you failed them, then you stayed on in the same class, and became a left-over.

Amy had already been a left-over for two years in the lowest class. Leftovers were looked down upon by the clever children, but Amy didn't seem to mind. She was bigger than the rest of us and her mother made her wear a white pinny to school, but she was gentle and kind and I don't think Amy ever felt a failure.

She had one great talent that no-one else could match. She couldn't add or subtract or spell or remember her tables, or even sew or knit, but she could do the most exquisite copper-plate handwriting.

Good writing was considered an essential in those days

and we all had a writing book into which we laboriously copied words and phrases. Most of us managed blots and smudges, misshapen letters and clumsy capitals, but Amy's writing book was a thing of beauty. Every letter was the perfect size, the perfect slant, the perfect tapering from thick strokes to thin and back. I only hope when she grew up, she didn't end up washing dishes or scrubbing floors for a living.

CHAPTER 10

For as long as I could remember, I had heard talk about compensation for Grandfather's accident. Sometimes the talk flared into arguments. The years were passing. If he didn't stir himself and do something, then he would never get a penny, let alone the hefty sum the family was certain he was due. But Grandfather was old and tired, and anyway, his union was handling it. He had faith in them.

Grandfather and Grandmother.

The first post came before I went to school. That morning, Mother picked it up when she went to bring up the jug of milk from the front step. There was only one envelope. It was addressed to Ernest Leopard, Snr.

Grandmother took it without hesitation. She opened any letter addressed to Grandfather or Eric or any of my three aunts. If any of them complained, she snapped back that they had no reason to protest unless they had something nasty to hide.

There was a cheque in the envelope. It was for three hundred pounds.

I didn't go to school that morning. Everyone forgot about me in their furious indignation. Three hundred pounds! It was an insult to an old man who would never work again. Somebody had to do something about it.

Grandmother did something. She levered her sagging bulk out of her armchair, put on her fur coat with the bunch of artificial violets pinned to the front, skewered her bird-of-paradise hat to her head and gathered up her handbag.

She took Violet with her, possibly because she was the quietest of her daughters, and they went in a taxi. The neighbours were very impressed.

Where she went and who she saw, I do not know, but it was hours before she came back. As she walked in the front door, I was bundled upstairs and Mother flew down again to join in the noisy argument that had already broken out.

Grandmother had failed. The union had done their best. Mr Leopard should think himself lucky to get three hundred pounds.

For the next two days, when I came home from school, I was told Grandmother wasn't well. She was very upset.

I wondered if Grandfather was upset too, but no-one mentioned him. Grandmother sat slumped in her armchair, lank grey hair falling across her face, her handbag clutched in her lap. I wondered if she was going to die, but every time a meal was put in front of her, she cleared the plate.

On the third day, she called for her fur coat and ordered Violet to take the morning off work and book a taxi.

I know it wasn't a school day, so I imagine it must have been a Saturday. Grandfather came up to sit with me and I read my comic to him, but half the time he didn't seem to be listening.

When I asked him where Grandmother had gone, he said, "I don't know, lass. I wish to God I did."

He found out that afternoon when she got back. Grandmother made no attempt to soften the blow. She had accepted that three hundred pounds was all the compensation he was going to get, so she had paid his cheque into her bank account, then gone round to the offices of the Orient Shipping Line and booked four passages. She was going to Australia on the next ship and she was taking her three daughters with her.

Mother ordered Father to take me to our room. I ran ahead of him, crying bitterly, apprehensive but not understanding.

He stayed with me, listening at the half-open door to the confusion below. Father kept out of family quarrels unless Mother screamed for his back-up. When that happened, he would eventually climb back up the stairs, white-faced and shivering, and lay on the floor to recover.

The house had quietened a little when he took me downstairs to go to the lavvy.

I could hear Eric in the basement pleading with his mother not to go. She had ruled him all his life. She had kept him at her beck and call, taught him to rely on her completely, and now she was walking out on him.

In the bedroom upstairs, Mother screamed at my aunts that they ought to be ashamed of themselves, and as we crossed the yard to the lavvy, Grandfather sat on the concrete crying.

Father didn't say a word to him. I was seven years old. There are some memories that never fade.

Grandfather stood beside me at my window the day they left. He watched the cabin trunks and suitcases full of new clothes being carried out. He watched Grandmother settle herself into the taxi. I don't know where Mother was, but Father was at work and Eric was in the pub getting drunk.

Grandmother had not deigned to join in the arguments that had raged for the past weeks. She had been too busy. Ornaments, pictures, all manner of oddments unearthed from cluttered cupboards, even the bead curtain in the passage, had been carted round to Uncle's shop in the High Street. Suddenly she hadn't cared what the neighbours thought. Money was more important than dignity. She needed every penny she could get to finance her new life.

"She will be all right," Grandfather said quietly as the taxi drove off. "She's taken the girls with her. They'll get work and look after her."

All my life I had been taught it was wicked to hate, but at that moment I hated my grandmother with such intensity I didn't even feel guilty.

Grandfather seemed to understand.

"Don't worry about me, love. God will look after me," he said simply.

That wasn't Mother's opinion. God didn't come into it. Her father, penniless, and her brother, an alcoholic, had been dumped on her. She would have to cook and clean for them while her mother and sisters swanned off to a new, carefree life.

As if living in poverty with a bald man wasn't enough for an attractive young woman to bear.

Her anger was beyond belief. In her frustration, she raved and shouted at the top of her voice, oblivious to the listening neighbours, and no-one knew how to calm her.

Grandfather prayed. When Father came home from work, he lay on the floor, white-faced and shaking, and Eric crawled back from the pub and fell into a drunken sleep in an armchair.

For two days, I didn't go to school and at night, Grandfather came up and put Cecil and me to bed.

The house was bare and lonely and unfamiliar. Eventually, Mother calmed, but her anger didn't go away. It was always there, just under the surface, ready to bubble up at the least provocation.

She scrubbed and cleaned and dusted, she washed and boiled and mangled. She shopped as best she could with what little money there was and every night, she put a meal on the table for Eric and Grandfather.

But, night after night, Eric didn't come back from the pub and his meal dried up in the oven.

It was Ernie who broke the news that Eric had lost his job. He had been employed as a painter and his boss was not the type to put up with an employee who staggered in half-drunk every morning.

Uncle Ernie and his wife, Ida, lived in rooms in a house a few streets away. Ernie was small and quiet and limped. Ida was a big, buxom blonde who loved flashy clothes and had a laugh that could echo from one end of the street to the other.

Mother couldn't stand her.

"Common as dirt," she said. "Straight from the gutter."

Maybe she was, but she was always the centre of attention in the pub.

Ernie came alone to break the news about Eric, but he and Ida had been talking. He had a proposition to make. He earned his living as a window cleaner and he had his own barrow and ladders, but with his gammy leg he always had trouble with upstairs windows.

He would be willing to take Eric on as a partner if he could put up enough money to buy more ladders.

Grandfather never hesitated. He sold the piano. Mother wasn't happy, but the old man was sure he was doing the right thing. Perhaps it was what Eric needed. The responsibility of running his own business might be good for him.

Grandma didn't need the piano anymore. She hadn't even

written. She was where she had always wanted to be, and he was left to care for Eric.

When the piano had gone, and the new ladders arrived, Ida had another idea. Ernie was paying rent to house the barrow at night. Why not park it in the yard behind Grandfather's house? The two of them, Eric and Ernie, could easily man-handle it through the passage and down the stairs into the yard every night and morning.

Grandfather agreed. The next week Ernie and Ida moved into rooms a few houses further along Swan Street and the pub at the corner became their local. The three of them, Ida, Ernie and Eric, drank there each night until closing time.

Eric's birthday was a few weeks later and Ida made a big thing of it, encouraging the regulars in the bar to sing "Happy Birthday."

It didn't end there. At closing time, she invited everyone to stock up with booze and come along to Eric's house to continue the festivities. The rowdy party went on until well into the early hours. The piano gone, they sang to an accordion accompanied by the spoons.

Next morning, there were drunks sprawled on the stairs and vomit in the parlour and all through the passage.

Grandfather placated Mother and helped to clear up. He would have a word with Eric, he promised. It would never happen again.

But it did. A few weeks later. Then a few weeks after that. Soon, every Saturday night, the house was invaded by a drunken party.

Mother raised hell, but Ida matched her in abuse. She could mind her own business. It was Eric's home as much as it was hers. She was only another lodger in Grandfather's house. It was up to the old man.

The lodgers in the top flat had enough. Poor and common, they might be, but they had some standards. They moved out.

Grandfather begged Mother not to do the same. He promised he would be strong. It was his house. He would put an end to the rowdy invasions. He was old, but he still had his strength and the raging temper he had fought so long to control. Reluctantly, he admitted to Mother that he was afraid.

If a gang of drunks goaded him far enough, he was afraid he might kill one of them.

For Mother, that was the last straw.

CHAPTER 11

There were few rooms to let at a price we could afford to pay, but Father did his best. He found one in a drab terrace house. It was a long walk from Swan Street and I had to change schools, but the room was clean and there was a gas-stove on the landing outside.

From the moment we moved in, Mother hated the place. Father pleaded with her to cope until he could find something better. He knew her, and he was afraid. While her anger still boiled, the least little provocation could cause an explosion.

My new school was much the same as the one I had left except I knew no-one. I was ahead of the other pupils in my lessons, and I sensed they resented it. Soon I learned not to shoot my hand up when I knew an answer, and to dawdle over my sums, so I wasn't the first to finish.

I didn't want any trouble. Strangely, I was happier at school than I had ever been, thanks to the teacher. She was young, pretty, and dressed all in black. Her mother had just died, and she looked sad.

When she took us for a drawing lesson, I felt she was my friend. Year after year, sitting at the window in Swan Street, I had drawn and coloured and painted on any scrap of paper I could find. No-one had ever noticed what I did, and in my mother's impatience to clear up, my efforts had all disappeared into the dustbin.

My new teacher was different. She praised and encouraged me. She had wanted to be an artist herself, she told me, but she hadn't had the chance. If I worked hard, things might be different for me.

Each afternoon, one pupil stayed behind for a few minutes to help the teacher clear up. When it was my turn and we were alone, she showed me some of her pictures. To me, they were exquisite.

As I made my way out of school, I was happy. I still wanted to be a singer and a dancer, but now I wanted to be an artist too. One day, I would paint beautiful pictures.

In a corner of the playground, a gang of girls from my class were waiting for me.

"Teacher's pet," they yelled and pulled the ribbon out of my hair. One of them slapped me, another tripped me up.

For the first time in my life, I saw red. I hit out at the nearest face. There was a scream and next moment the caretaker grabbed me and took me to the headmistress. I went home with a letter summoning my mother to the school next morning because I had been fighting.

Father cried when he saw the letter. Mother exploded. Her pent-up anger poured out in a stream of abuse that echoed around the neighbourhood.

Screaming that she could take no more and was going to throw herself into the river, she slammed out of the door. Father moved to go after her, but his legs crumpled beneath him and he sank to the floor, shaking pitifully.

We moved a few days later. Another school, another room in another unwelcoming terrace house, another landlady to irritate my mother, and mice, lots of mice.

By the third move, every penny my parents had saved

over the years had been spent on moving vans. The fourth move was at Christmas and our 'divvy' from the Co-op paid for it.

Then, early one Sunday morning, Eric arrived at the front door. He looked thin and agitated. Grandfather was ill. He begged Mother to come back and nurse him. There was no-one else. He wouldn't let Ida near him.

Mother didn't give in easily. For hours, she raved about the way she had been treated. Then she made him swear that none of his drunken mates would ever come back to the house again. And that included Ida.

Eric would have agreed to anything. He even put up the money for the moving van.

Father didn't say anything. He just looked ill.

It took weeks for Grandfather to recover. We were back in our old room, the same furniture back in the same places, the same view out of the same window. It was as though the past months had been a nightmare best forgotten except that I couldn't forget the teacher who believed that one day I might paint beautiful pictures.

By the time Grandfather was well enough to come down and sit beside the kitchen fire, the house had been scrubbed from top to bottom, mostly by Eric, while my mother stood over him. Ernie had learned that if he wanted the privilege of keeping the window cleaning barrow in the yard, then he would have to clean the passage night and morning.

My mother.

Mother was feeling better. I'm sure she enjoyed being in control.

The letter came out of the blue. It was nearly a year since Grandmother had left and there had been no word from her until then.

She and my aunts were coming back to England. They would be sailing in three weeks. The envelope had been sent by sea mail, so it was at least a month since it had been posted, which meant they were already on their way.

I braced myself, sure the letter would trigger an angry outburst or another argument. But there was nothing. Only a numb silence as the letter was passed from hand to hand.

"Why?" Mother demanded at last. "Why are they coming back?"

No-one answered. No-one knew.

"I suppose I'll have to buy her another piano." Eric sighed.

They arrived at Tilbury three weeks later. Grandfather felt someone ought to go to meet them, but no-one volunteered.

Father was a bag of nerves. He helped clean the house and begged Mother to make it a happy homecoming. It was a difficult thing to ask. She didn't believe in forgiving or forgetting.

To be fair, Mother did her best. She cooked a meal for the whole family, excluding Ida and Ernie, and laid up the big table in the basement kitchen.

The travellers arrived in a flurry of luggage and chatter, filling the house with confusion. I remember Trixie saying I had grown while she was away. That was all. There were no kisses, no hugs, no little presents.

The only time I had eaten at the kitchen table with all the family was at Christmas dinner each year. Then coloured paper chains and bunches of bright balloons had chased away the gloom.

Now, there was nothing to brighten the blankness of the grubby walls and shadows crept in from the corners of the room and settled above the circle of heads bent over their piled plates.

To me, silence was frightening. It was unnatural in our family and heralded trouble.

Mother held her patience for as long as she could before asking the question.

"Why have you come back?"

Grandmother looked up.

"Money." She was still eating. "Violet, you've finished. You tell them."

Violet did, with constant interruptions from Trixie and Edith.

She explained that work was scarce in Western Australia. All three aunts had ended up working as cleaners in the Perth Public Hospital. It had been hard work, long hours, and little pay.

Until one day, another cleaner had persuaded Violet to go to a fortune teller. Not one of those fraud ones you see in fairgrounds. This one had been a respectable woman living in a nice house in the suburbs. She only took clients by recommendation and she only charged two shillings a sitting.

The fortune teller told Violet that one day she would be rich. Hearing that, Trixie immediately booked a sitting. She was told the same thing. Soon, Edith was assured the hard times were nearly over and she could look forward to a life of luxury.

Thoroughly excited, the aunts took Grandmother for a look into the future. The fortune teller had been even more enthusiastic about her prospects. She was due to come into a great deal of money. When plied with questions, she had said vaguely that the money was somewhere across the sea.

That had been enough for Grandmother. It could only mean the Blackmore Estates and the money that had been put into Chancery when she was young. She had been a fool to give up on it. There must still be a way to prove she was the rightful heir. All she needed was to get back to England and find a good lawyer.

"And money?" Mother asked sharply. "What did you do for money?"

Violet told us Grandmother hadn't hesitated. She had written to Edmund and Albert, her two eldest sons living in Victoria. She told them she needed money for passages to

England and to hire a lawyer. If they could provide enough to cover that, then the moment she got her inheritance, they would both be entitled to a share.

I went to bed joyful that night.

Everything had changed. My life was going to be like a fairy story. No princes or princesses, of course, and no beautiful castles, but we were going to be rich. All the family. Very rich. And that meant there would be no more problems. No petty irritations, no arguments, no fights. Just happy ever after...

I had no idea what Chancery meant, just as I had no idea about my grandmother's history, but it didn't matter. We were going to be rich. I was nine years old and still believed in fairies.

Happiness is a strange thing. We want it so much that we bask blindly in the warm prospect of it, blissfully ignoring the obvious signs that it is about to be shattered.

I was back at my old school and glad to be there, but I didn't tell any of my friends about our impending wealth. Perhaps I didn't want to make them envious. Or perhaps I was afraid they would turn against me.

I expected Mother to be as happy as I was, but she didn't seem to be, and neither did Father. They talked together a lot in whispers, his face white and pinched and hers flushed with the old anger.

The rest of the family didn't seem happy either. As the weeks and months passed, there were long discussions about how things should be handled and angry arguments broke out about who knew best and whose advice Grandmother ought to take.

She rarely seemed to listen. Now and then she told them all to go to Hell. No-one told me anything, but she seemed to be having trouble with the lawyers.

Then, one night about six months after she came back from Australia, I was sent to bed early. Cecil was already asleep, and I crept halfway down the stairs in my nightie and listened.

The bedlam of angry voices in the kitchen was as wild as it had ever been in the old days, but Violet's voice topped the lot.

"We haven't got a hope. That's what they say. All of them. We haven't got a bloody hope in hell of getting anything."

It was a long time later that my parents came up. Mother was crying. She didn't even look to see if I was awake.

"I mean it this time," she screamed. "I've had enough. I'm going to throw myself in the river."

When I fell asleep, Father was still trying to talk her out of it, still pleading and barring the door.

CHAPTER 12

I was terrified that one day Mother really would throw herself in the river. While I was at school and Father was at work, she was left alone all day with my little brother.

What if she walked out and left him? What would happen then? Or if he started off down the stairs and fell through the long window like poor Hettie?

I couldn't talk to Father. He was ill with worry already. I wanted to talk to Grandfather, but since Grandmother had come back from Australia, he had changed. He seemed suddenly to have grown very old.

Trixie was my only hope, but she wasn't interested.

"Take no notice," she said. "Everybody gets fed up sometimes. Silly bitch. Next thing you know, she'll try putting her head in the gas oven."

I didn't go to school for the rest of the week. I told Mother I had dreadful pains in my stomach and stayed at home playing with Cecil.

On Saturday, I heard a furious row break out downstairs. From the moment she arrived back, Grandmother had resented the window cleaning barrow being hauled through her clean hallway. Now she had had enough. Ernie would have to find somewhere else to park his barrow.

Grandmother was adamant, but Ernie refused to give in. Eric hesitated in the doorway, reluctant to incur his mother's wrath while Ida stood on the pavement and hurled abuse at her equally abusive mother-in-law.

Finally, Ernie tried to force the issue, jolting the swaying barrow up over the doorstep and sending it careering along the passage. It slewed around. A wheel hit the wall and gouged a deep gash out of the rose-patterned paper. The impact tilted the ladders, and they scraped wildly along, gathering every one of Grandmother's pictures and flinging them in a shattered heap on the passage floor.

It was the end. Reinforcements arrived in the shape of my three aunts. Within minutes, and with a crescendo of screaming and swearing, the barrow was hauled out of the passage and tossed unceremoniously into the gutter.

It was only much later, when the confusion had died down, that Mother realised Father had not come home.

He only worked a half day on Saturday and was usually back before two o'clock. It was three o'clock already, and she was angry. By four o'clock, she started to panic. At five o'clock, she had pulled on her coat, ready to head to the police station, when he came through the front door, a big smile on his face.

He had been offered a flat. A really nice flat.

It was unbelievable, like the sudden happy ending of a cheap novelette, when, out of the blue, every wrong is righted and everyone lives happily ever after.

The manager of the coal depot, where Father worked as a clerk, had a daughter. Newly married, she needed somewhere to live, and he had decided to put a deposit on a house and let it as two flats. Being a thrifty man, he saw an opportunity to acquire a property which was paid for by two grateful tenants.

His daughter preferred the top flat, which left him in need of someone to rent the ground floor.

Of all the clerks in the office, his eye had fallen on my father. For all his faults, he was a quiet, inoffensive man, always polite and well-mannered. That, combined with the fact he was married with a family, made him the ideal candidate.

Father was delighted until he heard how much rent would be expected. He need not have worried. The manager was not one to allow a minor problem to spoil his plans. He had already complained to the head office that as the business was growing, he needed help. If Father chose to move into the flat, he could be promoted to assistant manager with a wage increase that would cover the extra rent and bus fares.

Looking back, it's strange how often it is the self-interest of others that shapes our lives.

A few weeks later, we moved out of Grandmother's house, out of Swan Street, out of the East End, into a paradise called East Ham.

The house was in a clean, suburban street where no children played because there was a garden at the back of each property. There was a garden at the front, too, just enough to grow a hedge, and behind the hedges, every window had a white lace curtain.

Compared to our old room, the empty flat seemed huge and strange. We whispered as we walked from the parlour to the bedroom and then to the kitchen. There was even a lavatory, just for us, and the manager explained that if, perhaps once a week, we wanted a bath, we could come to an arrangement with his daughter to use the bathroom in the upstairs flat.

The strip of garden on the right-hand side of the path was ours to plant as we wished, and as if that were not enough, Father was now the assistant manager of the coal depot.

Life was so calm, it seemed unreal. Mother was happy. For the first time, she and Father had not only a bed, but a bedroom to themselves. For the moment, it held nothing except the big brass bed, but we had very little furniture and other rooms were more important. A couple of extra wooden chairs to stand around the table would be enough for the kitchen, but the parlour was different.

Visitors were invited into the parlour and Mother intended to make it as attractive as possible. Of course, there had to be a bed in the corner for Cecil and me, but it was very narrow and could easily be disguised beneath a spread of cushions. Dolls, toys, books, all our childish treasures were kept in the kitchen in a box under the table.

The parlour became Mother's obsession. She had to have the same white lace curtains as all the neighbours, parquet patterned linoleum, a hearthrug, and a three-piece suite, the sort of thing she had envied in shop windows all her married life, something modern and expensive-looking.

Father suggested a second-hand shop in the High Street, but Mother was disgusted. She put a deposit on a burgundy three-piece suite covered in fashionable uncut moquette, a black curly pile hearthrug, and two small tables and arranged for the furniture store to spread the repayments over as many years as possible.

Father cried when she told him.

To give Mother her due, she worked hard to achieve her dreams. She made curtains out of old bedspreads and cushion covers from old dresses. Everything was sewn by hand. Sometimes, when Cecil and I came home from school, we found her singing as she stitched.

I don't know how much Father's wages increased when he became assistant manager, but he rarely seemed happy. Mostly, he looked tired and worn. In the evenings, he ate the meal Mother had prepared for him, then went straight to bed, and when he took off his wig, he looked old and shrunken.

There were times when he looked content, when he marked out little squares on our side of the garden for Cecil and me and helped us plant seeds in neat rows. And when winter came, he took us to the common and let us watch the skaters on the lake until Cecil turned blue with the cold and we had to run him all the way home before Mother saw him.

I was growing up and as the months passed, I understood more about my parents. Sometimes I wished Father would talk to me, but he was always a secretive soul.

I had already discovered it was a serious heart complaint that kept him out of the army when so many of his peers marched off to war.

Now I realised he was a gambler. He loved the "gee-gees" as he called them and although Mother refused to waste money on newspapers, I knew he brought old ones home from work and hid them under the mattress. Sometimes I caught him studying the racing pages.

I'm sure Mother must have known. Nothing he did, right or wrong, escaped her eagle eye and there were sudden flare-ups when Cecil and I would be banished to the kitchen away from the hiss of angry voices.

Occasionally, the mood changed and on Saturday afternoon, when Father came home from work, we would go to the shops and Mother would choose something new, a picture or a vase maybe, for the parlour. Then I would guess the "gee-gees" had been kind to him.

~

My new school was much the same as the one I had left, a big, three-storeyed building, boys at the top, girls in the middle and infants on the ground floor. The three layers never mixed, not even at playtimes. One group would be ushered inside before another was let out into the playground. Except for one day of the year.

On Empire Day, the entire school assembled in the playground. A rickety wooden dais was erected by the caretaker and on it sat the headmaster dressed as John Bull and one of the teachers wearing the flowing robes of Britannia, complete with gold-painted helmet and trident.

Any girl with a white dress was invited to join the choir singing loud, patriotic songs while boys gave an exhibition of military marching up and down the playground. As a finale, a local dignitary made a speech telling us how lucky we were to be British and calling for three hearty cheers for our Glorious Empire.

One thing made me unhappy.

I was always late for school. I was never there when the register was called and there was always a big black mark put against my name. Every day I had to stand in the corridor red faced, panting and ashamed, while morning prayers were said in the hall.

I tried to explain that I had to bring my little brother, Cecil, to school with me, but Mother never had him ready on time.

Inevitably, the harsh clang of the school bell echoed across the streets before she deemed him clean and polished and perfect.

Cecil was a blue-eyed, blonde little lad with a round face and she adored him, fussing over him more than she had ever fussed over me. I didn't care about that. I loved him too, but I did care about the school bell.

Every morning, I snatched Cecil's hand and ran along the street, across the main road and along more streets, and all the time my heart would be in my mouth while I prayed the bell didn't stop. There was an awful silence when it did, like the hush of impending doom, and we were late yet again.

I begged Mother to help me be early for school, but I'm sure she never understood my frustration. She didn't know how often I choked back tears as I dragged Cecil along the streets. Sometimes, when I complained, she would nod her head impatiently, but mostly she didn't seem to listen.

Sophie was always early. She lived across the road from us and was in my class. She had long golden curls, but they were natural and didn't have to be rolled up around old collars every night like mine. Her teeth were straight and white and her ears didn't stick out, not even a little bit.

Sophie was always clean and tidy. There was a perfection about her that Mother envied and that I, joining in wholeheartedly with every rough and tumble game in the playground, could never achieve.

Yet Mother tried, unashamedly, to model me upon her. When she heard Sophie was learning the violin, I was enrolled with the local music teacher and Father had to find the money to buy a second-hand fiddle.

It didn't matter that the last thing I wanted was to play the violin. Every evening, I was locked, protesting, into the parlour for an hour to practise.

I knew I would never be like Sophie, but I made up my mind to beat her in anything I could, so my mother would be proud of me.

I did. I came top of the class and landed the leading part in the school end-of-year play. Mother was delighted. She was so proud she paid the bus fares for Grandmother and my three aunts to come to see me perform. I played a Greek goddess, and I revelled in every moment,

Hilda in her school play.

Next day, I was surprised and a little apprehensive to be called to the headmistress's room. I need not have worried. A member of the local amateur dramatic society had seen my performance. There was a part for a child in the next play they were staging. Would my parents allow me to audition for it?

I walked my brother home from school that day with my head in the clouds. I was going to be a dancer and a singer and an artist and now I wanted to be an actress as well.

My parents were arguing when I got home. Mother sent Cecil and me straight to the kitchen and we were stuck in there for hours. Eventually, Father went to bed without eating.

When Mother slapped our meals down on the table, we ate them without a word. She was wearing her coat and hat and when she had bundled us into bed, she turned out the light and slammed the front door.

I laid awake for a long time thinking of the river and wondering if I should call Father, but I knew he would only cry.

The fingernails on my left hand were chewed and bleeding when I woke the next morning and there was a row of little holes across the sheet where I had gnawed at it in my agitation. It wasn't the first time that had happened, and I dreaded Mother discovering them.

She was in the kitchen making porridge. I could tell by the way she stirred it she was still angry, but I told her my news.

She didn't say anything. I thought she hadn't heard, so I told her again.

When she turned around, her eyes were red and puffy, but she didn't look sad. She looked angrier than I had ever seen her before.

"I heard you the first time," she snapped. "I don't know what they've been filling your head with at school. No! I don't care what anyone says, we're a respectable family and I'm not having you getting mixed up with a bunch of theatricals."

CHAPTER 13

The furniture van came a few days later while I was at school.

When I came home, the three-piece suite had gone from the parlour. So had the black rug and the two little tables. Only the linoleum was still in place. No-one wanted second-hand linoleum that had been tacked to the floorboards.

"It's all gone back to the shop." Mother answered my question without looking at me.

"Why?"

"Because we don't need it anymore. We're going back to live in Swan Street."

I couldn't believe it.

"But why?"

"Your grandmother is going back to Australia."

There was a finality in her voice I didn't understand. I pestered her with questions, but she pushed me aside and walked away.

When Father came home, they didn't speak to each other. They didn't speak to Cecil and me either, and in the awful silence, I knew it was true. We were going back to Swan Street.

We took back only what we had brought with us. All the little extras Father had bought to please Mother, the pictures, the vases, the brush and poker set that had stood beside the parlour fireplace, the beaded light shade, they were all sold to the second-hand shop in the high street, everything except the narrow bed that Cecil and I shared and the parquet linoleum.

Mother sat on the floor and prised all the tacks out of it, then carefully rolled it up and took it with her. Perhaps she resented leaving it for the landlord. I don't know. It was always difficult to follow the workings of my mother's mind.

We went back to the same room, the same dark varnished wallpaper, the same window staring down into the same street. Mother, despite her temper and her moods, had always done her best to make a home out of what little we had. This time, she didn't bother. The beds were put up and the table and the wooden chairs squeezed into the space that was left. Only the necessities, china, cutlery and saucepans, were unpacked. The rest, still in boxes, was pushed under the big bed.

Nothing had changed. Most of the time, Grandmother sat in her usual sagged heap in the basement kitchen, clutching her handbag on her lap. She sold everything in the house, every piece of furniture, every utensil, knick-knack, picture, everything. Dealers came to the front door and made offers, but mostly she ridiculed them, swearing they were trying to cheat her. She needed every penny she could get to finance the journey back to Australia.

Otherwise, everything was the same. Petty differences between my aunts flared into violent arguments. Eric escaped to the pub every night and staggered back, drunk. Grandfather, with his flickering candle, searched the house for Minnie, and in the backyard, Charlie's rickety cage slowly fell to pieces.

It was only when I went back to school that I felt happy. My old friends were glad to see me and so were the teachers. Even the headmistress welcomed me, saying it was good to have me back.

It was scholarship entry time. She had chosen a few pupils she felt were worth putting through the exam, and she added my name to the list.

I didn't tell Mother. I didn't think she would be interested, but I did tell Grandfather. He listened and smiled, and for a moment, he looked his old, cheerful self.

"Don't worry too much, love," he said quietly. "God will sort everything out. He always does in the end."

Nine of us were sent to sit the scholarship examination, four boys and five girls. Ours was a poor school in a poverty-stricken area, but the headmistress had her pride. Like a mother hen, she inspected both boys and girls. Boots were polished, hair combed, ribbons tied into neat bows, even fingernails were cut and cleaned.

In the privacy of her office, we were overhauled and inspected and not until she felt we were fit to represent our school were we handed over to the teacher who was to escort us on the tram.

In the days that followed, Mother changed. She barely spoke to Father, but she became more decisive and she waited in the passage each morning until the postman's rat-a-tat came at the door.

But she made no attempt to unpack the boxes in our room.

One morning, I was early for school. Cecil and I were waiting outside the big iron gates when the caretaker came to unlock them. We were the first children to be let in. It was the only time it ever happened.

No-one told me anything, so I had no idea why Mother had packed us off so early. Not that I cared. I was happy to be with the rest in the hall instead of standing in the corridor when the headmistress took her place at the rostrum.

She led the prayers as usual, then beamed around at us. She had some wonderful news. One of the children who sat the scholarship examination had triumphed. Hilda Spear had been awarded a scholarship to St Olaves School for girls.

I remember every head in the hall turning, everyone's eyes being on me, then the headmistress went on, "This is a significant achievement for a school like ours and to celebrate it, we are all, boys, girls and infants, going to take the day off."

The outburst of cheering was deafening. A teacher put an arm round me and led me out of the crowd and up to the headmistress. As I stood wide-eyed at her side, there were three hearty cheers for me before the children surged out of school.

The headmistress took me to her office.

"I know it's all confusing," she said gently, "but I want to explain. This is a marvellous opportunity for you. You will go to an outstanding school and there will be no expense for your parents. Uniforms, books, sports equipment, everything will be provided free. You will be able to learn languages, music, anything you want, and later on, who knows, you might even go to university."

She smiled at me.

"Now, I know you can't wait to go home and tell your parents. Don't forget to tell them your name will be put up in gold letters on the Honours Board in the hall."

I walked home in a daze, with Cecil at my side. He was excited and kept asking me questions, but I didn't have the answers. It didn't matter. It would all make sense later. I was revelling in the moment. For once, I felt important.

The streets were full of children, all heading home. Children I hardly knew waved to me, and mothers, surprised by the sudden invasion, stared at me from their open doors.

For the first time in my life, I had achieved something important, and it felt wonderful. At last, Mother would be proud of me. I was sure she would. The thought warmed me and I imagined her boasting to all the neighbours.

Only my grandparents were at home when we got back. Before I could stop him, Cecil raced down to the basement, shouting the news as he went. Grandmother was asleep and woke with a start, confused and irritated by the intrusion.

Hastily, Grandfather ushered us up to our room.

"Stay here. Your parents will be back soon," he said and went down to placate Grandmother.

I didn't care. I was too happy for anything to dampen my excitement. When my parents came home, I met them at the front door. I had won a scholarship. I was going to a big, important school. One day I might go to university. I tried to blurt everything out before I was hurried back upstairs.

My parents listened, and I told them everything I knew, everything the headmistress had told me, even about the gold name on the Honours Board. I only stopped when I was too breathless to go on.

I expected them to be pleased, proud, delighted, all the things I was feeling, but they were silent.

After a moment, Mother put her arms round me. It was something she never did, and it took me by surprise.

"Tomorrow," I went on, "you have to come to school and sign the papers. I'm going to have everything, books, sports clothes, everything."

There was a long pause, then Mother drew away from me.

"I'm sorry," she said.

I didn't understand.

"You only have to sign the papers..."

But Mother shook her head.

"You're a clever girl, but... I'm sorry. You can't take the scholarship."

My stomach lurched.

"But it won't cost anything. Nothing..."

"I'm sorry," Mother said again. "We're going to Australia with your grandmother. All of us. Everything's arranged."

I didn't want to go to Australia. I knew nothing about it except that it was on the other side of the world and it was part of the British Empire. Beyond that, it was a vague place inhabited by strange-looking animals.

I didn't want to go to Australia, and I didn't want to go to school either. The head mistress and my teachers were openly disappointed in me and my classmates plied me with questions. Why was I going to Australia? What was wrong with England? The children of the East End, like their parents, were aggressively outspoken and fiercely patriotic. From being the centre of attention, I became a traitor.

I loved England. I had been taught to love it. It was my country. But looking back, I see now that I knew little more about England than I did about Australia.

Except for the one brief stay at East Ham, which is in the suburbs of London, my knowledge of my own country was confined to Swan Street, the poverty-stricken area around The Elephant and Castle, one trip down the Thames to the sea and an excursion to the country to pick bluebells.

I knew so little, yet somehow, from the books at school, the pictures on Grandmother's walls, snippets of overheard conversations, and from my beloved Tiger Tim's Weekly, I had built up pictures in my mind. Endless green fields, dappled with wild flowers, stone churches, leafy woodlands and quaint villages, rivers lined with weeping willows where ladies with parasols drifted in punts, and huge breath-taking white cliffs lapped by the sea. That was my England, and I didn't want to leave it.

Neither did Eric. The last thing he wanted to do was to go to Australia. He argued, he swore, he drank himself into a stupor. Perhaps he saw it as a last chance to break away from his mother.

But he had been ruled by her for too long. In the end, crying bitterly, he gave in. She packed his clothes, sent him to get a haircut, then locked him in the house the night before we sailed to keep him sober.

Ernie could find another partner to join him in the window-cleaning business, she said. He could sell Eric's half and send on the money. But he never did.

No-one was interested in what I wanted. No-one listened, and no-one told me why we had to go to Australia. It was a long time, and I was on the other side of the world before I found out.

Father had never won on the "gee-gees". He had lost heavily, but, like all addicted gamblers, he had clung to the fantasy that his next bet would be the winning one. When he ran out of money, he found another way to keep gambling.

As a trusted employee, it was his responsibility to pay into the bank all the cash handled at the coal depot. The temptation had been too much. One big win was all it would have taken to change our fortunes and let him pay back the money he had borrowed from the firm.

But he didn't win.

The day he learned the auditors were due to check the accounts, he had been desperate enough to confess to Mother.

He was too weak to own up to his crime, and she was too proud to face the prospect of a husband in prison. Flight was the only answer. Mother's family was going to Australia. We must go too.

When Father enquired at Australia House, the waiting list for would-be immigrants was long. Too long. But there was another way. They could be nominated if a relative or friend already in Australia was willing to guarantee to be there to help them when they stepped off the boat, to provide accommodation and work, and to deal with any difficulties they might meet. If we were nominated, we could go to the top of the waiting list. We could even go on the same boat as Grandmother.

That was when Grandmother had taken over. Annie, the daughter she sent to Western Australia as a young girl, had married a farmer on the wheat belt.

He was poor, but Annie was a simple soul and had been content to share an earth-floored shack with the pigs and chickens, her two little daughters and her beloved husband.

But tragedy struck. Their land had been ravaged by locusts, and fighting to destroy them, her husband, Dermott, had used arsenic. Within days, he was dead from arsenic poisoning.

Left alone, Annie had been grateful for the help of the owner of the next farm, a widower. She had two little girls to care for and no husband. He had three small boys to bring up and no wife. His farm was successful and his house was large and comfortable. Soon they were married.

It was convenient. There was no love, but Annie didn't complain. She still loved Dermott and kept a portrait of him under the marital bed. When Jack, her new husband, was away working on the vast expanse of the farm, she hung Dermott's portrait above the bed and went to sleep content.

It was Jack who nominated our family. He did it for Annie, but with the clear understanding that it was purely a formality and my parents were to ask nothing of him.

Perhaps because I did not know the real reason for our flight, I didn't accept the inevitability of what was happening.

In all the stories I read, there was always a happy ending. The most depressing situation was overturned at the last moment and everyone lived happily ever after.

I wanted that happy ending for us. I prayed. I clung to hope. I earnestly believed something would happen. A miracle would give me back my scholarship and make my dreams come true. I reasoned, quite humbly, that I had never done anything wicked. Surely God could spare me one miracle? If you are a believer, you go on believing right to the end. You can't help it.

I believed until the taxis drew up outside our empty house, the pile of luggage was crammed inside, and Grandfather, tears in his eyes, handed Minnie over to a neighbour.

I knew then that he would never see her again, just as I would never see Swan Street.

CHAPTER 14

The sun shone brightly the day we sailed. The dockside was a noisy confusion of people, more people than I had ever seen before, all overshadowed by the huge bulk of the liner docked alongside. People were laughing, some hugging each other in last tearful embraces, some waving or throwing bright streamers up to the passengers lining the rails high above us.

Our luggage was unloaded from the taxis and piled into a huge net spread out on the dock. Our only other item of luggage was already aboard. The amount we could take with us as nominees was limited, but we were allowed a little stowed away in the hold, to provide a few household items needed for a fresh start in our new country.

As far back as I could remember, Grandmother's sewing machine had stood in a dark corner of the basement kitchen. She wouldn't allow anyone but her no touch it. Not that my aunts had ever cared. They didn't make or mend, they didn't even sew a button back on. My mother did. She made clothes for Cecil and me out of other people's old ones, all by hand, while the sewing machine stood there, dusty and unused.

When she was clearing the house, Grandmother tried to

sell it. The sale of our furniture and possessions had brought little. The contribution demanded towards our fares had been nominal, but it still left almost nothing with which to start a new life. My mother offered a pound for the sewing-machine. When Grandmother could find no better offer, she grudgingly took it.

The wood from Charlie's old run was used to make a crate round the machine. In the space above the treadle, Mother packed a doll and a train set given to us by Auntie Edie, two saucepans, a frying pan, and, optimistically, a few pieces of crockery plus two ornaments. One was a mother-of-pearl rose bowl presented to her when she was married by the staff of the restaurant where she had worked. The other was a Wedgwood biscuit barrel, a wedding gift from Auntie Edie. She treasured them both. They were quality, the only possessions she had of any value.

The crate containing the sewing machine had been sent to the docks a few days before, and was already stowed in the hold. Apart from that, everything we possessed was crammed into two tatty second-hand cabin trunks. They contained bed-linen, a blanket each, and our meagre family wardrobes.

There was something else packed carefully among the clothes. It was a clock that had stood, ticking loudly, on the mantelpiece of the kitchen all my life and I had been told its history many times.

Way back in the family tree, a newly married couple had argued. The young husband bought the clock as a peace offering to his wife. Unfortunately, he had chosen a clock topped by a large German eagle, but his wife hated Germans.

In her anger, she threw the clock across the room. It missed him but smashed against a wall. The clock mechanism and the ornate case survived, but the eagle was broken off.

Apparently, the sight of the hated German eagle smashed

to pieces on the floor calmed the young woman's anger. After kissing and making up, the couple tossed the remains of the eagle into the fire and the clock became a family heirloom passed on from one generation to another.

When my grandmother first went to Australia, with no intention of returning, she had handed it over to my mother. Now there was no-one left to pass it to. Ida and Ernie had not even been considered, so there was no alternative but to pack it and take it with us.

On the dockside, the pile of luggage had grown. There were shouts, waved hand signals, and the net closed around it, then rose high into the air and swung it away out of sight.

Father held my hand as he watched it go. He gripped so tight it hurt. I wanted to pull away, but he looked ill. Perhaps his thoughts were the same as mine. Everything we possessed was loaded on to this great ship. Now, wherever it went, we had to go.

A uniformed man pushed his way through the crowd and touched Grandmother's arm. "First class gangplank this way, Madame," he said respectfully.

For a moment, she hesitated. Then she pulled her fur coat closer about her and scowled at the man.

"Third class," she snapped.

Behind her back, my aunts were overcome by giggles, but for once I was sorry for her.

She believed she belonged in first class and she could never forget it.

About two-thirds of the liner was given over to first class accommodation. The remaining third housed the immigrants, the nominees and the few fare-paying third-class passengers.

Once aboard, there were routines to be observed and queues. After a long wait, we were examined by the ship's doctor. It was a cursory affair. We had to brush our hair back from our faces and push up our sleeves. He glanced at our foreheads and our forearms, nodded and passed on to the next family.

More queues, and we were given our cabin number, our place numbers at the long tables in the dining room and leaflets telling us about shipboard life, the community bathrooms, the laundry room with its big washing tubs and the drying room festooned with rope lines where wet washing must be hung to dry.

And everywhere there were people, talking, questioning and confused. Grandmother and my aunts took it all in their stride. They were seasoned travellers by now and had little patience with the preliminaries.

For my part, I wanted to escape. All my life, I had been kept isolated. I wasn't used to crowds. I longed to find the cabin that would be our home for the next four weeks, the place where my parents and Cecil and I could shut the door and be alone together.

But it wasn't going to be like that.

Third class cabin accommodation was strictly segregated, male quarters in one area, female quarters in another. Grandmother and my aunts were together in a four-berth. Grandfather and Eric were not so lucky. They had to share with two other men.

It was even worse for Father. Six-year-old Cecil was a male, so he had to sleep in the male quarters in a six-berth cabin. Five men and one small, frightened boy in a space just big enough to hold six bunks, three up and three down.

Looking back, the journey must have been a nightmare for my father. He was already a nervous wreck. For weeks he had carried on with his job knowing that, at any moment, his guilt could be discovered.

I didn't understand then what it must have meant to him to hear the sirens blast, to feel the throb of the engines starting up and to know the liner was pulling away from the dockside.

He had never spent much time alone with his children, but now he had sole charge of my brother from bedtime to breakfast time. Cecil, timid and tearful, wanted his mother, but women were not allowed in the men's cabin area.

That must have been difficult enough, but Father had his own problems. He couldn't take his wig off and put it in a box under his bed as he always had done. He was too embarrassed to take it off at all. Instead, he climbed into the upper bunk, still wearing it, then snuggled down under the bedclothes. Once out of sight, he could take it off and tuck it under his pillow.

Father had always groomed his wig before putting it on in the morning, confident that, if he took proper care, no outsider would realise his hair was not real. But there was no mirror in the cabin and every morning when Mother first set eyes on him, she would be horrified.

While other passengers headed to the dining room and breakfast, she would whisk him around some quiet corner, to comb his wig and make him 'respectable'.

Cecil and Hilda onboard the SS Orama.

Mother and I shared with four others. I slept on a top bunk, she on the one below me and beneath that, on the floor, was stowed one of our cabin trunks. The second had been put in Father's cabin.

If Mother had known we would be segregated, she would have packed accordingly, but rearranging the contents of the trunks, separating clothes and necessities into male and female and transferring them, was difficult, and since Mother was not allowed in the men's area and Father was not allowed in the women's, exchanges had to be made in armfuls at the boundary between the two.

There was no other storage space but the trunk under the bed. When we pulled it out to repack it, or even to change our clothes, it took up practically all the floor space and the other occupants had to sit up on their bunks until we finished. One of them was a large lady with a temper as fierce as Mother's. Our cramped journey was going to last more than a month, so I was careful not to upset her.

In the dining room, meals were served in two sittings at long community tables amid an endless barrage of chatter.

As I had been taught it was bad manners to speak at a meal table, it was a revelation.

After the evening meal, large bowls of apples and oranges were placed along the centre of the tables and we were invited to take one piece each, which we could eat up on deck if we wished.

Supper was a mug of thick cocoa and a dry ship's biscuit, so hard it was impossible to break. Grandmother, knowing what to expect, had brought with her a teapot, packets of tea, sugar, sweet biscuits and a small jug. Every evening, she sent Eric, teapot and jug in hand, down to the galley for hot water and milk. I am sure she enjoyed the envious glances of others as much as she enjoyed lounging back in her deck-chair, sipping at her tea.

~

For the first few days, the whole atmosphere of the ship was a novelty, then life settled into a pattern. Men drank in the bar or carried their glasses out on deck and stood chatting or watched groups of card players gambling for pennies and half-pennies.

For women, life had a more normal pattern, mending, knitting, and caring for their children or organising games to keep them occupied. Many of them spent hours down in the washrooms, scrubbing in the big tubs, hanging out their washing on the rope lines, ironing and guarding their possessions. Few had enough that they could risk an item being stolen.

For the first time in my life, bathing was a delight. There was no tin tub before the fire, no arguments about who should carry the buckets of water up and down the stairs.

Even at East Ham, cleanliness had been a misery. Mother had never taken to the young couple in the flat above and the fact they had a bathroom and we didn't rankled with her from the beginning. She had hated having to ask permission to use it and eventually the tin bath had come back into use.

The liner could not carry enough fresh water for baths, so when the taps in the bathrooms were turned on, seawater gushed out. It was lovely and hot and there was as much as we wanted. The fact it was salty, and it was impossible to get a lather no matter how much soap you used, didn't spoil the experience at all.

There were some passengers who were seasick from the moment we pulled out into the open sea, but most of them managed to get as far as the Bay of Biscay. Then the rush began from the dining room to the doctor's surgery.

Eric was seasick. So were Father and Mother. At mealtimes, the crowds thinned and there were queues outside. Mother was worried, but Grandmother merely shrugged.

"No one dies of seasickness," she said. "It won't hurt them not to eat for a few days. They'll be alright as soon as we get out of the Bay."

On Sunday, an announcement rang out during breakfast. The captain would be holding an interdenominational church service in the dining room at 11 o'clock. Everyone was welcome.

I had heard of Protestants, Catholics, Anglicans, Wesleyans and Spiritualists, but I had never heard of Interdenominational.

Grandfather explained that Interdenominational meant it was a church service for any religion. He didn't explain any more than that, so I went with him. No-one else in the family was interested.

I had not said my prayers since I left England, and it worried me every night.

As far as I was aware, God and his Angels lived in Heaven, and Heaven was in the sky above us. I knew it was not restricted to the sky above Swan Street, I imagined it spreading out around it, hidden only by the canopy of the sky, unseen but always there.

That was why I had looked up when I talked to God. As long as God was above me, watching over me, I had felt safe.

But now, nothing felt safe.

I didn't want to admit it, even to myself, but I had stopped praying because I didn't feel God was with me anymore. I had left him behind. And as the liner carried me far away from everything I had ever known, I was afraid he would never find me again.

CHAPTER 15

We passed through the Straits of Gibraltar and into the Mediterranean. Our first port of call would be Toulon.

As we approached port, Grandmother's mood darkened. She loved to be the centre of attention with someone at hand if she needed anything from her cabin or to keep her deck-chair reserved on the rare occasions she chose to stretch her legs. It irritated her that my aunts had taken up with young immigrant men and spent most of their time with them. Not that my aunts cared. They were quite candid. They were always on the look-out for "good-looking rich fellas", but if there were none, they would make do with whoever was available.

When the ship docked at Toulon, all three aunts, dressed in their best, went ashore with their new boyfriends, leaving Grandmother behind. She was furious. My parents, reluctant to spend money on trips ashore, took the brunt of her anger.

All her old prejudices resurfaced. She hated the French. Why would her daughters want to go ashore in a country where men openly pee-ed in the gutter? Sometimes with their lady-friends clinging to their arms?

I don't know where she formed that belief. I would have been too embarrassed to ask, but I do know there was a terrible row in Grandmother's cabin that night when my aunts returned and stewards were called to calm things down.

After Toulon the weather became hotter and sailors put up awnings across the decks. The crew were always friendly and did everything they could to make the journey as pleasant as possible.

In the evenings, cabin stewards kept a watch on sleeping children and a piano was wheeled from its locker on the upper deck. A sailor played lively tunes for anyone in the mood for dancing and ended with a rousing sing-song.

Sometimes Mother allowed me to stay up and sit with her as she watched the dancers. Perhaps she felt lonely. Father put Cecil to bed soon after the evening meal and we didn't see either of them again until morning.

The temperature increased as we crossed the Mediterranean and headed for Port Said and the Suez Canal. Passengers on the lower decks, close to the engine room, complained about the heat in their cabins at night and brought their pillows and sheets up to sleep on deck. No-one seemed to mind as long as everything was cleared away for the sailors to hose down the decks in the morning.

It sounded like fun. I longed to sleep under the stars, but Mother wouldn't hear of it. She wasn't sleeping with a crowd of strangers and she certainly wouldn't allow Cecil and Father to do such a thing, even though their cabin was one deck below ours and they were both feeling the heat badly. Father tried to reason with her, but she was adamant.

I had learned about Egypt at school and knew exactly what to expect. There would be pyramids, the Sphinx, the great

River Nile and dusky-skinned people who wrapped up their dead and turned them into mummies. It would be a land steeped in thousands of years of history, a kind of memorial to the past.

What I had not expected was that our arrival would be marked with a boisterous welcome. Before the liner came to a halt in the middle of the harbour, it was surrounded by a swarm of tiny, brightly painted bum-boats, all stacked high with wares, their owners shouting at the top of their voices to attract attention.

Ropes were tossed up to the decks and laughing passengers, tied them to the rails and hauled up baskets of fruit and sweets, carved ornaments, shawls, and all manner of other wares.

To me, the trust in the upturned faces of the people in the boats was incredible. Passengers could easily have emptied the baskets and walked away, but they didn't. They chose what they fancied, shouted down and haggled over the price, then sent the baskets back with the money due and the rest of the unwanted goods.

The noise was deafening. There were hundreds of little boats and hundreds of shouting sellers. Small boys screamed up to passengers, encouraging them to toss money into the water. The moment there was a flash of silver, they plunged in, disappeared down to the depths, then reappeared moments later, a bright coin held high.

Whenever there was a break in the cascade of coins, they climbed on to the nearest bum-boat, stripped off their clothes, wrung them out while waving happily to the passengers above, then put them back on and shouted for more coins.

It was wonderful.

Suddenly, a party atmosphere invaded the ship. Even my parents looked more relaxed than I had seen them for a long time. It was as though, in the novelty of the moment, happiness was infectious.

To my delight, after the mid-day meal, Mother decided we ought to go ashore. After all, we might never have the chance to set foot in Egypt again. Even Grandmother agreed to join the excursion.

A fleet of motorboats ferried passengers ashore, and as soon as we landed, crowds of eager brown faces, young and old, milled round us. Outstretched hands offered souvenirs, sweets, clothes, perfumes, and carved wooden animals. Flashing smiles encouraged us. "Cheap, very cheap!" "Buy for the pretty lady." "English money only." Their vocabulary was limited, but their persistence was relentless.

The children were the most determined, beaming as they fought their way through the crowd to us so they could perform astounding sleight-of-hand tricks. Some, as young as six or seven, begged us to put a coin in our hand and close our fist tightly over it. They never touched the hand, just waved their little fingers close to it, then turned and ran. In a flash, they were gone. And so was the coin.

The day was sweltering. I still hoped I might see the Sphinx and the pyramids, but there were only crowded streets lined with dark shops.

Eric offered to treat us all to a drink in a little cafe whose tables spilled out into the street, but the proprietor only accepted Egyptian money and Eric had only English. As if by magic, a fez-capped money-changer appeared through the curtain at the back of the café and Eric was given ten coins the size of English two-shilling pieces in exchange for his pound. Back on the boat, we learned from one of the crew the Egyptian coins were worth only sixpence.

"Don't worry," he said. "You got away lightly. The kids often steal the laces out of your shoes while you're sitting at the table having a drink. They're marvellous. You don't feel a thing. Then they come along with a tray of shoelaces and try to sell them to you."

By the next morning, we had left Port Said behind and were in the Suez Canal. It was incredible. A shining blue ribbon of water threaded across the dusty brown earth. Looking down from the deck, there seemed barely enough room for the huge liner to ease its way between the two banks. Groups of women working on the land looked up and waved as we passed. They were so close I felt I could reach down and touch them.

Hour after hour, we slid along. Only the gamblers went back to their cards. Everyone else lined the rails.

We passed a village sweltering in the sun, and as I looked behind us, the sliver of water disappeared into a haze as if we had been left suspended high in the air above a strange land, a part of it forever.

At school, our geography lessons had mostly been about the British Isles. I knew the continents and the great oceans and I knew that all the pink pieces on the world map belonged to the British Empire. Where exactly the Suez Canal was and where we were heading, I had no idea except that it was on the way to Australia.

Now, I know that once we left the Suez Canal, we went across the Red Sea, through the Gulf of Aden and out into the Arabian Sea. Loudspeakers told us our next port of call would be Colombo, the capital city of Ceylon.

Our journey had become an endless sight-seeing tour under a blazing sun where you stood still and the world was brought to you, but I could never forget that as every day passed, I was farther and farther away from everything I had ever known.

Sometimes I laid awake at night, wondering if poor old

Minnie was all right or whether she had pined for Grandfather and died. I wondered who had been given my scholarship. But mostly, I wondered if Australia was a place where I could become a dancer or a singer, or an artist or an actress.

We didn't go ashore at Colombo. Mother's mood had changed. The light-heartedness we enjoyed at Port Said had gone. Perhaps the fact we were only a week away from our destination was to blame. Soon we would start a new life. Gradually, she sank into a depression and whenever she was depressed, her anger flared.

She snapped at her sisters, argued with Grandmother, and barely spoke to Father. Most of her time was spent in the washrooms. All our clothes had to be washed and ironed and ready. Who knew what lay ahead for us?

But as Mother's depression deepened, Grandmother's mood lightened. She seemed almost cheerful. Her long-standing ambition would soon be achieved. She would reach Australia, bringing all her family with her.

CHAPTER 16

Auntie Annie was at the dockside when the liner berthed at Fremantle. With her was a man in a wide-brimmed hat. It was Jack. Uncle Jack to Cecil and me.

Mother told me I must be nice to him. It was thanks to him we had come to Australia.

I tried.

I would not have dared to be disobedient, but some instinct made me dislike Uncle Jack on sight. I suppose he was different from anyone I had ever met before. He was thin and bony and his clothes hung limply on him as though they belonged to someone else, and under the shadow of the hat brim, his face was dark brown and wizened. He reminded me of the prunes my mother soaked overnight before she stewed them.

There was no friendliness in his expression, no welcoming smile. Only impatience that the boat had been late docking and his voice was loud and sharp when he complained they had been waiting a long time.

Annie was different. She was chubby and cheerful and

put her arms around me and kissed me so heartily I couldn't believe she was Mother's sister.

It took Uncle Jack's car, a taxi and a small truck to move our family and luggage the twelve miles from Fremantle to Perth. The luggage included the packing case containing the sewing machine. Cecil cried when he saw it, and I understood. It made me think of Charlie and my little white-washed yard.

Annie had rented a furnished house for us in Nedlands, a suburb of Perth along the Swan River. Part brick, part weatherboard with a corrugated iron roof, it stood in a tidy little garden with a post-box, American style, at the gate.

Alighting from the taxi, Grandmother stared at it in disgust. "God Almighty! What's the silly bitch thinking?" she demanded. "There's not enough room to swing a cat."

Embarrassed, Mother shushed her as Uncle Jack's car drove up, but she was unabashed. "We'll need a bloody shoe-horn to get us all in," she growled.

There were only two bedrooms. Grandma would have one, she decided, and my three aunts could share the other.

Like most Australian houses, there was a veranda at the front and another at the back. There was a stack of stretcher beds in the garden shed, so Grandfather and Eric could sleep on the back veranda and Mother, Father, Cecil and I could sleep on the front veranda. There was no discussion.

I had never seen people sleep in full view of every passer-by in the street. Even in the poorest homes in the East End of London, where people slept three or four to a bed, there had always been some sort of privacy, a door to close against the world.

I expected Mother to explode, but she didn't. She looked stunned and later Father found her crying in a corner of the garden.

Next morning, Annie arrived early. She and Uncle Jack

were booked into a hotel in the nearby beach resort of Cottesloe, where they usually stayed when they were in town. They had to get back to the farm. It was a busy time, she explained, and Jack couldn't afford to be away for long. She hugged and kissed me when she left and I was sad to see her go.

My parents didn't have had much money left, and they were desperate to find work.

Mother asked if Cecil and I could stay at the house while they went looking for work in Perth, but she was told that Eric and my aunts were off on the same quest and Grandmother didn't feel well enough to look after children.

Mother cut some sandwiches, took us to the local school, and booked us in. She would be back, she promised, by the time lessons ended.

The school was a huddle of single-storey weatherboard buildings set in a waste of grey sand. Most of the children were barefoot, and none of them were friendly.

"They're Pommies," they said accusingly. "Listen to how they talk."

They didn't like Pommies, they said. Nobody liked Pommies. They only came to take work away from real Australians.

I didn't understand. I didn't know what a Pommie was, and I had no idea why I was being labelled one.

In any case, I had enough to think about. The work the children were doing in class was far behind the level in London and I soon realised shooting my hand up to answer every question made me even more unpopular. I learned to keep my hands folded in my lap.

~

My parents searched for work, any kind of work, but there was none to be found. Perth was already full of unemployed workers and more arrived every time a ship docked at Fremantle.

There were government schemes to help immigrants. Men were sent upcountry to build roads or to cut timber. The work was hard, the pay was minimal, but it was better than nothing.

But we were not immigrants. We had been nominated. That meant the authorities had no obligation to help us. If my family needed support, then it must turn to our nominator.

There was only one thing the authorities would do to help us. They would send us to an abandoned farm. Across the expanse of South West Australia, hopeful pioneers had struggled to hack down the bush and clear enough land to start a farm. They had felled trees, dug out roots, built shelters for their families and begged the bank to advance them enough money to buy seeds or potatoes or a few animals.

And after years of hardship, some had succeeded.

A great many more, however, had given up. Worn out and defeated, they had walked away from their dreams, taking only what the family could carry on their trek back to civilisation. Behind them, the bush crept back and wiped away all their efforts.

The authorities were willing to settle us on one of these lonely outposts. They would give us one-way tickets to the nearest rail siding and provide us with a cow and some chickens. After that, we would be on our own.

Mother was horrified.

At the end of the week, the landlord called for the rent. Grandmother demanded that, as my parents were sharing the house, they must pay half. Mother refused. Four beds on a veranda was not sharing a house, and anyway, if they did pay, we would have nothing left to buy food.

Another week passed, and still there was no work. None

for my aunts, or Eric or my parents. Grandmother was furious and raged at her daughters. They were not trying hard enough. As for my parents, if they were near to starving, they must demand help from Jack.

It was the last thing Mother wanted to do, but in the end, desperation forced her to contact Annie. Jack had said it was a busy time. Was there any work on the farm for my father? Just for a week or two until she managed to find work herself.

Uncle Jack refused outright. We had said we would need no help, otherwise he would not have agreed to nominate us.

Somehow, Annie talked him round. She had sent her two little girls to a boarding school in Perth. Jack's farm was over two hundred miles away, at Nungarin in the wheat belt, where there were no schools, and she had wanted them to have a proper education.

But the girls were unhappy so far from home and she had reluctantly given in and agreed to take them back. She would be down the following week to collect them and would take Father back to the farm with her.

I liked Annie. She was completely different from the rest of the family, perhaps because she had only been a child when she was sent away from them. She talked to me and asked all about the scholarship I had won and lost. No-one else had mentioned it since we left England. She made me feel important, not just a child among grownups who should be "seen but not heard".

As good as her word, she arrived a week later and seemed oblivious to the black mood hanging over the family. If Father could pack a bag of old working clothes, she would pick him up later. In the meantime, she was going to collect her little daughters, and she was sure Mother, Cecil, and I would like to go with her.

Mother could hardly refuse. Annie was our lifeline.

It was the first time I had been to Perth. I had been told it was the capital city of Western Australia and I suppose I was expecting a miniature London, but this was totally different. There were weatherboard houses with corrugated iron roofs, and veranda-fronted stores that looked as though they had come straight from the Wild West. Only the hitching rails were missing.

"Most of the schools here are Catholic and this is one of the best," Annie said as she rang the bell.

I had heard a great deal about Catholics. Grandmother hated them, and although I had never met one, I had grown up thinking of them as frightening and evil.

I was not prepared for the two smiling nuns who answered the door. Their black habits and veils, the white framing that left only their faces visible, the soft rustle of their footsteps, the beads that tinkled as they walked... It was all so unexpected I was speechless.

So, I am sure, was Mother. She said not a word as we followed Annie along a corridor, and were ushered into a room that was bare except for a small table and four wooden chairs. The stark walls were broken only by a small shrine with figures that I took to be Mary and the baby Jesus, and close to it, a picture of a big red heart that seemed to be bleeding. I tried not to look at that. I didn't understand it and it made me nervous.

A young nun in a white veil brought us tea and biscuits. She smiled but said nothing and when the door closed behind her, we were left in silence. I had never been aware of silence before. It seemed to be pressing around us, waiting.

Suddenly, the door burst open and a big, black-clad figure strode in. Annie stood up. Mother stood up, and I jumped to my feet. I don't know why, except that Sister Mary Emmanuelle was that sort of person. She was a presence. She was as broad and tall as a man with huge hands and big black shoes and when she spoke, her voice was deep and firm.

Briskly, she poured us a cup of tea, offered us a biscuit

and said how sorry she was that my cousins were not happy, but perhaps when they were older, they would like to come back.

The young nun in the white veil was summoned to take Annie to collect them and Mother, Cecil and I moved to follow them, but Sister Mary Emmanuelle waved at us to sit down again. She poured another cup of tea.

"Your sister has been telling me about your problems." She frowned. "What kind of work are you looking for?"

Mother flushed scarlet. She always guarded her privacy. I expected her to fly into a temper or walk out, but she didn't. Instead, she hung her head.

"Any kind. Any kind at all."

Silence filled the room again. Cecil and I didn't move. After a moment, Sister Mary Emmanuelle leaned forward and patted my mother's hand.

"I can't promise. Times are hard, but I will see if there is anything I can do to help."

She shook her head as Mother thanked her.

"Never mind that. There is one thing you can do for us. I understand your daughter won a scholarship in London. It would be interesting for us to compare standards with our own pupils. Come back tomorrow. Maybe by then I will have some good news for you and Hilda can take some of the tests our girls have just finished and see how they compare."

Annie drove us back. Father was on the front veranda, his bag in his hand. He tried not to cry as he kissed us goodbye and we watched silently as they drove away, Annie, Father and two little strangers who were my cousins.

Once the car was out of sight, Mother took Cecil's hand and mine and held them tight.

"Don't tell your grandmother," she whispered. "Don't tell any of them we've been with the Catholics."

Next morning, we dropped Cecil off at school, then Mother and I went back to the convent. Sister Mary

Emmanuelle was as good as her word. She gave Mother three names and addresses.

"Work of any kind is hard to find," she said, "but these are all good Catholics. Tell them Sister Mary Emmanuelle sent you. They will help you if they can. Now, off you go. Don't worry about Hilda. We'll keep her busy until you get back."

I hadn't expected Mother to leave me alone, but in her eagerness to find work, she went without a backward glance and I followed the big, black-clad figure across the convent gardens and through a gateway into the grounds of the Victoria Square Ladies College.

I had not seen the school in London that offered me a scholarship, but I had built up an imaginary picture and hugged it jealously to myself. Now I saw something that rivalled it.

The buildings were imposing, some stone, some red brick, surrounded by beautifully kept gardens, wide lawns and sparkling sprinklers.

Confronted with this sunlit reality, my fantasy images faded and I knew that in the future, whenever I conjured up a picture of what my scholarship school might have been, it would look like this.

Sister Mary Emmanuelle took me to a classroom, sat me down, and spread a pile of test papers on the desk in front of me.

"No-one will disturb you here," she said cheerfully. "I'll come back every little while to make sure you are all right. Just do as much as you can."

The door closed behind her, the tinkle of her beads died away along the corridor and I was alone.

I thought of my mother and prayed someone would give her work. Sister Mary Emmanuelle was a Catholic. I had been brought up to hate Catholics, yet she was trying to help us. I didn't understand. I only knew that she would be back and that she would expect me to be working on the tests.

They were not difficult, and soon I relaxed. Every little while I heard the warning sound of approaching beads, the quiet opening of the door, the awareness of the black-clad figure watching me. Then she would be gone again.

"You are finished?"

Sister Mary Emmanuelle came into the room and gathered up the papers. She looked through them carefully, then sat down beside me. "You didn't do the French paper or the Latin one."

"I'm sorry." I felt she was disappointed. "I haven't learned French or Latin."

"I see." She pulled a watch on the end of a heavy chain from her pocket. "Good gracious! Lunchtime."

I had lunch in a long dining room with the boarders and when I went back to the convent, Mother was waiting. She looked flushed and happy. She had been offered a job washing dishes in the Rosebud Café in the centre of Perth.

Sister Mary Emmanuelle seemed pleased.

"It's a beginning," she said, then hesitated and pursed her lips. She seemed to have a habit of doing that when she was trying to be tactful. "I have been talking to our Mother Superior. She would like to meet you."

The happiness faded from Mother's face.

We followed Sister Mary Emmanuelle along silent corridors and waited while she knocked on a door, then ushered us into a large room.

Mother Superior was seated at a desk, dressed all in white, her face as colourless as the veil that surrounded it. Her hands were clasped and rested on the pile of my test papers.

She motioned us to sit, and I could sense Mother's reluctance.

"Sister Mary Emmanuelle has been talking to me," she said, looking directly at me. "She told me about your scholarship and she has shown me the tests you have done, tests that were intended for girls a year older than you. You did very well."

There was a moment of silence and out of the corner of my eye, I was aware of Mother's hands clenching and unclenching in her lap.

"I understand you have not yet learned French or Latin," Mother Superior continued. "What about sports? Do you play tennis or netball?"

"Netball. Not tennis." I was still watching Mother's hands. "And I'm a good runner."

Mother made a sudden move as though to stand up, but Sister Mary's hand reached out sharply and stayed her.

"You must be wondering why we are interested in your daughter," Mother Superior said. "Let me explain."

She told us the Victoria Square Ladies College was recognised as one of the best educational establishments in Western Australia. Boarders came from all over the state. Standards were at the highest level and it had a reputation to uphold. Examination results were published in the national newspapers and competition with other colleges for prospective pupils was intense.

She sighed. "Unfortunately, the fact that many of our pupils come from wealthy families does not mean they are blessed with superior intelligence or dedication. But our standards must be maintained, so we are always interested in finding a gifted child like Hilda."

This time, Mother ignored Sister Mary Emmanuelle's attempt to restrain her.

"I'm sorry. You're wasting your time. We've got no money to pay school fees. Haven't you heard? The only job I managed to get this morning is washing dishes."

Mother Superior clasped her hands in front of her and nodded.

"Yes. I understand that was due to the efforts of Sister

Mary Emmanuelle here. Now, Mrs Spear, will you do me the courtesy of hearing me out?"

Mother didn't answer, but she sank back in her seat and her eyes dropped to her lap.

"The College is prepared to offer Hilda a twelve month trial," she explained. "There will be no fees. Everything will be provided, uniform, books, sports equipment, even day-to-day expenses like tram fares. And she can have a mid-day meal with the boarders, as many of the day scholars do."

"But you don't understand," Mother protested. "We're not Catholics. We're Church of England."

Mother Superior merely waved a hand.

"That is not important. In return, Hilda will be expected to study hard and attain high grades in all her subjects. That will mean catching up in French and Latin. And she will be expected to join in with all college activities, except, of course, religious devotions."

She paused, but Mother was silent, and after a moment, she continued.

"If, at the end of the year, Hilda has fulfilled the promise she shows now, then she will be welcome to stay under the same arrangement for the rest of her school life, even on to university, if that is what she chooses. All we ask in return is steadfast dedication to her studies, and that she continues to achieve high grades."

There was another silence before Mother Superior leaned forward. "I understand you also have a small son. Is there anyone who can look after him while you are working?"

I felt a pang of guilt. I had forgotten about Cecil.

"We have a primary section here where we take small boys as well as girls until they are old enough to start at a boys' college. If you accept our offer, your son could be educated here for the time being."

She held out her hand. "I hope things will get better for

you, Mrs Spear. Please think hard about our offer. It could mean a great deal to Hilda."

Mother was silent on the tram home.

"We didn't like you having to give up your scholarship," she said at last. "But there was nothing else we could do."

"Maybe God is giving me another chance," I said. I thought it might cheer her up, but she only sighed.

"If this is God's idea, I hope he's right behind me when I tell your grandmother."

She broke the news to the family that night.

"Over my dead body! No granddaughter of mine is going to be taught by bloody Catholics!"

All three aunts joined in at once. Voices rose, tempers flared and accusations flew. Grandfather did what he had taken to do every time a row broke out. He locked himself in the toilet.

Crying bitterly, Mother shepherded Cecil and me out onto the veranda and we sat on our beds in the darkness.

Once again, I was sick with guilt. This was all my fault. I didn't want to upset Mother anymore, but I had to know.

"Am I going to go to the college?" I asked.

Mother pulled a handkerchief from her pocket and blew her nose.

"Yes," she said, "but tomorrow we'll have to find somewhere else to live."

CHAPTER 17

There were only two days before Mother started work at the café. After that, she would be working shifts, eight in the morning until four in the afternoon one day, and four in the afternoon until midnight the next.

We walked all over Perth, asking people in shops, even stopping friendly looking strangers in the street to ask if they knew of a room to let, but with no luck. We ended up in a seedy area with narrow streets of rundown houses, each with its front door pushed wide open.

A big woman with blonde hair leaned in a doorway. She came across to us and asked if we were lost. When Mother explained we were looking for a room, she burst out laughing.

"Not around here, love. Not with kids." She winked broadly. "This is a turn-a-blind-eye area. You know. Red light. Best if you go back into town. Look for Adelaide Terrace. There are some lodging houses along there. You might be lucky."

We soon found Adelaide Terrace. The houses, two-storeys high with a veranda, all looked the same. Mother chose number seven.

The woman who answered the door was tall and thin, her grey hair scraped up in a bun and her accent richly Irish. Yes, she did have an empty room, but it was small. We could see it if we liked.

She led us up the stairs and opened a door at the end of a landing. The room was tiny.

Two stretcher beds, one on each side, left barely enough room to walk between them. Just inside the door stood a wash-stand topped by a jug and basin set, and opposite was a table and one chair.

"The children will have to share a bed. The lavvy is down in the yard. At the end of the landing, there's a kitchen and a bathroom. Anyone can use them. You just put a shilling in the meter if you want to boil a kettle or need hot water for a bath. And if you have to do any washing, there's a tub and a clothesline in the yard."

She smiled pleasantly. "I'm Miss O'Leary and my sister is Mrs McGuire. Now, how long do you want the room for?"

"I'm not sure." I sensed Mother's embarrassment and my eyes dropped to the floor as I listened to her explain she had no money until she started work in two days' time.

I waited for Miss O'Leary to throw us out, but instead, she sighed.

"All right. It's twelve shillings a week and you'll start paying on Friday."

~

The next morning, Mother took Cecil and me to an ornate gate in the wall encircling the Convent. A brass plaque announced The Victoria Square Ladies College, established by The Sisters of Mercy.

Cecil clung to her hand, tears in his eyes, and I pretended I was not afraid.

I was eleven years old, in a strange country, half a world away from everything I had ever known, and now my brother and I were being handed over to a community of black-robed figures who were hated by most of my family. Even Mother had echoed the cry that Catholics were evil.

The initial excitement about going to the college had faded as I lay awake in the narrow bed beside Cecil, listening to footsteps on the landing and the voices of lodgers in other rooms.

It was impossible to sleep. Each time I closed my eyes, I could see Grandmother's angry face.

Now I flinched as Mother pushed us through the gate.

"Don't worry. They won't hurt you," she said. "They only want you because you're clever. They'll make you into a lady and then I'll be proud of you. Just do exactly what they tell you."

Sister Mary Emmanuelle was waiting for me. Cecil was whisked away by a white-veiled novice and soon my clothes had been stripped off and wrapped in a neat brown paper parcel for me to take back to Mother. Then I was kitted out in a bottle green tunic, a blazer with a shield and the College motto emblazoned in red on the pocket, a white blouse and a broad-brimmed panama hat. There was no tie. Instead, a red bow was pinned beneath my chin.

I was allocated a locker in the sports room, already full with the items I would need, including a swimming costume, a tennis racquet, a white dress, and red and green sports kit. I had even been given a leather suitcase to carry home the books I would need for homework each evening.

I was ready to be introduced to my classroom and my new classmates, but first there were rules to be learned.

School started at half-past-eight in the morning and finished at five, with an hour's break for lunch and a visit to the chapel. On Saturdays there were art lessons from nine until twelve in the morning and in the afternoon, there was netball, tennis and athletics practice. Every evening there would be at least two hours' homework.

I would be expected to respect all breaks for devotions during lesson times, and while Catholics prayed, I would sit with my head bent and my hands clasped.

During the daily Catechism classes, I would go with other non-Catholics to a common room set aside for study. Shouting or any raising of voices was strictly forbidden. During sports matches against other colleges, we were allowed to encourage our own team, but pupils must always remember they were young ladies, not hooligans. For the same reason, once inside the College buildings, everyone walked quietly and sedately. No-one ever ran.

The girls in my class were all older than me. Some I liked on sight, some I didn't, but they accepted me without asking questions. I was simply a new girl arrived from England. No-one called me a Pommie. I am sure it would have been severely frowned upon if they had.

Whenever I was asked about my family, I simply said my uncle owned a big farm up on the wheat belt and my father was helping him. My mother preferred to stay in Perth with my brother and me.

That was all. I soon realised the less I said about myself, the better, and I worked out a variety of different routes to walk home so that no-one guessed where Cecil and I lived.

The room at the lodging-house was cramped, and with no ceiling, just the corrugated iron roof above our heads, it was stiflingly hot during the day. When it rained, the noise made conversation impossible.

There was no cupboard space, only a wire-netted safe

standing in the corridor outside where we could keep food away from the flies.

My uniform was a great worry. Mother had always fought to keep me looking the best she could. Now she was even more determined. She was going to show her family. I was going to be a lady.

The moment I came home from school and the room door closed behind me, I had to strip off the bottle green outfit, sponge away any spots, then fold each piece, the white blouse, the tunic, the blazer, even the bow and gloves, into smooth folds and lay it all out safely under the mattress. The panama hat sat in splendour on top of the water jug on the washstand.

As a dishwasher, Mother earned very low wages, but there were always people hanging around the back door of the café, begging for work. When she came home exhausted, I prayed that her anger would not return. If she lost her temper, and her job, what would happen to us?

But I need not have worried. She was too tired to be angry. Mostly, she just sat on the edge of her bed and cried.

Sometimes the owner of the cafe gave her titbits to bring home to us, overcooked biscuits, slices of stale cake or the occasional fish head so she could make soup. Mother had always hated accepting charity, but she took everything gratefully.

Often, she had no shilling to put in the gas meter in the kitchen to cook or to make a cup of tea and we were reduced to listening at the crack of our door until another lodger put in a shilling and went away without using it all.

At school, I worked hard, determined to keep my part of the bargain, but homework was difficult, especially in the evenings when Mother was at work. I had to feed Cecil and get him into bed and asleep before I could start.

I always felt the shadow of Sister Mary Emmanuelle hanging over me. If I stepped out of line in any way, homework handed in late or shoes not perfectly polished, she would come down on me like a ton of bricks.

She was big and over-powering, and occasionally stern and frightening, yet behind it, I always felt she was my friend.

Sometimes the college arranged treats for special occasions. Ice-cream was sold in the playground to raise money for charity or there were raffles for bars of chocolate. The other girls had pocket money. I had none. But Sister Mary Emmanuelle would always pass close to me and slip a couple of pennies into my hand. She never even glanced at me as she did it. And when I was chosen for the Junior Netball team, she nodded at me and wrinkled her nose in a grimace of satisfaction.

There were eleven non-Catholics who studied in the common room each day until Mollie and Susan Palmer arrived. They were twins and swelled our number to thirteen, which, for some reason, focused attention on us.

Sister Mary Emmanuelle broke the news. She didn't exactly say that the Reverend Mother was concerned our group was growing up as little heathens with no religious guidance at all, but she certainly implied it.

She told us the authorities at the Protestant Cathedral had been contacted. In future someone would be sent once a week to instruct us.

He arrived the following Monday, a weedy young man with horn-rimmed spectacles. He was escorted by Sister Mary Emmanuelle and looked ill-at-ease.

I felt sorry for him, especially when Sister Mary Emmanuelle settled herself comfortably in a chair behind him. Girls were not allowed alone in a room with a man, not even a priest.

His name, he said, was Mr Mackenzie and we were to call him Sir. Our ages ranged from Nora, who was four years old, to Katie, who was seventeen.

For a moment, he stared round, then he asked how many of us had been confirmed? None. And how many of us had been baptised?

The question caused some confusion. I, for one, had never heard of baptism, but I told him that I had been christened. Several of the class had never heard of baptism or christening.

Poor Sir. He went pink with embarrassment at our ignorance, and Sister Mary Emmanuelle shook her head in disbelief.

The first thing he must do, he announced, was to initiate us into our own church. He would arrange baptisms for those who needed them as soon as possible, and he would begin preparing the older ones among us to be confirmed. As it happened, there was to be a mass confirmation service in the cathedral in a few weeks' time.

Our lessons were only half-an-hour each but Sir put his heart into them, and I must admit, I enjoyed his teaching until he announced that, for the confirmation ceremony, we would all have to wear a white dress.

To most of the girls in the class, money was not a problem and there was a lot of giggling about new dresses for the occasion.

Obviously, there was no money for me to have a new white dress, and in any case, as my mother observed gratefully, I already had one. Back in Swan Street, she had made it for me out of one of Grandmother's old nightgowns, so that I could be in the choir for the Empire Day pageant. It was plain and simple and would have to do, even if I had grown a bit.

The confirmation ceremony was going to be an impressive event, with two hundred children taking part. We would proceed down the central aisle of the Cathedral in two lines, then take it in turns to kneel on a white velvet cushion in front of the bishop.

I was an attentive pupil, and by the afternoon of the confirmations, I knew exactly what was expected. I would dearly have liked Mother to have been there among the other parents, but she was at work.

I had never been inside a cathedral before and the sheer size of it was overwhelming. It was so big, so grand, and every face in the congregation turned to watch as we made our way down the aisle to the solemn music of the organ. I was only one of two hundred, but I felt important.

Then it happened. A voice rang out.

"I can see your bum."

A boy in the other lane was grinning at me.

"No, you can't." I snapped. "You're lying."

"Well, if I can't see your bum, I can see your drawers."

His words echoed around the cathedral, and Mr Mackenzie hurried across. He glared at the boy and walked between us all the way to the velvet cushion. When I finally knelt before the Bishop I was scarlet with embarrassment, certain that every eye in the congregation was on the girl who was showing her drawers.

Once the ceremony was over, I ran all the way back to the lodging house. Miss O'Leary met me in the hall. She could see I had been crying and sat me down on the stairs beside her.

"What is it, girl? What's happened?"

I told her, and she put her arm around me.

"Well, what are you crying for?" she asked. "You haven't done anything wrong. You went to your Cathedral to please your God. He's not going to get upset over a little thing like that, is he? He loves you. He made you, every bit of you."

She chuckled and gave me a squeeze. "Even your bum."

She was honest and kind-hearted, and her words made me feel better. I had always thought of God as a remote figure in flowing white robes. Suddenly, he seemed real and approachable. After that, I started saying my prayers again. I whispered them in bed at night when the light was out and neither Cecil nor Mother could see or hear me. They were not the real prayers my Catholic classmates said, although I did start with the Lord's Prayer to make them seem respectful. No, it was more a one-sided chat with a secret friend. It made me feel better. After all, there was no-one else I could talk to.

From that day on, Miss O'Leary became my friend. She and her sister lived downstairs in the kitchen. There was a bed in one corner and a curtain draped across another corner, behind which hung their meagre wardrobe. Every other room in the house was let out, some to lodgers who stayed for weeks, but many to one-nighters. Mostly they were men. Casual labourers, Miss O'Leary said, who had come to the city to spend their hard-earned pay after months in the outback. Most of it went on drink, judging by the coarse jokes that accompanied their attempts to climb the stairs by the dim light of a fifteen-watt bulb.

Every night I was woken by staggering footsteps heading down to the lavatory in the yard. I would lay awake listening until the footsteps climbed the stairs again and ended with the click of a room door.

They never woke Cecil, and I couldn't tell him how much they frightened me. Perhaps I had seen too much drunkenness back in Swan Street. I longed to lock the door of our room and feel safe, but I dare not. Every other night, Mother worked late at the Café and she had made me promise I would never lock her out.

As I said, after the incident at the Cathedral, Miss O'Leary became my friend. Sometimes she pottered up in the evening when Cecil and I were alone, just to be sure we were all right, and occasionally she invited us down to play cards with her and her sister.

They were a strange pair, direct, outspoken, toughened by sun and hard living, quite capable of tossing a lodger out into the street if he broke too many rules, yet always neat and tidy in their old floral dresses and men's boots, their hair scraped up into grey buns on the top of their heads.

They taught us to play poker and brag, gambling with old buttons instead of money, and always gave us a cup of hot cocoa and a biscuit before they sent us back to our room.

Father had been gone for nearly five months when he arrived on the doorstep. Miss O'Leary brought him up to us.

For a moment, it was hard to recognise him. His skin was dark brown and blistered into strips. The sun had bleached his wig to the colour of straw and sweat had rotted it into holes.

And he was so thin.

He had been sacked. He was, according to Uncle Jack, a useless office bastard. His only jobs had been to drive the team of horses and to look after the cows. And he couldn't do either. Jack's animals had been trained by being sworn at. Every command was an expletive. That was all they understood. Father never swore and he couldn't bring himself to utter the foul-mouthed profanities that Jack demanded.

He had slept in a shed with the other hands and had been paid one pound a week. From that, Jack had deducted the cost of a hat, a pair of boots, the cost of the petrol for driving Father to a doctor when his arm was poisoned, plus the doctor's fee, and his rail fare back to Perth. He brought home nine pounds.

Miss O'Leary called Mother downstairs. She was sorry. She understood the problem, but she couldn't allow two grown-ups and two children to live in such a tiny space. Luckily, she did have a bigger room. But it was sixteen shillings a week.

I spent that evening mending the wig, hiding up the repairs and trying to make it as presentable as possible. Father seemed pleased with the result. I think he was just happy to be back with us.

Hilda, holding a neighbour's child, with Cecil outside their boarding house.

Soon after my twelfth birthday, Sister Mary Emmanuelle called me to her office. She looked serious, and I was worried. I had worked hard on my French and Latin. My tennis was improving, and I had been chosen as a reserve for the Under 13 netball team. I prayed I was doing well enough.

I would sit for my junior examinations in a few months, she said. I was considerably younger than the rest of the class and it had been decided I should sit only six subjects, English, Mathematics, History, Art, Latin and French, and I would not be going up to the next grade the following year.

My heart sank.

"It's difficult doing homework," I blurted out, "but my father is back now. He can look after Cecil when Mother is working. If I could stay back for an hour after school..."

Her hand rose to silence me. "You really must learn to listen," she said severely. "I was about to say you will not go up a grade, but as you are progressing well, you will retake the junior examinations next year sitting all thirteen subjects."

The new room was bigger and a little more comfortable, but the extra rent made life difficult. Cecil and I had a mid-day meal at the college and Mother ate what she could at the café, so the few pounds Father had brought back with him was kept to provide him with a meal each day.

That worried him. He was happy about the college, but he felt he had let us down and all he could think about was trying to find work. Every day, he queued wherever work might be offered.

One day, he was lucky. There had been an accident at a timber mill. Several men had been injured, and they needed replacements. Mother didn't want him to go, but if you were offered a job and refused it, then you were blacklisted. He went.

After two weeks, a truck delivered him back. He had collapsed.

A few days later, the owner of the Rosebud Café called his staff together. He told them he had sold up and was going back to Italy. Unfortunately, the new owner had a large family and would need no staff. He thanked them all and gave them an extra half-crown on top of their final wages.

After that, it was difficult to concentrate on schoolwork. I tried to focus my mind, but I couldn't stop worrying. What would we do without any money coming in? With nothing to pay rent? Nothing to buy food?

I watched my mother grow more agitated as the days passed, and I was afraid.

One afternoon, Sister Mary Emmanuelle took me to one side.

"Well," she demanded. "Are you going to tell me?"

I told her. She frowned and shook her head and went away. Two days later, she came to me with a slip of paper.

"It's a restaurant. They want a waitress. There'll be plenty after the job, but she is to tell them that Sister Mary Emmanuelle sent her."

Next afternoon, when we came home from school, Mother was smiling. She had been given the job. Better still, she would get tips on top of her wages.

The relief was enormous.

CHAPTER 18

A few weeks later, I sat the junior examinations and passed my six subjects.

I was relieved, but Sister Mary Emmanuelle did not seem surprised.

"Now that's out of the way," she said, "you can start on your new subjects."

I must have looked apprehensive because she shook her head.

"Don't worry. You've already started botany and geology. With your maths ability, you should have no trouble with algebra, geometry, or trigonometry. That just leaves geography and English literature."

On the strength of my success, Mother decided we deserved a treat. There was a fireplace in our room and I was despatched around the corner to the greengrocers to buy an empty apple box. It cost two pennies.

The tricky part was smuggling it into the house and up the stairs without being caught by Miss O'Leary.

I felt like a criminal when the room door closed behind me. A successful criminal.

We broke the box up, lit a fire in the hearth, and gathered

round it. The night was warm, but that didn't matter. We were happy.

Memories flooded back from a past, thousands of miles away, a past that was gone forever. A fire had always been a special treat. We huddled together in front of it, the room behind us in darkness, and imagined pictures in the leaping flames.

Looking back, it is amazing how much happiness a two-penny box could bring. It was well worth the effort of scrubbing the hearth out afterwards and secretly disposing of the ash, so no-one would guess we had broken the rules.

Poverty is a strange thing. It can cut people off and keep them apart, or it can bind them together into a brotherhood.

In those days, poverty was a fact of life for many in Perth. The men who queued, hour after hour, for work then trudged home disappointed, became familiar faces to one another. The women who fought for a chance to wash dishes or scrub floors gradually forgot their roots, Aussie or Pommie, and became one of the hungry army, struggling to exist.

Newcomers were assimilated into the ranks and learned the secrets of survival. Firewood was doled out free to the unemployed, but waiting lists were long. Charities had special days when they handed out old clothes at church halls. There was a kindly old dentist who pulled out aching teeth on the spot and expected no reward. In the back room of a popular hairdresser's, women could have a free perm done by students provided they signed a form promising they would not make a claim if their hair frizzled up and fell out.

And if you wanted a night out to help you forget your miseries, all you needed was a silver three-penny piece. Most cinemas closed on Sundays, but one in the middle of Perth opened with all proceeds going to charity. The staff were volunteers, and the program consisted of an old film, a travelogue, and a newsreel.

The box office was closed. The only payment was a silver coin dropped into a collecting box. I never saw anyone donate more than a three-penny piece. No-one minded queuing for hours and the cinema was always full. From the day Father heard about it, Mother put a three-penny piece aside as often as she could manage. It made something exciting to look forward to.

The majority of girls in my class came from wealthy families. Their parents owned farms on the wheat belt, or gold mines, or were government officials, doctors, lawyers or the like. They didn't boast, but they took good living for granted. They always had plenty of money for new clothes, holidays and luxuries.

For some of them, the highlights of their year were the parties held on board visiting liners berthed overnight at Fremantle before they continued their journey to the Eastern States.

Perth was a young city striving to outgrow its hillbilly beginnings. There were a few big stores, a racecourse, and a university was being built. The team of workmen had been specially brought over from Italy and were bitterly resented by the local unemployed.

But there was nowhere suitable for glittering receptions, lavish parties and high-class social gatherings, except on the visiting luxury liners.

Pupils from Victoria Square Ladies College. Hilda is second from the right on the bottom row, wearing a white belt.

Not all my classmates came from wealthy families. Among them were other charity cases like myself. Poor students who had some special ability the College could foster for its own benefit.

One of them was Margaret. A nervous girl who had been born on a small-holding a few hundred miles south of Perth, where her parents struggled to make a meagre living for their five children.

The local priest had noticed Margaret had a remarkable

intellect and contacted the Sisters of Mercy in Perth, telling them she was just the sort of pupil Victoria Square Ladies College needed. As a result, Margaret had been brought to Perth, kitted out in the bottle green uniform and allotted a bed in the boarders' dormitory.

Soon she was top her class in every subject. No-one could compete with her, but she never looked happy, and she never talked to anyone. Other boarders told us she cried herself to sleep every night and only wanted to go home to her family.

At first, I didn't realise Yvette was a charity case, too. She had been friendly towards me from my first day, but never asked questions. She told me nothing about herself, except that her father was at sea and she lived with her mother, who was French. Quiet and beautifully mannered, Yvette was always in the background, an onlooker, a little apart from the rest. She was not clever in class, usually close to the bottom when test results were read out.

At first, she puzzled me, until I competed in my first Sports Day. I had seen her playing netball, and she had been very good, but when it came to athletics, running, jumping, hurdling, she was incredible. Sport was taken seriously and an ex-army instructor put us through our paces every week. Yvette was the apple of his eye. Already she was equalling state records, and I soon understood why the College wanted her.

Yvette became my best friend and my greatest challenge. Try as I might, I could never beat her at sports. I always came second.

~

I didn't find my new subjects too difficult and life at the college was good. I loved sport, and I loved learning. There were times, however, when I stopped and thought about how time was passing and how far I had strayed from my dreams.

Deep down, I still longed to be an actress, or an artist, or a writer.

I had given up my dream of being a dancer. No-one at the college danced, except the senior girls, when once a month, a contingent of spotted youths from the nearby Christian Brothers College was marched in, escorted by unsmiling priests. For an hour, the hall was given over to the correct etiquette of asking a young lady for a dance and the clumsy efforts to master the intricacies of the waltz.

Reluctantly, I had also given up my dream of being a singer. The college had an operatic society which performed annually at His Majesty's Theatre in the centre of Perth, but the volatile Italian countess who taught singing was unimpressed with the quality of my voice. During the production of Hansel and Gretel, the operatic rejects, of which I was one, were cast as gingerbread men. Dressed in brown outfits with huge buttons down our fronts to suggest outsize currants, our only appearance was to come bursting out of a wooden oven and line up behind the leading lady as she sang.

Unfortunately, in the week before the show, I strained my foot playing netball but decided to tell no-one in case I was replaced in the team.

On the first night, patrons of the college and dignitaries from the cathedral filled the front row. Backstage, the gingerbread men waited anxiously for their cue.

As the music reached a crescendo, the first gingerbread man bent and clambered through the oven door onto the stage.

Following close behind, I bent to follow, but my foot hurt and I stumbled. Lurching forward, I grasped the wooden door to regain my balance, but the oven shuddered and collapsed on the row of squealing gingerbread men behind me.

It was my only appearance with the operatic society. I was told I was no longer needed.

But I was not ready to give up my theatrical dreams entirely.

I had already suggested to the English teacher that the college ought to have a dramatic society, but her response was luke-warm.

Now I tried a different approach. I found a few like-minded friends and asked for permission to start an out-of-school-hours debating society that would meet once a month. This time, our suggestion was welcomed. A debating society was considered educational.

To my surprise, the debating society proved very popular. More popular than we had dared to imagine and from the first night there was a large audience of both boarders and day scholars. The only trouble was that the debaters, inexperienced and in awe of the audience, did not have much to say. The proceedings did not last long, and we were left with an eager but disappointed audience.

I went to see to Sister Mary Emmanuelle. I pointed out that it was a shame to waste a willing audience or lose the enthusiasm for the debating society before it had a chance to develop. Perhaps a few willing volunteers could put on a light-hearted sketch each month as a finale to round off the evening?

I never underestimated Sister Mary Emmanuelle. I am certain she read me like a book, but she agreed.

"Of course, I shall have to read the sketch before it is performed," she said. "And this must not interfere with your studies."

I was over the moon. At last I could take a step towards my dreams. I was going to be an actress. Not only that, I was going to be a writer.

The debating society audiences enjoyed my sketches and so did Sister Mary Emmanuelle, although she seemed concerned I might be stretching myself too far. When I sat the junior examinations again and scored highly in all thirteen subjects, she was delighted.

Everybody seemed to be. I was called in to see Mother Superior. She had the newspaper with the results of all the Colleges in front of her and congratulated me.

I was a credit to Victoria Square Ladies College, she said, and no doubt I would go on to university. Perhaps I would become a doctor or a lawyer. Wouldn't my parents be proud of me then?

I smiled and nodded. I didn't have the courage to tell her I didn't want to be a doctor or a lawyer.

With Mother at work and Cecil and me at school, it was hard for Father being cooped up in one room. He was a quiet, self-conscious man who found it difficult to mix with others at the best of times. Now, with a tatty wig and second-hand clothes, he became even more of a loner, walking the sun-baked streets to pass the time.

One day, he wandered into a church where a jumble sale had finished. The volunteers were clearing the junk that had been left behind and he was struck by the number of books waiting to be thrown out. He offered to clear them and was even given an old suitcase to carry them away.

Down by the river, he sorted them, putting the newest and most attractive back in the suitcase and dumping the rest a few at a time in dustbins on his way back to the lodging house.

When we came home, he excitedly told us his new plan. He was going door-to-door. For twopence, anyone could exchange a book they had already read for one out of his case. It would be a portable library service.

Mother was doubtful. She couldn't see him being

successful at knocking on doors, and the books he had to offer were hardly exciting.

I'm sure she expected him to become disheartened quickly, but strangely enough, he wasn't. It was mostly women who opened the doors, and perhaps there was something pathetic about him that appealed to them. Some not only paid the twopence but gave him a couple of extra books. Gradually, his case became heavier.

News travels fast among the hungry. Father had thought up a money-making scheme that needed no capital, just an old case and a load of junk books. Soon, others were competing with him.

Father tried going further afield, but the case was too heavy for him to carry. He decided he needed something extra, another line that was bright and cheerful, to attract the eye when he opened the case and make his efforts stand out from the others.

He begged some offcut material from a dressmaker, and Mother and I did our best. We made pincushions, needle cases, oven gloves, and anything else we could manage.

But there were too many men knocking on the same doors. There were arguments. Even fights, and Father found it increasingly difficult to carry the heavy suitcase for any distance.

Even Miss O'Leary was concerned.

"Keep doing this, man, and you'll drop dead," she warned him. "As sure as God made little apples, you will."

~

It was a few weeks before Christmas when one of the other lodgers told Father about the reforestation work. Men were being taken on to plant freshly cleared land with new trees.

He applied and was accepted. Perhaps he was beginning to look more like an Australian workman, burned brown by the sun, skinny, wearing old clothes and a broad-brimmed hat that had been given to him at a charity handout.

It was the first time our family had been separated for Christmas. Worse, it was Mother's turn to work at the restaurant on Christmas Day.

Miss O'Leary did her best. She contributed a pad and coloured pencils, two children's books, an apple and orange to help fill Cecil's stocking, and she invited us down for dinner with her and her widowed sister in the little kitchen where they both lived. All four of us wore paper hats, and we played snap and other children's games after the meal.

CHAPTER 19

By my fourteenth birthday, I had made it into the Senior Netball Team and the Senior Tennis Team, and what pleased me even more, I had won first prize in an art competition run by the West Australian Agricultural Show. To my mother's delight, the prize was ten pounds.

I got on well with the nuns who taught me, but I was always aware of Sister Mary Emmanuelle. She never fussed, but I knew she watched over me. If I appeared run-down, she summoned me to her office where she kept a big jar of cod liver oil and malt secreted in a cupboard. Every morning and afternoon, she would shovel a spoonful into me until she felt I was sufficiently recovered.

The tree-planting didn't last long. Father came back worn and depressed. Life wasn't worth living. He was a failure. There was nothing ahead for him, no work, nothing.

Rather than filling Mother with sympathy, his misery sparked her anger. The unreasoning rage I dreaded was unleashed. There was nothing ahead for her, either, she screamed. She might as well end it all now.

The other lodgers called Miss O'Leary and she marched

upstairs. Hammering on the door of our room, she bellowed there were to be no arguments in her house. If my parents wanted to fight, they would have to do it walking the streets. She was a strong character, and they went, slamming the front door behind them.

I was ashamed and frightened, but Miss O'Leary put her arms around Cecil and me and comforted us.

"Don't worry. They'll come back when they've got it out of their systems," she said.

She was kind, but she didn't understand. The river was only a few streets away. I was still afraid. If it hadn't been for Cecil, I would have run after them.

It was past midnight when they came back and climbed into bed without a word.

Next morning, Mother went to work, Cecil and I went to school, and Father set off with his suitcase of books. I don't think he knew what else to do.

Later that day, a door-to-door competitor, a Welshman, came across him sitting on the edge of the pavement beside his case.

"God Almighty!" The Welshman tried to lift the case. "Your guts'll fall out carrying that and you can't be making more than peanuts."

He sat down beside my father and opened his own case.

"Look, boy, this is the sort of stuff women buy."

The case was packed with cosmetics, stationery, handkerchiefs and oddments of haberdashery.

Father explained he had no money, but the Welshman shook his head.

"Look, as one Pommie to another, I'll do you a favour."

He took Father to a big corrugated iron shed on the outskirts of town. It was a warehouse stacked to the roof with goods of every description. A man was busy packing suitcases and handing them back to their owners.

"You take a caseful out, and when you come back, you pay

for what you've sold. You never know exactly what you are going to get, but it's all good stuff." His Welsh friend patted him on the back. "They don't take just anybody here, but don't worry. I'll introduce you."

That evening, Father looked self-conscious as he opened his case to show us what he had been hawking from door to door all day. It was full of ladies' knickers.

~

During her time at the Rosebud Café, Mother had been friendly with Nora, one of the waitresses. A Lancashire woman, she was married to a South Australian called Carl.

Out of the blue, Nora sought out my mother at the restaurant. She and her husband had been offered a house. Nothing big or special, but with Carl still unemployed, they couldn't afford the rent. They were looking for someone to share it with them.

The house wasn't big or special. It was one of a row of five corrugated iron and weatherboard shacks on the fringe of the ever-growing tip where lorries dumped rubbish, and on which a new causeway across the Swan river would one day be built.

There was a little weed-filled garden front and back and the neighbours looked friendly. One kept an ancient horse that snuffled over the fence at us, another had a hand-scrawled sign in her window announcing that she was a spiritualist and could summon the dead at any time for a shilling.

Miss O'Leary was sorry to see us go. She and Mrs Maguire came to the front door, handkerchiefs in hand, to see us off. Most of their lodgers didn't stay for so long.

Although the house was small, to us it seemed spacious. We had a bedroom, a shared kitchen, a toilet and a square lean-to with a large metal bath in the middle.

The packing case containing the sewing machine and one of the cabin trunks was still in the shed at the back of Grandmother's house.

My parents hired a carrier and went with him to fetch them. I think Mother hoped to see some of her family. Perhaps she thought the past could be put behind them, but only Eric and Grandfather came out. Grandmother sent a message saying she didn't want to speak to her.

Mother came back disappointed. I wished I could have gone with her to see Grandfather. I still loved him and missed him.

Father was out every day with his case, and soon he was a regular at the warehouse. As his Welsh friend had predicted, every time he visited, his suitcase was topped up with different lines. Most of them were ordinary, run-of-the-mill things like stationery, toothpaste or cleaning powders, but sometimes there were cosmetics, brightly coloured scarves, even prettily embroidered blouses. His sales increased, and we all helped him count his take at the end of the day.

But there were problems, too. The couple we shared with quarrelled constantly. Sometimes saucepans and frying pans flew, and we had to wait for tempers to cool before we could venture into the kitchen to cook a meal.

Then there were the flies and mosquitoes that invaded us from the tip. There was no netting on the windows or the doors, and although mosquito sprays were on sale, they were much too expensive for us to afford.

It was difficult to sleep, but Father did his best. He found some wire and rigged hoops across the beds. From them we hung strips of rag dipped in paraffin, or kerosene as the Australians called it. The fumes kept the insects away, but the rank smell wafting from the rags dangling inches above our faces made us feel sick.

No one told me what happened between Nora and Carl. All I knew was that one day they packed their bags and headed back to South Australia, leaving us to pay the full rent of the house.

Even with the money Father was bringing in, it was not possible.

When the landlord called at the end of the week, Father explained what had happened, and to his surprise, he was understanding.

No one realised it at the time, but the world was on the threshold of what would become known as the Great Depression. Times were tough for tenants and landlords alike.

Genuine tenants found they could no longer pay their rent, so they moved out and in no time, squatters moved in. Things were getting worse, and squatters were becoming more destructive. Many had no respect for property. If they were short of firewood, they pulled off cupboard doors or levered up floorboards. No-one dared leave a house empty.

The landlord asked my parents what they could afford. They told him and he appreciated their honesty. It was better to accept half rent than to have squatters. All he asked was that we looked after his property.

It seemed our luck had changed at last. Cecil and I had a bedroom to ourselves. We cleaned the house from end to end, unpacked the crate and Mother set to work on the sewing machine and made curtains out of old sheets. We even pulled the weeds from of the garden. For the first time since we left London, we had a home of our own.

About a month later, Father ran into his Welsh friend again, heaving a suitcase and sweating profusely.

"Bloody books!" He sighed. "But what else can you do?"

He stared at my father's case.

"You're not still carrying stuff from the warehouse, are

you? Haven't you heard? It's all nicked. The police are there, picking people up when they go in for a new load."

Father came home ashen-faced and shaking. That evening, as soon as it was dark, I looked after Cecil while my parents climbed across the tip and buried the suitcase and its contents deep in the rubbish.

~

Father had had no real job for the four years we had been in Australia and Uncle Jack had refused us any more help. We had not heard from Annie again. I think she knew she could only push Jack so far, and rather than admit failure, she had chosen to keep her distance. I still liked her, though, and wished life had been different.

Mother was tired and worn. Her anger still simmered and sometimes spurts of temper erupted out of the blue.

Unable to find work, Father badgered the authorities and eventually announced he had been put on the Unemployed Register. That meant he was entitled to State Sustenance Allowance. We would receive free firewood and seven shillings a week each for him and for Cecil. Nothing for Mother because she was working and nothing for me because I was past school leaving age.

As happened so often in my life, I felt guilty. I should have been working. I should have been bringing in money to help the family.

I tried to talk to Mother, but she flew into a temper. I was not leaving the college. She had sworn to her family I would grow up to be a lady, and nothing was going to change that.

One morning, a government truck drew up in front of the house. Two men tipped an enormous tree trunk over the fence and drove off. Our free firewood had arrived.

Our only means of cooking was a wood- burning stove.

Until then, we had scavenged wood from the tip, but now we had a huge supply, all in one lump.

Father had never used an axe. The man next door loaned him one, but he didn't explain about using wedges to prise strips off the trunk.

Gathering his energy, Father raised the axe into the air and swung it at the tree trunk. He was clumsy and out of his depth. The axe bounced off the wood and split his leg open.

Blood spurted everywhere.

The neighbour carried Father into our house and tried to reassure Mother. He had lived in the back country most of his life and had experienced many such emergencies. The bleeding had to be stopped. To do that, the leg must be held up in the air.

He disappeared next door and came back with a hook and some rope. He screwed the hook into the wall of the bedroom while my father lay on the floor moaning. Then he tied the rope around Father's ankle and hoisted his bloody leg high in the air.

"That should do it." Our neighbour looked pleased with himself. "When you're out in the bush, you can't just stand back and wait for a doctor. It's a case of do something or die."

The bleeding didn't stop, and my father didn't die.

In the end, Mother sent for a doctor. It cost four pounds and took months to pay off.

CHAPTER 20

One afternoon, Trixie appeared on our doorstep. She told us Grandmother was ill, and she thought Mother ought to come.

I went with her, but by the time we reached the house, the old lady had been rushed into hospital.

The family was in a state of consternation. They told us Grandmother had been getting worse for some time. She had severe gastric problems and although her doctor had put her on a strict diet, she refused to listen. She had demanded steak, oysters and rich fruitcake, and my aunts had supplied her with everything she wanted.

The consternation was not caused by Grandmother's condition, however. The doctor had moved her into the nearest hospital, which happened to be a Catholic establishment, staffed by nuns.

When Grandmother realised, she was furious but too ill to do anything about it. She demanded one of her family stayed by her bedside to protect her.

My aunts and Eric visited her during the day, but the years of listening to Grandmother's hatred had left an indelible mark. None of them were prepared to stay the night under a Catholic roof with black-clad nuns hovering nearby.

There was only one person in the family who loved Catholics, Violet sneered.

By the time I reached the hospital, Grandmother was unconscious. The doctor was kind and explained there was nothing else he could do for her. I nodded, and he put his hand on my shoulder for a moment before leaving.

As the hours ticked past, I sat beside the bed, watching the shallow rise and fall of her breathing. I was with her when she died.

When I got back, the family had already heard the news. Grandfather and Eric were crying. The aunts were arguing. Trixie had claimed Grandmother's fur coat. Violet had her gold watch and her bird-of-paradise hat. Edith was sorting through her jewellery, looking for her treasured necklace with the huge amber pendant.

~

The family knew Grandmother would have insisted everyone wore black for the funeral. To me, it seemed she was still controlling us, even from her coffin.

None of the neighbours had much love for a family who argued at the top of their voices night and day, but they rallied round. Offerings were dumped in a heap on the kitchen table to be sorted through and tried on.

I was given a shapeless black coat and an ugly black felt hat. Looking in a mirror, I hated my reflection, and it seemed an extension of the hate I felt for my grandmother. Another wave of guilt crashed over me.

My cousin, Maybelle, arrived at the cemetery in a bright red dress which, knowing her family's circumstances, was probably all she possessed. No-one in the family ever spoke to her again.

We had a post-box on our gate, the same as everyone else, but no-one wrote to us. Father was the only person who looked inside it after the postman passed by each day. His leg was almost healed, and he was growing restless.

Then one morning, a Post Office van drew up outside and Mother was handed a parcel. The sender's name was on the outside. It was from Auntie Edie. Cecil and I crowded round excitedly. Only Father stood back.

The parcel contained six pretty dresses and an envelope. Mother opened it and read out the letter inside.

"Dear Hilda and George. It was so good to hear from you, although I wish Fate was being kinder to you. Still, I am glad you feel you can turn to me when things are at their worst. You asked for twenty pounds, but I am sending you thirty. Please see it as a gift, not a loan. The dresses are only second-hand, but I hope little Hilda will be pleased with them. I hope they fit. Love, Edie."

Mother didn't understand. Neither did I. Father looked shame-faced as he explained. With nothing to do except wander the streets, he had spent a lot of time at the newspaper stand in the library, and he had worked out a gambling system.

Mother exploded. How dare he! After everything he had promised.

Father begged her to listen, but it was a long time before she quietened enough for him to go on. He told us he had checked his system with the racing results in the newspaper day after day, and it had worked. If he had had money to gamble, he would have been hundreds of pounds in pocket already.

"No! I won't have it! Not again!" Mother was beside herself.

"Please…" Again, he managed to calm her. "Just let me explain how it works. Tell me where I could be wrong."

She listened, her face grim. So did I.

The system only bet on favourites, and sooner or later, a favourite always came up. The secret was to increase the stake money so that when you won, you got enough back to cover all your previous losses and make a profit as well.

Father had been planning for months. Now all he needed was enough money to back his system, which was why he had written to his sister asking for a loan. He had thought it best not to tell her why he needed it.

"I can start with a small stake," he explained. "That will give me a chance to build up. There won't be any expenses. No entrance money. Nothing. I can work from Scotsman's Hill."

I had heard of Scotsman's Hill, but I had never been there. Trotting was a favourite form of racing in the West. The horses pulled lightweight carts behind them, carrying the drivers.

The trotting ground was just around the corner from the tip. At night we could see the glare of lights in the sky and hear the music and the excited buzz of bookies and the thousands of people who turned out to watch and bet.

Scotsman's Hill was at the far end of the tip, a huge mountain of rubbish that overlooked the beautifully kept trotting ground. From the top of it, you had a panoramic view of the racecourse.

But Scotsman's Hill was only for the poor. Anyone could go up there, and provided you could climb to the top of the rubbish tip, you had everything you could want, hotdog stands, sweets, drinks, popcorn vendors and bookies who welcomed even the smallest bet.

Hundreds of people, many of them families, spent their Saturday nights up on Scotsman's Hill, enjoying the music from the loudspeakers, gambling a few pennies at a time and shouting encouragement down to the races below.

"Please. Let me have this one chance." Father's parting words rang in my ears. He had gone, and I was sitting with Mother.

Her anger was spent, and her eyes were raw from crying. I was about to suggest we went to bed when she turned to me.

"He's tried gambling before," she said. "Only it wasn't his money. It belonged to the firm he worked for. That's why we had to leave England and come here before the police caught him. That's why you had to give up your scholarship."

She looked at me, but I was too shocked to react.

"What do you think we should do?" she asked.

I was fifteen, and for the first time, she was treating me as an equal. It wasn't fair. I didn't want to take sides, but I knew she was waiting for an answer.

I said the only thing that came into my mind. "It isn't really our money. It belongs to Auntie Edie, and she sent it to him."

The next Saturday evening, Father set off for Scotsman's Hill.

He came back smiling. His system was working. He had won three pounds. The next week, he lost two pounds, but he was unconcerned. It was all part of the system. He would soon make it up.

And he did. He came back seven pounds better off. Mother never asked for a penny. She seemed determined to give him this one chance.

"If only it would work," she said, out of his hearing. "He's an office man. He tries but he can't do the heavy labouring they expect of him here. His heart won't stand up to it."

For his part, Father was happier than I had seen him in years. The next Saturday, he was jovial. Why not make it a family outing? Why didn't we all go up on Scotsman's Hill and enjoy the excitement?

But that was asking too much of Mother. She told him he would be better on his own. He could concentrate on his calculations and she would have supper ready for him.

But the supper was cold when he came back. It was after midnight and he looked ill. He would not be returning to Scotsman's Hill. He had lost everything.

~

The letter came a few months before I was due to take my leaving examinations.

Sister Mary Emmanuelle was still dosing me with cod liver oil and malt each day. She said little, but I knew she was anxious I should do well.

For myself, I was not greatly worried about the exams, even though I was considerably younger than any of the others in the class. What I was worried about was my family. A new sense of responsibility was weighing me down.

I could have been working for nearly two years, bringing in money to make life easier for them. Instead, I was still studying and everyone who cared about me had their sights set on me going to university, then spending years studying to be a lawyer or a doctor.

It wasn't what I wanted, but it was what my family needed. It would be a future that would make all their sacrifices worthwhile. The time was coming when I would have to decide.

~

Mother was apprehensive when she opened the letter, but it was just a few lines summoning my parents to a meeting.

Father was afraid the authorities had changed their minds about paying the sustenance money.

That afternoon, when Cecil and I came home, it was obvious something serious had happened. My parents had not been the only ones summoned. Dozens of couples had been seated in rows to listen to a speaker.

Australia was a vast country with a tiny population, they had been told, and the need for immigrants to swell that population was as great as ever. But they had to be the right kind of immigrants, healthy, hard-working, ambitious pioneers, the kind that could make Australia a great nation.

"And we're not that kind of people," Father said bitterly. "The government has decided they can't afford to keep us. They've made a list of all the people who are on state handouts and they're going to send us back where we came from."

"I won't go," Mother wailed. "I won't go and they can't make me."

I looked at Father.

"It's no good," he said sadly. "We may as well face it. There's nothing here for us... but we can't all go."

"Why not?" Cecil asked.

"Because they won't take your sister."

Mother was angry and crying at the same time.

"She's nearly sixteen now. They say she's healthy and well educated, the sort they want here and they won't send her back. We have to go without her."

~

I had to tell someone. Sister Mary Emmanuelle listened with her head bent. I couldn't see her face, but her big hands were clasped together on her desk.

She was silent for a long time, then she looked up at me. "Does your family want to go?"

I nodded.

"And you?"

It was all so sudden, I couldn't think clearly. I couldn't imagine life without my family. In all the years I had been in Australia, I had been cocooned in the hard-working peace of the convent. Outside of that, I had known only the blanketing isolation of poverty, hardship and frustration.

I had no friends who knew about my life beyond the college walls and nothing would have made me turn to my mother's family for help.

All I really knew about Australia was second hand, schoolgirl chatter, boastful accounts of holiday trips, extravagant parties I had never experienced, shopping trips to stores I had never entered. Yet, if my parents left, I would have to stand on my own, find a place to live, and get a job. Suddenly it didn't matter about examinations and university, doctors, lawyers or anything else. I had come to a crossroads and life would never be as I had known it.

I was not a Catholic. No-one had made any attempt to change that, and I was glad. My relationship with God was free and uncomplicated by rituals, doctrines or fear, but at that moment, he seemed very far away.

Sister Mary Emmanuelle was still watching me.

"Do you want to go back to England?"

"I want to be with my family," I said, "but the authorities have decided I have to stay here."

She stood up.

"Go home. You are more use there at the moment. I will go and see Mother Superior and together we will speak to the Bishop. Have faith. He has a few influential Catholics among his flock."

A week later, another letter dropped into our post box. Mother read it aloud.

'Regarding the arranged repatriation of the family to England, representations have been made from several quarters, and after official consideration, it has been decided to include daughter, Hilda Anne Spear in the repatriation order.'

The relief was enormous. I tried to tell Sister Mary Emmanuelle how grateful I was, but she brushed my thanks aside. What had happened was no fault of mine. I had kept my part of the bargain and the college was proud of what I had achieved.

"They say you'll be sailing in ten weeks, so there's no time to waste."

She was as good as her word and as practical as ever. Who knew what lay ahead for me? I would be given good references, but I needed something more practical. Some of the older girls were taking secretarial courses, and I was to join them. In ten weeks, I must master the rudiments of shorthand and typewriting.

There was more. We would arrive in a cold country at the beginning of winter. She arranged with a charity for the whole family to have the pick of whatever warm clothes they could offer.

I wanted to kiss her, but you don't kiss people like Sister Mary Emmanuelle. You just thank God they exist.

CHAPTER 21

We sailed from Fremantle ten weeks later. There were the usual streamers and cheers and noisy goodbyes from the dockside, but there were no familiar faces among the crowd. No-one had come to wave us goodbye.

I had been determined to see Grandfather before we left. Mother and Cecil went with me. Eric had found a job somewhere up country and my three aunts were at the hospital working.

Grandfather seemed a lonely figure sitting on the veranda puffing at his pipe, yet he looked to be in better health. There was a calm about him, a peacefulness that I had never seen before.

He had joined the congregation at the local Anglican church. He told me he was glad of the company, but he still communed with his God in the same direct way he had taught me.

"Poor Annie," he said, "she wouldn't have liked it, but nothing can irritate her now, can it?"

I understood. He was relishing a tranquillity he hadn't known since he met her. He was a good man, and he had earned his peace. I knew he was old, but I hoped he would live a long time to enjoy it.

The S.S. Largs Bay was a one-class liner. Her sailing list included paid passengers and a large contingent of 'repats' from all over the country.

To be honest, once onboard, no difference was made between the two groups. The crew were cheerful, the facilities, sports equipment, and the like were available to all, and we were grateful. Dressed in charity clothes and with less than ten pounds in Mother's purse with which to start a new life in England, my family still clung to their dignity. To them, repatriation was a slur labelling us as rejects and the last thing they wanted was to publicise the fact.

There were those among the 'repats' who felt as they did, but there were others who were angry. They called protest meetings in the lounge and argued noisily that nothing was being done to help them. Australia was tossing them out to save money and the British Government was taking no responsibility. We would walk off the boat on the other side of the world and be met with absolutely nothing.

Although we kept away from the meetings, we knew they were right. The biggest problem would be to find somewhere to live.

Mother had flatly refused to contact Ida or her brother Ernie, and she had dared my father to ask Auntie Edie for help. In her eyes, Auntie Edie was a lady and Mother felt she looked down on her. I think she had always been ashamed of her family.

It was difficult to think of anyone else we could turn to, but eventually Mother had remembered a girl called Lizzie, who worked with her at the restaurant in London before she was married. Lizzie's mother had let rooms.

It had been a long shot, and in the letter Mother wrote, she did not mention our true circumstances. She only said we were returning to England, but her effort succeeded. The mother had died, but the letter found its way to Lizzie. She was now married with a teenaged son, but she was delighted to hear from her old girlhood friend. She and her husband lived in an area of London called Tooting. We were welcome to the spare room for a few nights until we could get ourselves organised.

We were six days out from Freemantle and due to call at Colombo the next day when something happened that stayed with me for the rest of my life.

There was another meeting of repats going on in the lounge. One or two loud-mouths were making a great fuss, calling for joint action of some kind. The captain had promised to come down and speak to them.

Father was agitated. He would not admit to being a repat, but he felt he should attend the meeting. We ought to know what was going on.

Mother couldn't control her emotions any longer. She flew into a rage and forbade him to leave the cabin. When Father objected, she ranted uncontrollably and by the time he gave in, she was white and shaking. She looked so ill Father called the ship's doctor, who gave her a sedative to make her sleep until morning.

Father and Cecil went to bed soon afterwards, and for the first time, I was left alone.

Up on deck, a band played and as I stood against the rail watching, a young man picked his way between the dancers towards me.

Would I like to dance? He said he had noticed me several

times during the past days, but I had always been with my family and he had been hesitant to intrude.

I had never danced with anyone except for a few clumsy steps when the college boys came to the convent for their lessons. I stumbled, I stepped on his toes, and soon we were laughing together.

He bought me lemonade, and we stood at the rail and talked. His name was Kit Bridgman. He was eighteen and had been on holiday, staying with relatives in New South Wales. Now he was going home to his father's tea plantation in Ceylon.

He asked about me, and I told him what I wanted him to know. That I was almost sixteen, had been at college in Perth and was now travelling home with my family. In the unexpected pleasure of the moment, I didn't give a thought to my faded cotton charity dress or my scuffed school shoes.

We were together all evening. He was easy to talk to, and I felt as though we had known each other for years. We danced the last waltz, then stood looking across the dark water to the lights of Colombo.

"It's been a lovely evening," he said at last, then he held my hand and kissed my cheek. "I am going home and so are you. It would have been lovely if things had been different, but I know I shan't forget you."

When I came up on deck next morning, the little boats were ferrying passengers ashore and he was gone. But I have never forgotten him. For the first time in my life, someone made me feel important. I had laughed and danced and talked and not felt guilty about anything.

And it was true what he had said. I was going home, back to where I had begun my dreams of being a dancer and a singer and an actress. I could start afresh without being committed to anything. No doubt, if I had stayed in Australia I would have gone to university and ended up studying to be a lawyer or a doctor. I knew myself too well to doubt it. I would have done what I thought was right for those around me, for those who would become dependent upon me.

But Fate had intervened. It was not my decision, but I was going home. It was going to be hard, I had no doubt about that, but as the days passed, my spirits lifted and I knew I was right to believe in miracles.

~

Our route was the same as the outward journey, but in reverse. We crossed the Arabian Sea, the Gulf of Aden, the Red Sea, and the Suez Canal, before reaching Port Said.

We didn't go ashore at any of the ports. There seemed little point, as we had nothing to spend.

It was after we left Port Said that my father found the wallet, tucked down the back of one of the chairs in the lounge. He may have been a gambler, but he was honest. He immediately handed the wallet, stuffed with notes, to the purser.

"The owner's a lucky man," the purser said. "Leave me your name and cabin number. He's bound to give you a reward."

We waited eagerly. After two days, Father went back to the office. The purser looked embarrassed. Yes, the wallet had been claimed, but the owner had simply stuffed it into his pocket and walked away without so much as a 'thank you.'

We passed Gibraltar and crossed the Bay of Biscay. The protest meetings continued, and they became more militant as we neared our destination. We didn't attend any of them, but it was impossible to miss the raised voices. The meetings had become the talking point of the ship.

It was rumoured the captain thought there might be trouble when we landed, and to placate the ringleaders, he sent out a message asking his company to pass on to the government the intensity of feelings on board.

"Don't suppose it'll do much good for the poor devils," our cabin steward said innocently, "but you can bet your bottom dollar there'll be police at the dockside just in case."

He was right. There were groups of police discreetly stationed at intervals along the dockside as the liner berthed, but as the passengers crowded the railings, their eyes were all on a single figure among the crowds below.

A large woman in a shapeless lime-green coat had rolled up a magazine to form an improvised megaphone and was bellowing through it. At first it was difficult to distinguish what she was shouting, but gradually it became clearer. "Hilda! Hilda! "

"Oh, my God!" Mother whispered. "It's Lizzie!"

Half an hour later, we made our way down the gangplank. Our cabin trunks were already on the dock and the hold luggage was being heaved up in great slings.

We had been passed by the Passport and Customs officials set up in the ship's dining room while a noisy meeting of the militant repats was going on in the lounge.

Looming clouds shrouded the sky as we stepped onto English soil, but whatever the future might hold, I was glad to be back.

Lizzie pushed her way through the crowd and enveloped Mother in a bearhug.

"Jesus Christ! Never thought I'd see you again, girl! Had a good trip, did you? What the hell made you go to Australia?"

She asked questions and plunged on without waiting for answers.

"Sid would have come with me, but he's in Glasgow. So's my son, Reg. They're at a meeting, but Charlie's outside with his van. Don't worry. It's big enough to take all of you and your luggage as long as you don't mind the smell of vegetables. You remember Charlie? My brother, the one that got nicked for picking pockets. He's straight now, mind you. God, it's good to see you, girl."

All four of us climbed into the back of the van with the luggage. The smell of onions and oranges was unmistakable. Charlie seemed cheerful enough, but he didn't say a word. He didn't have a chance. Lizzie sat in the front and talked over her shoulder the whole way. It was like being swept into a new life on a tidal wave.

Lizzie's house was one of a terrace tucked away in a backstreet. Charlie helped heave the cabin trunks up to the spare bedroom and offered to store our crate in the shed where he garaged his van until we got settled. By that time, Lizzie had a meal on the table.

"You and George and the boy can go in the spare room and the girl can go up in the attic," she announced. "Reg sleeps up there. They'll be company for one another."

I didn't understand then why Charlie chuckled at that, but Lizzie scowled at him. "None of that," she warned. "He knows I'll be watching him."

When the meal was over, Charlie went and Lizzie beamed.

"I thought you might be knackered. Mightn't want to go down the pub tonight, so I got in some gin and plenty of Guinness."

My parents glanced awkwardly at each other. They never touched alcohol normally, but they could hardly refuse. Lizzie had made us so welcome.

"Sid'll be sorry he wasn't here," Lizzie said as she poured her third glass of Guinness, "but he'll be back tomorrow. He's been to Cardiff and Birmingham, too, this time. Always takes Reg with him. Says we've got to get all the young people with us."

"He travels a lot, does he?" Mother asked politely.

"You name it, he goes there. Went to Poland last year. And Russia."

"What does he do?"

"He's a fundraiser. It's his job to get the money in. Contributions. You know. You can't have a revolution without money."

She grinned cheerfully.

"If Sid could hear me, he'd knock my block off. You won't say a word, will you? He's heart and soul in it. So's Reg. Reckons we'll all be as happy as pigs in shit when the workers rise up. Me, I don't know. I ain't really joining in. Let 'em get on with it. Still, it would be nice to sell off the Crown Jewels and all the palaces and things as long as we all got our fair share of the dosh."

Father said nothing. He just looked stunned.

Later, up in the spare bedroom, he sat on the edge of the bed, his head in his hands. "What the hell are we going to do now?" He never swore, but he was past caring. "We've got ourselves mixed up with a load of bloody Communists!"

CHAPTER 22

Next morning Lizzie was her bright, breezy self. She was going shopping. Would I like to go with her?

I agreed, knowing that once they were left alone, my parents would be out looking for other accommodation.

As soon as her shopping was finished, Lizzie headed for a pub. How old was I? Nearly sixteen? Good. Near enough.

She ordered me a glass of guinness.

"What kind of work are you looking for?" Lizzie asked. When I told her I had been at school until I left Australia, she looked amazed.

"My God! Well, you're going to need a job, aren't you? Your Mum and Dad look as though they can do with all the help they can get."

She frowned, then stared round at the pub customers and banged her empty glass on the table to attract attention.

"Listen, you lot. I've got a girl here looking for a job. She's not fussy. She'll do anything, won't you, love? Any of you lot got any bright ideas."

She waited while heads were shaken, then grinned. "Don't worry. I know plenty of other pubs. We'll do the rounds."

Sid and Reg came home that afternoon. Sid was a dour, angular man, his heavy brows drawn into a permanent frown. He was polite, but that was all. We were Lizzie's friends. He talked to her, not to us.

Reg was different. He was seventeen, with lank hair greased back from his face and bad breath, but he brimmed with self-confidence. All the girls fell for his charms, he assured me. If I behaved myself, he might take me up West for a night out with his pals.

I didn't want to go, any more than my parents wanted me to, but Lizzie was thrilled with the idea. A night out was just what I needed, she assured me.

Lizzie was rough and ready, loud and completely devoid of tact, yet the more I was with her, the more I liked her. She was just as God made her, no frills, no affectations. If anyone had suggested she had a heart of gold, she would have set about them with a rolling pin, yet, if she had found a family of stray dogs, she would have taken them in whether Sid liked it or not.

She hadn't found stray dogs. She had found us. She was happy, and we were grateful.

I went. I was the only girl with nine rowdy young men, all unashamedly looking over Reg's new girlfriend.

I had never been on an Underground train before and Piccadilly Circus, Leicester Square and the Strand, with their bright lights, thronging crowds, kerbside musicians and horn-honking traffic, were a new world. I had only been to the West End of London once before in my life when my aunts had taken me to the music-hall.

I thought we might be headed to see a show, but I was wrong.

"We'll have a good blow-out, then we'll do the rounds and have some fun," Reg promised.

We went to Lyons Corner House in the Strand, where my aunts had taken me for a dignified afternoon tea when I was small. The place hadn't changed, waitresses in black dresses with white aprons and frill-edged headbands, little tables with snowy white tablecloths and a band playing soft background music.

A man in a dinner suit at the door was visibly nervous at the sight of us. He explained there were no tables available for large parties, but my companions thought that was hilarious. In moments they had crowded him aside, pushed tables together and gathered up empty chairs while waitresses stood back apprehensively.

The man in the dinner suit pushed the waitresses forward.

"Serve them. We don't want trouble with them again if we can help it," he muttered.

Reg and his friends had plenty of money to spend, but nothing on the menu appealed to them. They shouted orders for drinks and demanded the lousy music from the band be jazzed up. When the food appeared, they protested it was cold and there wasn't enough of it. Arguments broke out and people at nearby tables moved away.

Two more men in dinner suits headed across the dining room towards us. I could see trouble coming and told Reg I wanted to leave, but he was too busy enjoying himself.

Twenty minutes after we walked in, we were all thrown out, but none of them seemed to care. It was all a great joke.

I wanted to go home, but Reg wouldn't hear of it. Now we were really going to have some fun, he told me.

I didn't know the expression then, but Reg and his gang's idea of a fun night out was a 'pub crawl' round the West End. Bursting in through the swing doors, downing a few pints, creating confusion, then moving on. Cheerfully at first, then, after a few stops, the mood changed. I didn't drink anything, which irritated Reg, and he never let go of my arm.

A few more stops, a few more pints, and my companions were staggering. People stood well back for them to pass.

"Up the workers!" Reg shouted at the top of his voice.

It was a signal. They all began singing 'The Red Flag'.

The police were waiting for us at the next pub.

I tried to explain that I was nothing to do with them, but Reg was still holding tight to my arm. "She's my girl," he mumbled. "Where I go, she goes."

At the station, they put all nine of them in the cells to cool off for the night, but they listened to me. It was obvious I hadn't been drinking and I don't doubt I looked scared and upset.

A policeman took me home, and my parents were horrified. Jack said nothing, but Lizzie was furious.

"He promised me he'd look after you. Just wait till I get my hands on him, the little louse! I'll tan his arse," she swore. "I don't give a damn how old he is or how many bloody revolutions he's planning to start."

Lizzie was genuinely upset about what had happened. Next day we hardly saw anything of her, but when she came back in the late afternoon, she was beaming. She had found us a flat.

"It's a lousy, poky little dump," she confessed, "but I reckon it's as cheap as you'll get."

It was in Balham, on the third and fourth floor, overlooking a busy street market. The ground floor was a tobacconist's shop. Above that was a ladies' hairdresser and above that was the flat. Two tiny rooms, one fitted with a gas cooker and a sink, and above that, an attic, its walls sloping almost to the floor. It had been divided in two by a shabby partition.

"I told you. It's a lousy, poky little dump," Lizzie repeated, "but it's only twelve shillings a week. You'll be better away from my lot. Reg is a bloody nuisance. Can't keep his mouth shut. Thinks it's a game. One day, he'll land us in the shit. Sometimes I wonder if it's all worth it."

We took the flat. Charlie moved in our possessions, including the crate with the sewing machine, and Lizzie donated a rickety table and two worn mattresses.

We had a home, and all we had to do was to find twelve shillings a week to pay for it.

I needed a job, and I was told the Labour Exchange was the place to go to find it. I hoped Father would come with me. He had grown up in England and must have known about such things, but he said he didn't feel well enough.

Since we had landed, the life seemed to have drained out of him. In a way, Mother was the same. They had no drive, no enthusiasm. I had seen our return to England as a new beginning, a chance to make my dreams come true, but I was still young and they were worn and disillusioned.

It occurred to me that coming home had always been the dream at the back of their minds. They had never settled in Australia, never felt they belonged there. Unconsciously, perhaps, they had clung to a hope that one day they would be back where they began and everything would be good.

That was why they had built so much on me. When that day came, I would have finished my education and been qualified for a profession. I would be able to earn a good living anywhere and the family would return to England and live comfortably.

But it had all happened too soon. We were back in England. Life was no easier, and I could provide nothing for them. As happened so often in my life, I felt I had failed them.

I went to the Labour Exchange on my own. I told them all about myself and showed them my certificates and my references. They registered me and gave me a National Insurance number, but when it came to finding work, they seemed stumped.

Australian examination standards meant nothing to them. In the end, they told me that Avery's, a firm of scale makers, needed a filing clerk in their London offices. They phoned and arranged an interview and I ran all the way home to get enough money from Mother to buy a return ticket on the Underground.

I found it at last, a big office block. A middle-aged woman took my certificates and references and frowned at them.

"An Australian, eh?" she said.

I shook my head. "No. I'm English."

She stared at me and handed back my papers. "Well, these are Australian. You're very brown and you talk funny. Still… maybe you'll fit in. You can start next Monday."

I was on my way home before I realised I hadn't asked how much I would be paid.

I had a job and a few days free before I started. There were things I had to do.

I knew my suggestion would be badly received, but I felt we ought to tell Auntie Edie we were back in England.

Mother objected at once. There was no point in contacting Edie until we had made the flat nice and comfortable. When I pointed out that we had no money to do that, she flew into a raging temper. She would not be embarrassed. She would not have people looking down on her.

When no-one would argue with her, she sulked for days, not speaking, not even bothering to prepare meals, then she gave in.

Father phoned his sister, and she came at once. Auntie was such a gentle soul, it was difficult to imagine how Mother could dislike her so much.

It was clear that Auntie Edie was appalled by the state of

the flat. We were sitting on the cabin trunks and sleeping on the mattresses on the floor, but she was the essence of tact.

For years, she had been a companion to an elderly lady who had just died. It was an amazing coincidence, she said. Now that she was alone, she was moving out of the house into a flat. She had been wondering what to do with the excess furniture. We could have whatever we needed.

She waited until my mother was out of the room, then hugged and kissed the three of us with tears in her eyes. And she was as good as her word. Two days later, a moving van blocked the street market outside. She had sent what she felt we needed, a dining table and chairs, two armchairs for the little room that would become a lounge, beds, even curtains, bed linen and blankets.

We had a home, and we were grateful, but there were drawbacks. We had no bathroom, just a kitchen sink, and the toilet was way down, past the hairdressers, past the tobacconists, and one flight further down than that, in a basement lit only by a dangling light bulb that swung at every draught sending eerie shadows into the dark corners. It reminded me of Grandmother's basement kitchen and had the same dank smell.

I hated going down there at night after the tobacconists and the hairdressers were closed. It was eerie. We were just around the corner from the Balham Underground Station and the tube line ran right under the building. We were told that, when the line was being laid, they had discovered an underground stream and the tunnels had been brought closer to the surface to avoid it.

Certainly, whenever you sat on the toilet, you could hear the trains rattling under you. At night they seemed louder and you could feel the toilet seat shake.

The tobacconists had already been broken into several times, and I worried there might be someone lurking down there. We made it a family excursion down to the toilet before we went to bed.

Another thing I wanted to arrange was a school for Cecil, but I found we had a rebellion on our hands. My brother had been christened Cecil but now he told us it was a stupid, sissy name and he had been ridiculed and mocked long enough by his classmates. He refused to start at a new school until his name was changed. He would be Tom, Fred or Harry. He didn't care what he was called, but not Cecil.

Mother had always boasted he was a beautiful child with a beautiful name. Normally, in her eyes, he could do no wrong, but this was different, and she was furious.

I suggested George. It was Cecil's second name and also his father's. In the end, Mother gave in, and encouraged by my brother's victory, I admitted I hated my name too. Mother had never made any secret that she disliked Hilda. She rarely used it and had taken to call me Dinah after her favourite character, the cat in Alice in Wonderland.

I was not keen on being called after a cat. If I was to succeed in my dreams, I needed a new name, one I could be proud of. I abbreviated Hilda Ann to Diann and then to Diana.

I decided to go with Mother to the local school. She was still in a difficult mood and I didn't want some simple thing to rouse her anger and give my brother a bad start.

Again, I felt guilty. I had been given the chance to get a better education than most and I wanted my brother to have his chance too. I asked about scholarships.

The headmaster was pleasant, but firm. Clearly, I didn't

know the English system. Children sat an eleven-plus examination, and the brightest won their place at grammar school. The examinations had already been held for the year, which meant George had missed out.

I couldn't believe it. Surely, under special circumstances like his, there was still a chance for him to sit the exam and gain a place?

The headmaster was patient. I was wrong. True, there were cases now and then when an obviously clever pupil had, for some reason, failed. To cover this, another examination was held two years later. If a headmaster felt a pupil could compete successfully with the grammar school standard at thirteen, and proved it, then he could be considered for a transfer.

"It doesn't really work, though," he said. "Myself, I have never put a child forward for it. It wouldn't be fair to build up their hopes only to destroy them. Two years at grammar school and pupils are further advanced at everything, and are learning new subjects, like French and algebra."

"But, if my brother was good enough in two years' time, you would put him through the examination?"

He shrugged. "It's not likely, is it? He would need special coaching and tuition."

"I can do that. And if I can get him up to a high enough standard, you promise you will put him through the examination?"

He hesitated, then promised. In fact, he did more than that. He lent me textbooks and offered to be available for any advice he could give.

CHAPTER 23

I started work on Monday morning.

It is strange how quickly we fall into the pattern of the throng.

I ran for the Underground train in the morning, afraid like everyone else of being late, then worked all day sorting a mountain of invoices into a wall of neatly labelled pigeonholes. I ate my sandwiches amid the chatter of the staff restroom before hurrying back to my pigeonholes, then ran to catch the train home and stood tight-packed, shoulder-to-shoulder all the way.

It was the same every day.

At the end of the week, when I had signed for my pay less my National Insurance stamp, put aside the cost of my next week's fares and the tasteless cups of tea that helped my sandwiches down at lunchtime, I took home eight shillings.

I took home eight shillings and the flat cost twelve shillings a week. I had to do better.

Lizzie dropped in one evening to see how we were doing. Her concern was genuine, and she bounced with excitement at the transformation in the poky little flat she had found for us.

I was unpacking one of the cabin trunks when she arrived and had just taken out some of my sketches. She pounced on them with delight.

"My God, girl, you ought to be an artist. Here. Let me have 'em for a bit. There's someone I want to show 'em to."

Lizzie had worked at the restaurant long after Mother left. She still breezed in at intervals to see the staff and to joke with regular customers. One of them was Mac, a well-known cartoonist.

She came back beaming from ear to ear.

"He liked 'em. Said you've definitely got talent. Said the first thing you've got to do is get yourself into art school."

I had no idea who Mac was, but his opinion boosted my confidence. I wanted to be an artist, and a published cartoonist thought I had talent. All I needed was to be trained. But I couldn't think about my dreams yet. First, I had to get a better paid job, start coaching George, and find work for my father.

But Father beat me to it. Not with a job for himself, but with possible work for Mother. In a newspaper at the library, he found an advert for female outworkers. It was perfect, he told me. She would be able to work from home.

Mother was not so sure. Her moods were still erratic, so I offered to go with her to an interview.

We came back on a crowded tram with bulky parcels of padding, wooden coat hangers, metal hooks, lengths of brightly coloured satin, rolls of ribbon and reels of cotton.

"He's a very nice man." Mother told me. "He's given me half a gross of coat hangers to cover to see how I get on."

Father's eyes gleamed when he saw the pile of materials. I

tried to explain the magnitude of the work involved, but he was too excited to listen.

To complete a coat hanger, an outworker first covered a hook with ribbon and screwed it into a curved piece of wood. Then, she stripped lengths of padding, cut them to size, bound them round the hanger and stitched them securely with cotton. Next, she cut lengths of satin, turned their edges, and hand sewed them to the padding without leaving any visible stitches. Finally, she cut a piece of ribbon and tied a neat bow around the hook.

Father nodded happily. "And what's the pay like?"

"There are seventy-two of them and when they're finished and delivered back, we will get three shillings and sixpence."

I didn't want to think about how many hours of work it would take, but in our circumstances, even three shillings and sixpence - less bus fares - was worth having.

We all worked on the hangers. Mother, Father, George when he wasn't at school, and myself when I came home from work. We had them finished in five days. Parcelled up, they made a formidable package to take on a tram, but Father volunteered.

He was gone a long time. When he returned, we heard him bumping and puffing up the stairs. He had brought back a whole gross this time. One hundred and forty-four hangers waiting to be covered. He was so worn out he went straight to bed.

~

We could never afford newspapers. I tried to keep up with the news of the day by looking over people's shoulders as I huddled close to them in crowded Underground trains and if anyone discarded a newspaper, whether it was on a seat or in a dustbin, I pounced on it.

That is how I came across the advert. 'Wanted. Young lady to take charge of a new office opening in West End. Shorthand, typing. 78 p.a.'

I didn't know what 78 p.a. meant, so I asked one of the other filing clerks.

"Blimey!" She sounded impressed. "That's thirty shillings a week!"

I phoned and made an appointment in my lunch-hour. The office was on the fourth floor overlooking Oxford Street and it was cluttered with ladders, buckets, paint tins and tools. A workman was putting up shelves while another painted the ceiling.

A third man, neatly dressed in a suit, welcomed me and explained that he and his wife were the owners of a company manufacturing high-class children's knitwear in Lancashire. They were opening a London office, but their plans had been delayed.

He looked apologetic as I glanced around the room. There was no furniture, no desk, no typewriter, just a telephone on the floor.

Everything would be finished in a few more days, he assured me. Could I do shorthand?

I could. It wasn't really a lie. I had worked hard during the six half-hour lessons.

What about typing?

Yes, of course. That was a lie, but he had no means of testing me, and at that moment, I would have told him anything to get the job.

When I showed him my examination certificates and references, he seemed amused. He wasn't looking for someone excelling in netball or tennis and he doubted I would need much Latin or botany, but I did seem to have a pleasant personality, and that was important.

I knelt on the floor and wrote my name and address on a

piece of paper he gave me. He had to return to Lancashire that afternoon, but he would let me know.

I returned to my pigeonholes with a heavy heart. Thirty shillings a week. It had been too much to hope for.

A few days later, a letter arrived and as I opened it, I braced myself for another disappointment. Instead, I found I had been offered the job.

The letter told me that a Mr Barker would meet me at the office on my first morning.

When I arrived, the place had been transformed. The clutter and confusion were gone. A desk had been placed by the window and on it stood a telephone, a typewriter, a wire tray marked IN and another marked OUT. Three plaster models of children stood naked in the middle of the floor, and in the drawers beneath the desk were stationery, a telephone directory, a kettle and a teapot.

Mr Barker was a lot older than I expected. He was just starting too, he told me, and he hoped we could help one another.

I hoped so, too. I was delighted at the prospect of thirty shillings a week, but I was scared as well, especially when he explained he had been hired as the rep for London and the county of Middlesex. He would travel round in his car with his samples, then every afternoon, he would telephone in his orders and his general report to me. I would take it down in shorthand, then type it out and send it off to Lancashire before I finished work for the day.

The cupboards and drawers along one wall of the office were already stocked with the latest range of children's knitwear. I would be expected to change the outfits displayed on the models every day.

I didn't understand the importance of that until he explained he would be visiting all the top London stores and meeting the buyers. Obviously, he could only carry a limited number of samples in his suitcase, so he would encourage them to call in at the newly opened office, where I could show them the whole range.

He was very eager. I didn't know then that he had been out of work for a long time. Reps had to be young and dashing to impress the women buyers, but he was tall and thin, with years of experience but very little hair and a cough that interrupted his sales patter. Poor Mr Barker.

I never told him I was terrified each afternoon when the telephone rang. I took down all his reports in scrawled longhand, buying time by asking him to repeat things, claiming the line was bad or my pencil had broken. And when he rang off, it sometimes took me an hour to turn out one sheet of typing without any mistakes.

Perhaps he guessed, if only because the typing paper ran out so quickly and my handbag bulged like a football with the rejected pages I took home rather than leave in the waste bin.

Mr Barker dropped in every morning and once he was gone, I changed the clothes on the models, dusted every surface, made myself cups of tea and practised my typing. Pigeons and sparrows came to the open window, and I fed them scraps from my lunch. That still left hours with nothing to do. To break the monotony, I sometimes locked up the office at lunchtime and went for a walk.

The West End theatres fascinated me. I studied the posters and walked past the queues waiting for matinees. The buzz of excitement was exhilarating. I still wanted to be an actress, but I knew it was not possible. Not yet. But why shouldn't I write a stage play? With the innocence of youth, it didn't seem a difficult task.

I saved up my pennies and as soon as I had ninepence, I told the family I had to work late at stocktaking on Saturday afternoon. I hated lying, but I couldn't tell them the truth. If Mother had known I was going to see a West End matinee, she would have been furious. I didn't want to upset her. I just wanted to see a play.

Outside the theatre, I queued for an hour, then paid my ninepence and chased up the stone steps to the gallery with the rest, racing to get a good seat.

It was wonderful. I had never seen a full-length play before. I enjoyed every moment and resolved to start work on my own play as soon as possible.

In the meantime, I was doing my best to teach George. He learned well, but it was difficult because Mother always joined in.

Sometimes, we went up to the attic rooms, but in summer they were stiflingly hot. There was an outlet to the roof, and we opened it when the weather was warm, or even climbed out on to the roof and sat together looking down on the street market below as we studied.

I enjoyed teaching George and our lessons reminded me how much I missed learning myself. I signed up for a weekly French conversation session at the local adult school. It was not only a chance for me to brush up on my French, it was an opportunity to meet people. Mother didn't approve, and I always felt selfish because I knew I ought to be at home covering coat hangers, but it was enlightening to talk to others and hear their thoughts about the world beyond the narrow confines of my home and the office. People talked about Germany and the Nazis and the fear there might be trouble ahead.

I didn't mention such things to Mother. She never looked at the newspapers I brought home. Father spent most of his time at the library, supposedly looking for work, but probably enjoying the racing pages. Either way, I don't think the affairs of the world interested him much.

When George reached thirteen, his headmaster was as good as his word. He spent an hour talking to him, then entered him for the second-stage examination. He passed easily.

"I wish him well at the grammar school," the headmaster said, "but you do realise there will be expenses, uniform, sports equipment and so on. Will that be a problem?"

Mother never hesitated.

"Of course not. He will have whatever he needs."

Out in the street, she scowled at me.

"Don't fuss yourself," she said. "You had your chance. Now he's going to have his. Your father will have to ask Edie. I'll bet she's got plenty tucked away."

CHAPTER 24

Perhaps it was contacting Auntie Edie and talking about George that sparked the idea. I don't know. But for some reason, Father began thinking about his own mother. He hadn't seen her since his parents divorced when he was a tiny boy and he had no idea where she was or even if she was still alive. Neither had Auntie Edie.

He became obsessed with the idea of finding her. Mother didn't object too much, so I agreed to help him. We knew little except that she had gone to live in Maidenhead after the divorce and she had remarried. That was all.

It took me nearly four months. Four months of letters, phone calls, and help from kind people I did not know. A girl looking for a grandmother she had never seen seemed to touch a sympathetic chord.

At last, I could tell Father that his mother was alive and living in Bray in an almshouse owned by the Fishmonger's Association. I wrote to her, and a reply came back by return of post in a neat, round, almost childish hand. Please, could we come and see her? It would make her so happy.

At first, Mother baulked at the idea. It would mean four

train fares and we would have to take her a little present. It sounds harsh, but I understood her resistance. We were living right on the edge. We spent every evening sewing coat hangers, but there was never a penny to spare.

Auntie Edie had been happy to buy George his uniform and his sports kit, but there were other things he needed, simple things like handkerchiefs, socks, and a second-hand bag to carry his homework books.

In a way, we were lucky to live overlooking a street market. Facing us, across the road, was a fishmonger's shop, and on Saturdays, we could watch the prices drop.

There was no refrigeration as there is today, and fish that had been on display for hours would not be saleable by Monday. It was better for the fishmongers to sell it at a loss, but timing was important. Sixpence a pound… five pence… four pence… When it reached threepence a pound for cod, Mother rushed downstairs and across the road to the shop. We didn't have fish on Friday at our house. We had it on Saturday.

It was the same with the butcher. Outside his shop, on a tier of rails, hung his weekend joints, mutton, lamb, beef, pork, all neatly labelled with their weight and all open to the dust and flies. As Saturday progressed, the rails emptied and by the time evening approached, a crowd gathered round the shop door.

The butcher and his assistant, in their aprons and straw hats, waited until the crowd was big enough, then the performance began. The remaining joints would be held up and auctioned, starting with the price on the label, then slowly going down. Sometimes joints went for only a quarter of the original price. The secret was to wait until the big bidders had made their purchases, then pounce on a bargain before the butcher decided to shut up shop.

In those days, shops were geared to suit their customers

and most had little to spend except at Christmas when the saving clubs paid out.

At the far end of the market, one shop developed its own way of trading. The brothers who ran it bought cheap surplus lines from warehouses. They sold everything, bed linen, clothes, china, toys, even paint and tools at amazing prices. But if you saw something you wanted, you had to buy it straight away, as they might never stock it again.

For most people, buying on impulse was difficult, so the store became known as the Lay-by Shop. Customers put down a deposit of whatever they could afford and were given a card. Payments were entered on the card and when, at last, the full price was paid, the purchase was complete and they could take their goods home.

There was probably a time limit, although I did know of one woman who took a year to pay off a blanket. I do know that no purchase was too small because I once put sixpence deposit on two pairs of lisle stockings (there was no nylon in those days) and it took me six weeks to pay off the remaining two shillings.

But despite the shortage of money, I wanted to see my grandmother. I had no idea of her age, and I was afraid she might die before I met her.

I discovered I could save a few pennies on my rail fare by getting a workman's return ticket on the Underground. It meant travelling early. I didn't start work until nine, but the ticket got me into the West End before eight, which meant I had an hour to wait.

On the first morning, I wandered the streets until I found some seats in a quiet square. I carried paper and a pencil in my handbag and each morning I sat writing notes for my play until one day an elderly gentleman sat down beside me.

He politely suggested, as he was sure I was a nice girl, that I move away, so I was not mistaken for one of the prostitutes who touted there.

Early one Sunday morning, there was a loud hammering on our street door. It was Lizzie. She was scarlet with exertion, but she beamed at the sight of us.

"Got something for you. Couldn't get it up the stairs. Too heavy. You'll have to help me."

George and Father came back carrying an ornate wooden cabinet about fifty centimetres wide and eighty high.

"It's a wireless set," Lizzie announced. "Sid's got himself a new one. You can get France and Germany and God knows where on it. He says he needs it now things are hotting up, so I grabbed this one for you."

She chuckled at our blank expressions. "I'll show you how to work it. You'll have to take the batteries to the shop every couple of weeks to get them recharged, but it don't cost much. There's two of them in the back and they weigh a ton."

The wireless delighted Father. He spent hours twiddling the knobs, and when the batteries died, he struggled to the shop by himself to get them recharged.

In the evenings, we all sat and listened as we worked. It was exciting to feel we were connected to the outside world.

I made sure to listen to the news, although at times it was depressing. The King was very ill. No-one actually said it, but everyone seemed to think he would die.

We were listening the day he did. The announcement was interrupted by knocking on the front door. A messenger had been sent by the outwork firm with a huge parcel of black crepe. They needed thousands of black armbands at once. Could we work through the night?

We did. We worked that night and the next night and the

next, taking it in turns to pedal the sewing machine and fold and pack the bands.

During the day I fell asleep at the office but when we were paid it was my mother who said, "Well, that should pay to go and see your grandmother, shouldn't it?"

We went to Bray the following Sunday. Walking through the iron gates to the almshouses was like stepping back into the distant past. Tiny grey stone cottages stood in a square around a flower filled garden with an ancient pump in the middle.

She was waiting for us.

I was a little apprehensive. The only grandmother I had known had frightened me and filled me with guilt because I couldn't love her. I hoped my new grandmother might be like Auntie Edie.

In appearance, she was just like Edie, but there was more to her than that. From the moment I set eyes on her, she was the perfect grandmother. Small, chubby with pink cheeks and snow-white hair, she didn't hesitate for a moment. She folded each of us in her arms and kissed us as tears rolled down her cheeks.

My cheeks were wet too. Suddenly, it hit me how many years of happiness had been wasted by not knowing her before.

She had afternoon tea ready for us and served us in the garden outside her cottage. Other old folk watched from their doorways and she smiled and waved to them.

"They're all my friends," she said. "They helped me carry out the table and chairs. The cottage is too small to get you all inside."

One old fellow came close and hugged her. "She's good to us," he said. "She helps us when we need it."

There was nothing shy or awkward about her, but she had an innocent, childlike honesty. She told us about her divorce and how much she had missed her children, but when she had asked to see them, her ex-husband had written a letter saying they were happy and well cared for and had no desire to meet her.

Some years later, she had married again. He was a fishmonger, a kind man, and she learned to help in the shop and go with him in the early hours of the morning to the fish market to buy stock.

Soon she had a baby girl. Her new husband adored her, and, in her own words, she was grateful to be happy again. But it was not to last. When her daughter was six, she ran to greet her father when he came home. He scooped her up in his arms and lifted her high in the air, but the ceiling of the cottage was low. She hit her head and died three days later.

"He never got over it," she said. "We had fourteen years together, but he never forgave himself."

After he died, she ran the shop by herself until it became too much for her. The Fishmonger's Association offered her the almshouse, and she had been grateful.

She sighed and patted my hand. "I hope when you fall in love it will be with someone who really loves you, and that it will go on forever."

I always remembered her words and I think they made me cautious and determined to wait for my own Mr Right.

CHAPTER 25

A week later, we received a letter from Grandma telling us how happy our visit had made her. I wrote back at once, saying that I would come to visit again as soon as I could.

It was lovely to hear from someone so cheerful. At work, Mr Barker was increasingly depressed. His sales were poor because, although the knitwear designs were beautiful, they were too expensive to compete with other brands. To keep him going, he had taken on another line of children's coats. I saw them when he opened his case, but he begged me not to tell or he would be sacked.

I didn't tell. I didn't need to. We both received letters on the same day saying the office had not been as successful as expected and was being closed. The firm thanked us for our efforts and said they would give us excellent references.

I was sorry for Mr Barker, and he was sorry for me. His daughter worked at Thomas Cook. They preferred to employ people who were recommended to them, and if I liked, he would ask her to speak for me. I did like. Thomas Cook was a world-wide travel agent. It sounded exciting.

Mr Barker was as good as his word, and I received a letter inviting me to an interview.

I decided not to tell my family I had lost my job straight away.

I took my references, the Australian ones and those from the knitwear company, to my appointment at Thomas Cook's Head Office in Berkeley Square. The staff manager offered me a two-week trial. The wage was twenty-two shillings and sixpence a week.

It was a big drop in income, but I was told it was the standard starting rate for new staff. Wage increases were given annually, and I was lucky. One was due in the new year. In the meantime, I would need to fill in a detailed questionnaire about myself and provide six photographs.

After two weeks, I moved upstairs to the Salaries and Records Department and was told about the benefits of working for a world-famous firm.

I was entitled to a cheap season ticket to reduce my travelling expenses. Unfortunately, it couldn't be used on the Underground, which was the only travelling I was likely to do. There were also other perks, which meant I could get discounts on toiletries, cosmetics, cleaning goods and confectionery if I bought them through the company.

After a few years' service, I would be able to buy furniture and other household necessities on hire purchase. Some staff even took out health insurance and a mortgage through the company.

"Once our staff have proved their worth," the manager said happily, "we provide everything for them. We look after them for life."

I had a strange sensation of being suffocated, as though the walls of the room were moving in on me. It may have been ungrateful, but the thought of my employer controlling every aspect of my life filled me with dread.

For a moment, I wanted to run, but I told myself I was

being ridiculous. I had been offered a steady position in a dependable company. I didn't have to go home and tell my family I had lost my job. Instead, I could tell them I had found a new one.

In the circumstances, I should have been thankful.

Every day, the newspapers printed articles about the growing threat of Nazi Germany, but like so many ordinary people absorbed with their own problems, I didn't take the prospect of war seriously. The world had suffered the appalling tragedy of the 1914-1918 conflict with its massive losses. Surely it could never happen again? The current crisis was part of the never-ending power struggle in Europe. It would blow over. It had to.

On my way home from work each evening, I walked through Green Park, past the gates of Buckingham Palace, and made my way to Victoria Underground Station. The extra walk saved me a penny on my fare.

There were always lots of other workers on their way home, but one evening, things were different. Crowds thronged the Mall, restless and chattering. It was obvious something had happened, but I had no idea what it could be.

As I pushed my way through the crowds outside Buckingham Palace, a terrific roar went up. People surged forward, thousands of them, and I found myself pinned against the palace gates. The crush was frightening, and I struggled for breath. All I wanted to do was escape, but it was impossible.

"Listen," someone cried. "Listen to him. This is history."

Another roar went up as the Prime Minister appeared on the palace balcony. The crowd quietened, and I was able to turn my head enough to see Neville Chamberlain hold up a piece of paper and wave it.

A message blared from loudspeakers, but perhaps because I was confused, or perhaps because my ear was pinned against the gates, I couldn't understand a word. Voices shouted the message back through the crowd, and soon the cheers were deafening.

"He's done it!" a woman screamed. "He's made Hitler sign. There's not going to be a war after all."

It was nearly the end of November when we received a letter from the trustees of the almshouses. Grandma had had a heart attack. She had been found collapsed on her cottage floor and by the time she reached hospital she was dead. They had found our letter among her possessions.

I went with Father to the funeral. It was a bitterly cold day and the small church was nearly full. Looking around, I recognised some of the people who had peeped at us from their doorways, the old folk who had been her friends. It struck me then that they had known her so much better than I ever would.

When the service finished, an old lady came across to us.

"I spoke to you when you came to see her," she said. "She was so happy that day. She talked about you all the time after that."

I nodded politely and smiled. At that moment, words were beyond me.

I couldn't believe I had found my Grandma and lost her again so quickly.

It was nearly five years since I arrived back in England. I was twenty, and I had done none of the things I dreamed of doing.

George was progressing well at school. I helped him in every way I could and I was proud of him, but I felt I had made no progress myself.

Sometimes, family responsibilities weighed heavily on me. I loved my parents, but our roles had reversed. I was no longer the child. Instead, I had become the adult, and now I saw things differently.

All my life, I had been scared by Mother's outbursts. I had hoped that if I was good enough, she would change. The vicious rages would stop and she would be calm and content. But now I understood her moods were governed by more than bad temper. They came from a deeper level that was far beyond her control.

Father was a weak man. Life had not been kind to him and he had made many mistakes, but he was neither cruel nor immoral. The harshness of life in Australia had crushed his spirit, and he had aged far beyond his years.

I didn't blame my parents for their failings. They were what life had made them. I was young. I could have walked away and left them to survive as best they could, but I knew I would not.

Apart from outworking, the only work Father had done was as a scrutineer for general elections. He was responsible for handing out the voting papers, but as he was only needed for one day every few years, it did little to help the family finances.

Some days, Mother seemed happy, but on others, she barely spoke for hours on end and turned on anyone who came near her. Sometimes she would stare into space, forgetting what she had been doing, then talk loudly about her father and sisters. She wanted to know how they were doing. To please her, Father wrote a letter to Violet.

For myself, my main concern was paying the bills until I received the increase in wages I had been promised. The family was surviving on what I brought home, but every week was a struggle.

My job consisted mainly of filing, and once a week, I stuck a National Health stamp onto a National Health card for every Thomas Cook employee in London. The stamps came in big rolls, and on my first day, my superior supplied me with a sponge roller and a china dish of water 'to make things easier for me.' Without those, I presume, I would have had to lick every one of them.

The wages, the actual counting of cash and putting it into neat brown bags, was handled by the manager of the department himself, a pompous little man called Mr White.

When the new year arrived, we were called in to the office, one at a time, so Mr White himself could tell us how much our raise would be.

"I am very pleased with you," he told me. "Keep up the good work. You have been given five pounds."

I imagine I said thank you as he handed me my wage packet, but I certainly said nothing else.

I was confused. I had expected a raise, not a bonus. Back at my desk, I stared at the brown envelope until the penny dropped. I had been awarded five pounds per annum, which worked out at less than two shillings a week.

The Manager's office was rather like Grandmother's parlour. You only entered by invitation. However, once the ceremony of presenting each member of his staff with the news of their increase was over, I didn't wait for an invitation. I was angry. If I had stopped to consider, I might have been more tactful, but I didn't.

It only took seconds for me to tell Mr White how I felt about my raise. Less than two shillings a week was barely an increase at all, and I would be looking for another job.

He stared at me from behind his horn-rimmed glasses and my anger cooled. I had been too hasty. I should have found another job before handing in my notice.

"I see," he said at last. "Well, I can't give you any more money unless you take on more responsibility. You seem intelligent, so perhaps you have been wasted sticking on stamps."

He frowned as he thought.

"If I put you in charge of the Staff Guarantee Fund, you would have to learn to use a comptometer and your wage would be thirty shillings a week. Would that suit you?"

He didn't wait for my answer but explained that every Thomas Cook's staff member from all over the world had to pay a set amount of self-insurance into the Staff Guarantee Fund on a sliding scale, from five pounds a year for those handling cash, like booking clerks, right down to the native porters in countries like India who only paid a few coppers a year.

Records were kept in huge ledgers that were ceremoniously chained to a big trolley every night and wheeled away to be imprisoned in a safe in the basement, then brought up again the next morning. Details from every page in every ledger had to be fed into a comptometer and the results checked with the bank accounts at regular intervals.

I think he expected me to be impressed by my new job. I had never worked on a comptometer before, but it didn't sound too mind-blowing. As far as I could make out, all you had to do was to press the right buttons, then crank down a big handle and go on to the next page.

I accepted the job with as much dignity as I could muster, then went home walking on air. It wasn't just that I would be earning thirty shillings a week again. It was much more than that. I had stood up for myself. I had no real qualifications, no special skills, but I had faced up to authority and I had won. I was proud of myself.

It was a long time, before a letter came back from Violet. Air mail was costly, so she sent it by sea mail and it took over a month to reach us.

Eric was dead. No-one had seen him since he had gone north to take a job on an outback sheep station. He had died of lockjaw. That was all Violet knew.

Grandfather had wanted to bring him back and bury him beside his mother, but the rest of the family had decided it wasn't worth the cost. He would have to stay where he was.

It seemed a sad but fitting end. In his short life, Eric had never really mattered to anyone.

Trixie had married because she was in the family way, but she hated her mother-in-law. Violet, too, had married. Her husband was an Italian, and she wasn't sure if she liked him, but he had a big house overlooking the sea at the beach resort of Cottesloe near Perth, and he also had a vineyard. As for Edith, she was getting more difficult every day. Sometimes Violet thought she might be going mad.

We had hoped a letter from her family might cheer Mother up, but, sadly, it had the opposite effect. She should never have left her sisters to rush into marriages with any Tom, Dick or Harry. She was their eldest sister. She should have been there for them. As for Edith, she cried over her for days. She knew what it was like for people to think you were mad when you were perfectly normal.

Soon after that, the tobacconist's shop below our flat was broken into again. This time, the thieves got away with cigars, cigarettes and tobacco, but they also broke down the side door that opened into our passage. Perhaps they thought it led to a storeroom, but it actually gave access to the whole building.

Mother was terrified and insisted we needed a dog, a very big dog.

Father and I were despatched, to the Battersea Dogs' Home, with an outsize collar and chain. If we didn't come back with a vicious dog, she vowed, she would never sleep again.

There were cages full of strays at the home. Some were new arrivals, waiting for a health check, others were kept aside in the hope their original owners would come looking for them. The rest were in three crowded cages.

An attendant took us to see them. "Choose whichever one you fancy," he said. "Then give me a shout."

We stared into the cages. There were dogs of every shape, size and breed, big dogs, small dogs, dogs huddled into corners, dogs collapsed in weary heaps. The only thing they had in common was an expression of abject misery.

I looked helplessly at my father. "She wants one that will scare off burglars."

We were still trying to decide when the attendant came back.

"They're all fed up. Wouldn't you be?" he said when we explained our problem.

Letting out an ear-piercing shriek, he rattled the bars. Here and there, a head raised and turned towards us with weary disinterest. Only one, a small black and white mongrel, stood up and gave a bark.

The attendant tapped my arm. "If I was you, I'd take that one. You ain't going to do no better."

Dogs were only allowed upstairs on trams and the other passengers watched curiously as we carried the dog up, weighed down by the heavy chain.

As I sat down, it leaned sadly against my legs. There was nothing about it that appeared either big or vicious. I had an awful feeling we were going to be making a return trip to Battersea.

Mother was waiting at the front door as we came round the corner, the dog trailing behind us, tail between its legs, on the end of the chain.

She stared at us in undisguised disgust. "What the hell do you think you're playing at? Dragging the poor little devil along on that chain! You've got no brains, the pair of you."

With that, she scooped the dog up in her arms and marched inside. By the time we reached the flat, she was feeding it scraps. The relief was enormous.

CHAPTER 26

Sometimes, when I had a spare moment, I reviewed my progress in life. I was keeping the family's head above water, but I wasn't getting anywhere with my own dreams.

There was no hope of me getting into art school. The possibility of being a singer or a dancer had long dropped behind me, but I still clung to the hope that one day I could be an actress.

I had seen posters for a local dramatic society and thought I could spare one evening a week from the outworking. I wrote to ask if I could join the society and received an invitation to their next meeting.

I went with high hopes, but they were soon dashed.

The secretary of the society had not been able to decipher the signature on my letter, but guessed from the handwriting I was a man. The society was always on the lookout for men, but did not need any new women members.

I was reduced to my last dream.

If they didn't need an actress, did they need a writer? I told them I would be happy to write an original play they could stage for their next production.

My offer met with mixed reactions. If I provided a finished script, the committee would read it and decide whether it was suitable.

I returned home triumphant. At last, I had an opportunity. If I was to succeed, all I needed to do was to write a first-class script.

But it wasn't easy. There was nowhere I could find enough peace to concentrate. Even in my lunchtimes, when I crossed the road into Green Park and settled myself on a quiet bench, the sheep that were supposed to keep the grass down preferred the smell of my sandwiches and crowded hopefully around me.

I had never been one for making friends. I liked people and enjoyed company, but there were too many parts of my life I wanted to keep hidden away.

However, there was one person at the office who became close to me. He was a quiet man, about ten years older than me, who also kept his private life strictly to himself. He was Irish and a Catholic. He lived with his parents and he was a good listener. That was all I knew about him, except that everyone called him Fitz.

Sometimes he would take his sandwiches to the park and sit beside me and one day I confided in him I was writing a play.

He listened with genuine interest. There was a sincerity about him that made me confident I could trust him. I had no-one else to confide in and it meant an enormous amount to me that he took me seriously and gave me advice.

I was trying to start at the top of the tree, he told me. He could understand my ambition, but the chance of an unknown writer completing a successful stage play was almost negligible. On the other hand, dozens of short stories were published every week in magazines and newspapers. Why not start by writing and submitting short stories?

I thought about the advice Fitz gave me, and I knew he

was right, but I had never read a magazine. I had often glanced at them in a newsagents. They looked attractive, but I had never had money to spare for such luxuries, and no-one left magazines behind on Underground trains or tossed them into waste bins.

I toyed with the idea of asking Fitz if he had any old magazines he could pass on to me, but I hesitated. Looking back, I suppose that seems ridiculous, but all my life I had been taught never to ask favours and never to allow anyone to become too friendly.

It was lovely, though, to sit in Green Park and chat with Fitz, casually commenting on the passing crowd and swapping sandwiches like naughty schoolchildren.

I was twenty-one. Fitz was older, but that wasn't a barrier to our friendship. He was quiet and thoughtful and gently attractive, but he was also Irish and a Catholic. If, at the back of my mind, I ever imagined he might become more than a friend, I knew it was impossible with a family like mine.

As the years passed, Mother was becoming more like her own mother, critical and unreasonable. She would gush over strangers, especially men, when they were first introduced, but later she would criticise them, tearing apart everything she saw as a fault.

In a moment of clarity, I realised Mother did not want me to have a life of my own. Any attempt to do so was blocked by tears or by temper. I was the family prop, the breadwinner. Again and again, if I made a plan, even for something as simple as a theatre visit with friends from the office using the free tickets we were given as a perk, she would tell me about the wonderful spinster women she knew who were content to devote their entire lives to caring for their parents.

If I reacted to such pointed remarks, her anger flared, and she became tearful, or belligerent by turns.

Occasionally, Fitz and I talked about serious things. Not

often, the lunchtime sessions in the park were mostly happy moments to treasure, but Fitz worried about the future. He had no faith in the peace treaty signed between Hitler and Chamberlain. He read all the papers and believed we were drifting into another war.

Myself, I didn't believe it. Perhaps I didn't want to. I had enough problems, and no matter how anxious I allowed myself to become, there was nothing I could do to change things.

The rut I was in was getting deeper. George's school needs became more expensive. Fares on the Underground went up. So did gas and electricity. The landlord put the rent up a shilling a week and the newspapers broadcast the growing threat of war.

~

For me, lack of money wasn't a temporary problem. It was the pattern of my life, a blank encircling wall I could never scale. Every penny I earned, every penny the family raised by working far into the night, was needed to feed us and keep the roof over our heads.

The only hope I could see was for me to get a better paid job, but every time I considered it, Mother grew agitated. Why take risks? A better job with more money sounded good, but what if it wasn't permanent? I might find myself out of work. It wasn't as if I had any real qualifications, no training, no trade. All I was fit for was an office job, and none of them paid well.

Looking back, it all sounds petty, but then it was real and frightening. Despite her moods and tantrums, I still loved my mother. I didn't want her to be unhappy, and I carried the constant fear that one day she really would harm herself.

Living with constant tension was exhausting, but I knew

that if I gave in and promised not to do anything hasty, she would calm down and life would become bearable again.

Sometimes it seemed life offered me nothing, not even hope. I had given up all my dreams, save one. No matter how disheartened I became, I was still sure, deep down, that I could be a writer.

I wrote whenever I could snatch a moment. While I ate my sandwiches in the park, in bed until I fell asleep, in crowded Underground trains, often jammed against other standing commuters. When there was no hope of writing anything down, I would plan the next sentence, then repeat it over and over in my head until the train rattled into my station and I could scribble it safely into my notebook.

But I had a problem. Every time I borrowed a book on writing from the library, it stressed that editors would not consider submissions unless they were typed. I had no money to pay for typing, and when I helped myself to some typing paper and made an excuse to stay behind at lunch-time, hoping to manage a page or two on the office typewriter while no-one else was about, I was almost caught and vowed never to risk it again.

Help came from an unexpected source.

As I walked past the Lay-by Shop one day, I noticed the window was full of ladies' lingerie. There, between the frying pans and bars of cheap soap, were sets of pretty pink petticoats and knickers trimmed with lace all neatly boxed. The price was two shillings a set.

I hesitated for days before I took the plunge and bought a set out of my next week's Underground fares and put ten more sets on lay-by.

The deed was done, and I was a bag of nerves. I need not have worried. I took the box of lingerie to work next morning and by lunchtime I had sold it for three shillings and sixpence and had orders for five more. By the end of the week, I had enough money to put down a first hire-purchase instalment of seven shillings and sixpence on a typewriter.

When I told Father what I had done, he begged me not to tell Mother, but there was no alternative. I had committed myself to finding eleven more monthly instalments and there was only one way I could do that. I put a card in the window of the nearest newsagents announcing that I was a typist.

I could only type with two fingers, but I told myself it didn't matter. I would offer a weekend only, next-day service. That way, I could type all through the night if necessary until I got it right.

My first customer was an elderly man who needed a reference typed out in a hurry. He would wait, he said.

I settled him into our tiny lounge and left Father to talk to him to pass the time. In the kitchen, I struggled to make a good job of the reference, but I was terribly nervous and I knew my customer could hear the hesitant two-finger tapping. I sent Mother in to turn on the radio in the hope of distracting him, but every few minutes she came back to enquire if it was done yet and my nerves went to pieces. I wasted a pile of paper and when I did hand over the reference, I was so ashamed of it I didn't charge the man at all.

It was 1939 by now and many people were certain war was approaching. I still wouldn't believe it.

I had my precious typewriter and the card in the newsagent's window brought in a spasmodic trickle of customers, barely enough to cover the next monthly payment, but enough for my clumsy efforts to eat up every spare moment and leave me no time to write.

On the third of March, the Prime Minister made an announcement over the radio. He had given Poland a guarantee that if Germany invaded, Britain would come to her aid.

We were swept along by a destructive tide, yet people clung to hope. France and England were allies, two great nations side by side. Hitler's army had already tramped over many borders, but his forces must be stretched to the limit. He was no fool. He would back down.

~

On the first of September, German tanks rolled into Poland. On the third of September, our Prime Minister made another announcement. It was not a great speech attempting to rouse everyone to a patriotic fervour. It was a flat declaration that we were now at war with Nazi Germany.

I never heard the end of Churchill's speech. Air-raid sirens blared out across London. I remember it was a warm day and our window was open. In the street market below, a shopkeeper had brought a radio onto the pavement and crowds were milling round it. The blast of the sirens caught them by surprise. Faces turned upwards, scanning the sky, then people ran…

The warning ended as suddenly as it had begun and the silence was terrifying until the all-clear sounded and we knew it had been a false alarm. A small English plane was scuttling home from France as fast as it could when it was detected by our own defences. In the tension of the moment, the whole country had been put on alert.

For fear of bombing raids, the government ordered that all children must be evacuated from the cities immediately. Pupils over five years of age travelled to the country with their schools. Babies and children under school age went with their mothers.

It was an enormous task. Railways were taken over and fleets of buses commandeered. For days, no-one went to work. There was no hope. Railway stations were deluged with harassed teachers and tearful children. Each child carried a small case full of clothes and wore a box around its neck containing a gas mask. No-one knew where the children were going, not even the teachers taking them or the white-faced parents waving them goodbye.

George went, his name and address pinned to him like the rest and a postcard in his pocket to let us know where he had been taken. Mother cried all night. She cried again a week later when the postcard came back. George was in Sussex. He had been paraded in the village hall with the rest, while the locals chose which children they preferred to have billeted with them. Few had chosen teenagers.

George and his classmates slept on the floor in the village hall that night, but the billeting officer told them he would take them from door to door the next day to persuade, or if necessary, order villagers to take them in.

The proclamation of war caused chaos at Thomas Cook. No one was going to travel abroad while it lasted. Not for holidays, at least. Bookings stopped overnight and there was no choice but to close everything down.

Thomas Cook had branches in every town and every country. There were thousands throughout the world. In Berkeley Square, where I worked, they had several floors of offices, a huge staff restaurant and hundreds of employees.

I was moved from the Guarantee Fund to a little office of my own. Managers were told to sack their staff, the newest and least important first, then work through the various grades until only a skeleton staff remained. My job was to hand out National Insurance cards and take back privileges like cheap-rate season tickets.

It was a depressing task, especially as I knew my last duty would be to sign my own dismissal notice.

Some of the younger staff were eager to be off, volunteering for whichever of the armed forces they had chosen. Others were upset and bewildered as they queued at my desk. A few were lucky. As whole floors of the building became empty, they were taken over by government departments. One was the Children's Overseas Reception Board, hastily set up to evacuate children from the danger areas, mostly to America and Canada.

At first, I thought I might be able to get a job there, but the tide of hopefuls leaving my desk and hurrying upstairs soon killed that hope.

~

We were at war, and everything had changed. Yet, in the pattern of everyday life, nothing changed, except there were no children playing in the streets, and people queued to top up their radio batteries for fear they might miss an important announcement.

Every titbit of news was passed on, even to strangers. Everyone was waiting, drinking in the horror of the news from Poland and fretting there must be something useful they should be doing. Youngsters joined up, and veterans who thought they had seen the last of military service re-joined their old regiments.

My parents had lived through one world war and the thought of another was more than they could bear. Father was the worst. He seemed to think the disastrous web of war had been woven solely to torture him. He cried pathetically for hours at a time and shook so much he couldn't hold a cup to his lips.

He was fifty. Thousands of young men were being called up and plenty of men older than him were queuing to volunteer, but he shuddered every time we turned on the radio and listened to the news.

"They can't take me now," he sobbed. "Not now. I wouldn't be any good to them!"

I knew he had been rejected from military service in the First World War because of a heart condition, and I reassured him he would not be called up for active service now. At most, he would be sent to work in a factory, but my words had little effect.

Women were called up as well as men. I was twenty-one, and I knew my time would soon come. What would happen to my parents then, I dreaded to think.

I worried every time I went to work and left them alone. I tried to find out if I could get Father evacuated out of London with Mother as his carer, but the authorities were swamped with school children, hospital patients, the blind, the disabled, the list was endless. There was no hope.

~

Lizzie dropped by one evening a few weeks before Christmas. I was glad to see her. Usually, in her breezy, whole-hearted way, she was a cheery presence, but that night she was depressed. Reg had volunteered.

"Couldn't wait for them to call him up," she said. "Didn't want to miss anything. Says he wants to be a bomber pilot and blow the Germans to bits. You'd think it was a bloody great bean feast he was going to, not a war."

We asked about Sid, but she only shrugged.

"Can't very well have a revolution now, can he? People've got too many other things to think about. He's trying to get a job in munitions. There's good money in munitions."

~

It was a miserable Christmas. George was still evacuated, the weather was bitterly cold, and all the news was depressing. Poland had been overrun. Soon, we were told, Hitler would turn his attention to the west, probably to Holland and Belgium. German submarines sank British food ships and talk of rationing was on everyone's lips.

Violet sent us a Christmas card, but it didn't arrive until the end of January. Edith had married and had a baby boy. Her husband, much younger than herself, was eager to join the Australian army, but Edith flew into raging fits of temper every time he suggested it and swore if he did, she would kill the baby.

Violet was worried about Grandfather. At eighty-five, he had moved in with his girl-friend who was also in her eighties. She owned a motor-bike, and he had taken to ride pillion on it.

Mother was horrified, but Violet seemed resigned to the old fellow's behaviour.

"He says they are thinking of getting married," she wrote, "because tongues are wagging about them living in sin."

My job at Thomas Cook was coming to an end. All the younger staff had gone, and those who arrived at my desk were older men and women, employees with years of service behind them who had, no doubt, thought they were settled for the rest of their working lives.

One morning, Fitz was in the queue. He had volunteered for the Air Force and that morning he had heard he had been accepted for an officer training course.

I suppose I had known it would happen, but it still came as a shock. He was my friend, the one friend with whom I felt relaxed and comfortable.

"I've been thinking about you," he said. "I know it won't be long before you are called up, but in the meantime, why not try to get a job in Fleet Street? There must be vacancies in magazines and newspapers with so many of their staff going into the forces. If it was only for a while, it might be a chance for you to get your foot in the door when the war's over."

He was so sincere. "Don't stop writing if that is what you really want to do," he said. "I'll send you my address as soon as I can. You will write to me, won't you?"

A week later, I received my notice from Cooks and handed myself my cards. I had been thinking a lot about the advice Fitz had given me, and I headed straight for the library.

There were so many newspapers and such a long list of magazines. Many of them I had never heard of, but in the end, I settled on The Sketch. That night I handwrote a letter, then typed it with slow, meticulous care, introducing myself and asking if there were any vacancies for which I could be considered.

A reply came back by return of post with an invitation for an interview, not with The Sketch, but with Illustrated Newspapers Ltd.

I was confused. I had never heard of Illustrated Newspapers, but an interview was an interview. I gathered up my references and prayed they would be enough.

I need not have worried. The white-haired man who greeted me was quiet and reassuring, with an air of relaxed efficiency. I learned later that he was William Nisbett, the Managing Director. He seemed untroubled that I had no experience of the world of publishing. I didn't need it. There were no vacancies for editorial staff, but if I wished, I could start the following Monday in the accounts department. My wage would be three pounds, ten shillings a week.

It seemed to amuse him I had thought I was applying to The Daily Sketch Newspaper, whereas I had actually written to The Sketch, a weekly magazine.

"Oh, well," he said pleasantly, "I am not complaining. Perhaps their loss will be our gain."

I went home walking on air. It wasn't just the big increase in pay. The important thing was that I was going to be a writer. I knew I was. One day I would make the transfer from accounts to editorial. The fact I had accidentally chosen the wrong publication seemed like another little miracle. In the meantime, the one thing I wanted to do was to write and tell Fitz my wonderful news.

But I never did. Sadly, I never heard from him again. He was my closest friend, and I missed him terribly. I always wondered what happened to him.

~

The Weekly Sketch was not the only magazine published by Illustrated Newspapers. There were many others, the Illustrated London News, the Sphere, the Tatler, the Sporting and Dramatic News, which became Sport and Country, and a glossy monthly called Britannia and Eve.

I couldn't believe my luck. I felt I had stumbled into a world of glamour and excitement even when I was given a desk beside a grumpy, elderly spinster who was to teach me my job.

The building was a bustle of activity, and everyone was cheerful. Everyone, that is, except my tutor. Miss Gardner described herself as "a maiden lady who lives alone." She had been working at the same desk for as long as anyone could remember, and in her own estimation, she had earned the right to special treatment.

Miss Gardner worked at her own pace, ignoring everyone around her, and stopped now and then to devour slices of cold porridge, which she made herself twice a week.

Her job, and now mine, was to cost the latest issues of the various magazines. That meant gathering the relevant figures from different departments, listing and analysing them, then entering the results in the correct forms.

I longed to be sent round the different departments gathering figures. I wanted to get to know everybody. But it was out of the question. Gathering figures was Miss Gardner's job and had been for over thirty years. Every Monday, after morning tea, she struggled her feet back into her shoes, with much grunting and complaining, and pottered off, sometimes for hours, leaving me to tot up endless columns of figures.

When she finally returned, I watched as she worked on the figures before handing them into the accountant's office. After that, I went back to totting up columns while she sat back for the rest of the day and concentrate on her porridge.

I didn't mind. News of the war, talk of the war, pictures of the war surrounded me, but I knew that one day it would all be over. One day I would be a writer. I just had to be patient. In the meantime, the increase in my wages was like a gift from heaven.

The outwork factory closed. I heard a rumour it had been turned over to making ammunition, but no-one was sure and we were not supposed to talk about such things. Government posters were everywhere warning Careless Talk Cost Lives.

To be honest, I was grateful to see the end of outworking. I finally had some free time in the evenings and at weekends to concentrate on writing. Remembering the advice Fitz had given me, I tried my hand at short stories.

I hated the misery the war brought to the world, but at least it was a time packed with incident and emotion, when everyday folk were transformed into heroes by a uniform. There was so much to write about. Our troops were gathering across the Channel, and France had built a huge fortified barrier, the Maginot Line which, we were sure, would repulse an enemy onslaught.

Germany had her own defences, the Siegfried Line, and the two great snaking lines of destruction faced each other, waiting. No-one could foretell the future, but every music-hall in Britain echoed the boastful refrain, "We're going to hang out the washing on the Siegfried Line. Have you any dirty washing, Mother dear?"

One Friday, Miss Gardner arrived late and sneezed incessantly. At three o'clock, she struggled into her coat and announced, "I'm off."

The others in the office were amused by my surprised expression.

"You won't see her for a few days," they explained, "or even a week. She's always the same when she gets a cold. She puts herself to bed until she feels better."

The accountant came to see me on Monday morning. He was a tall, thin man with a permanently worried look.

"I'm sorry about Miss Gardner," he said, "but she'll be back soon. I don't suppose there's anything you can get on with until then, but don't worry about it."

That was all. The rest of the office staff were busy with their ledgers and filing cabinets, answering the telephone and dealing with the queries brought by boys from the messenger pool. No-one took any notice of me, so I sat feeling uncomfortable. I was being paid three pounds ten shillings a week, and I was doing nothing.

I slid into Miss Gardner's seat and opened her desk. I had watched her carefully, and it all seemed straightforward. All I had to do was gather enough courage to begin.

I spent the next few hours finding my way round the building, knocking on doors and introducing myself as Miss Gardner's assistant, collecting the weekly figure sheets. No-one objected. In fact, everyone was pleasant, even in the rush and bustle of the editorial offices.

With all the figures gathered, I spent two days analysing them and filling in the relevant forms. No-one queried what I was doing. The next morning, I tapped on the door of the accountant's office and presented them to him.

I am not sure what reaction I expected, but he merely blinked at me from behind his glasses and nodded.

The following day, Miss Gardner came back to work and when I told her what I had done, she was not happy. From that day on, she barely spoke to me.

As the weeks went by, more foods were rationed and blackout regulations were strictly enforced. When daylight faded, no chink of light was allowed to escape from any window. On the continent, the German army pushed its way into Holland and Belgium and in London the fear of air-raids grew.

Street lights were no longer lit at night and even car headlights had to be masked so that only downward slits of light were visible. Kerb edges were painted white to help pedestrians and the speed limit for cars was reduced to twenty miles per hour in the dark.

For my twenty-second birthday in April, Father and Mother bought me a chiming clock out of the household money. It was the last thing I was expecting, but Mother had always wanted a chiming clock.

That evening, Lizzie brought round a birthday card and their family cheese ration. Neither she nor Sid ate cheese. In return, we gave her two eggs and some potatoes.

Lizzie seemed happy enough. The Local Defence Volunteers, later renamed the Home Guard, had just been formed. Spurred by the German advance into France, a million men of all ages had volunteered at once, and Sid had been among the first.

Lizzie was indignant when I looked surprised.

"Well, you don't think he's going to let some ruddy foreigners take over his country, do you?" she demanded. "Though what the hell he's supposed to do with a broom handle, I don't know. That's all they've given him."

Like everything else, paper was in short supply. Daily newspapers were cut down to a few sheets, but they still found room to report the successes of the invading German forces. Like an oncoming tide, they swept their way through the Low Countries and into France.

There was a general confidence that things would change once the Maginot Line was reached. That would stop the Germans.

But it didn't.

Soon, our newspapers talked of Hitler's plans to invade Britain itself. There would be air raids, they warned, but first, to soften us up, the Germans would drop thousands of incendiary bombs on our cities.

Like so many others, I queued to join my local firewatchers group. It was to be a reserve force to support the Fire Brigade.

Most of the volunteers in my group had day jobs, but after work, we hurried home, swallowed a meal, then reported to a derelict shed on a piece of waste ground at the edge of the local common. There, we learned to use stirrup pumps, fill sandbags, coil hoses and crawl in one end of a shed and out the other after a smoke bomb had been set off inside it.

To do this, we had to don a pair of dirty, smoke-blackened overalls to protect our clothes. Unfortunately, there was only one pair of overalls. One small, middle-aged lady had to turn up the legs so much the crutch hung down below her knees and as she crawled through the shed, she crawled right out of the overalls.

Turning back to retrieve them, she became disorientated in the thick smoke and had to be rescued and resuscitated. She was a nice lady, but we never saw her again.

I am sure most people still believed that once the Germans were met by the combined force of the French and British armies, they would be pushed back. During a war, the man in the street doesn't really know what is happening.

At that time, the government and the military screened all news and even letters home from servicemen had chunks cut out of them in case useful details might fall into enemy hands. As a result, a great deal of what was happening never found its way into the newspapers or on to the radio. Inevitably, ignorance bred rumours, speculation, and fear.

The news Winston Churchill had taken over as Prime Minister brought a huge sense of relief. Now, surely, we had a leader who was strong enough to face Hitler.

The nation's spirits lifted and there was a feeling that no matter how bad things looked, they could be changed. There was still hope. The German advance could still be halted. It may have been unrealistic, but the people believed what they were told. They certainly never dreamed that France would fall and our troops would be stranded on the French beaches.

The evacuation of Dunkirk has gone down in history, but at the time, the impact it had on the population was overwhelming. We were used to seeing sparse, censored news reports and suddenly newspapers were awash with stark reality.

Our army was trapped. Thousands of men crowded on to open beaches, hopelessly exposed to the mercy of the German bombers overhead.

It was the end of all hope.

Then we read the incredible news that hundreds of boats, fishing boats, pleasure boats, every kind of vessel, no matter how ancient, were heading across the Channel, a death-defying flotilla of rescuers determined to save "our boys."

We understood the risks they faced because journalists and newsmen travelled with them and their reports and photographs were splashed across every front page.

I knew people who admitted they prayed then, when they had never prayed before. And there were many who shed tears in the streets as they read about the little boats struggling to bring back their human cargo.

~

Lizzie came to see us about a week later. She looked sad and a lot older.

"It's Reg," she said. "He's gone. One of his mates came to see me. He was on the beach with the rest. The Germans were bombing them. He tried to push his way onto one of the boats, but it was already full. He fell in the water and drowned. They didn't bring him back because there were too many living ones waiting."

What do you say to a woman who has just lost her only son? We didn't know, so we made her a cup of tea.

When she was leaving, she turned to Mother.

"I have to say it. He was a useless little swine. No thought for anyone but himself. If he'd lived, he'd probably have ended up in prison or someone would have hung him. As it is... Well, he's died a sort of hero, hasn't he? Perhaps God does know best after all."

CHAPTER 27

Evacuation wasn't easy for George. He was moved from billet to billet, some comfortable, some cramped, some downright unfriendly. Food was scarce in the country as well as in the city and there were those who grudged being forced to take in a hungry fifteen-year-old.

However, once he sat his final school exams, it would be time for him to come home. Far from pleasing Mother, the prospect tormented her. She had always doted on George, and she didn't want him to come back to London. The thought he might be killed in an air-raid was too much to bear.

After Dunkirk, people's perception of the war changed. We were no longer part of an alliance. Now, we stood alone, and the next step for the Germans would be to invade us. We all knew that. Hitler's Operation Sea lion was about to begin.

New regulations were issued every day. The ringing of church bells was banned. Signposts were removed, and the broomsticks and pickaxes of the Home Guard were replaced by real weapons. First Aid classes were crammed with volunteers, while hospitals geared up ready to deal with casualties. Foreigners were rounded up and packed into internment camps, and RAF fighters could be seen attacking German bombers above our heads.

I was desperately worried about my parents, but there was little I could do. Life had to go on as usual. I made them promise that every time the air-raid warning sounded, they would go down to the safety of the basement. I even packed a bag with food and drink and a torch and stood two blankets beside it ready. But I couldn't be sure. Mother hated the basement and if she lied when she said they had taken cover, I knew Father was too intimidated by her to tell me the truth.

Mother was afraid of the basement, but I, too, had a fear. The Underground was the cheapest and fastest way of getting to work, but the escalators descending deep into the ground and the long dark tunnels, had always stirred in me a sense of claustrophobia.

Now my apprehension grew. There were times when the trains stopped between stations and there would be a long silent wait in the tunnel. No-one knew what was happening, but the fear was there. Was it an air raid? Had a bomb dropped on the station ahead? Or the one behind? Were we trapped?

I told myself I was being ridiculous. There was enough horror in the world without imagining more, but sometimes the relief when the train started again was so acute I feared I would be sick.

But many people didn't feel as I did. To them, the Underground was a haven. Every night, bombs dropped on London. People were killed and injured, homes were destroyed, and rows of houses became yet another sprawling bombsite.

Air-raid shelters were being built, but in the meantime, deep under London, the platforms of the Underground seemed a safe refuge.

Hundreds of people thronged down to them every night, whole families, old and young, clutching food and drink and warm bedding, some carrying young children who had not been evacuated despite all the warnings. Some even clutched their pets.

At first, it was chaos, but rules were quickly established. White lines painted along the platform edges preserved a strip beside the trains for passengers to board and alight. Shelterers could not cross it and were not allowed down until the evening rush hour subsided, which meant long queues gathered outside the stations as dusk fell.

There was a time limit, too, on leaving in the morning, but that was more difficult to enforce. Early morning travellers, running for a train, often had to negotiate crying children woken from their sleep, or even tiny tots squatting on their potties.

~

One morning, as I left home, the postman handed me an envelope. I recognised the writing at once. George had promised to write as soon as he finished his exams.

It was a difficult time for teachers and examiners. Village children had to share with the pupils from evacuee schools and classrooms were often used on a rota system. When there wasn't enough space, children were taught in church halls, or even barns. Providing the facilities for an examination was a nightmare, and we had been warned there might be delays.

I read the letter quickly and tucked it into my handbag.

By the time I reached the Underground station, the majority of the overnight shelterers had already left. At the foot of the escalator, I recognised two figures I had seen before, an old woman and a boy who might have been her grandson. In one hand, the woman carried a shopping bag, under the other arm, a pile of bedding.

She was leaned against a wall, gasping for breath.

"It's her asthma," the boy said when I asked if she was all right. "She gets it when she's worried. I'll make her rest when we get home."

I was in good time, so I rode up back up the escalator with them. At first, the old lady wouldn't part with the bedding, but when I persisted, she let me carry it.

At the top, she stood to catch her breath, and after a moment, she gave me a funny little smile.

"Bloody silly, isn't it?" she whispered. "Tonight, we'll have to do this all over again."

~

It was a bad day at work. The air raid sirens blared out again and again. Sometimes the warning only lasted a few minutes before the all-clear sounded, but each time we had to clear our desks of papers, snatch up handbags and other personal possessions, and hurry down to the safety of the basement.

No-one really knew what was happening, but rumours spread that bombs had been dropped on the suburbs and there were many dead and injured.

Going home, there were hold-ups on the Underground and by the time I reached Balham, the shelterers had been let in and were making themselves comfortable for the night.

We only lived around the corner from the station, but the sirens went up the moment I stepped out into the street. I ran the rest of the way. I wanted to be back with my parents and I had to break the news that George was on his way home.

That night, I insisted we slept in the basement. There

were several loud crashes, one of them startlingly close, and I was glad I had had my own way.

Next morning, as we climbed the stairs to our flat, there was chaos outside. A bomb had fallen on the main road in front of the Underground station. The bridge beside it, carrying the overhead railway lines, had collapsed and a bus, blasted out of control, had run forward into the huge crater, only its back end visible above the shattered road.

Worst of all, the blast had smashed the retaining walls that diverted an underground stream. The released waters had flooded the whole station and the tunnels on either side of it.

Hundreds of people drowned in the darkness that night. Firemen, police, and wardens had raced to the scene, but there was nothing they could do to rescue them.

I knew we couldn't stay in the flat after that.

I was used to my mother's moods, but this time, I understood her reaction. I had never liked the basement either. The gloom, the smell, the vague vibrations of the trains below us, had created an atmosphere that made my flesh creep. Now there was nothing but an oppressive silence and the thought of dead bodies floating in the darkness beneath our feet.

The raids were getting worse, but I knew Father would not have a hope of persuading Mother to shelter down in the basement. And I would be away for longer each day. The flooding had closed other stations along the line and the overhead rails were down too. The only chance of getting into London was to start walking and pray some passing vehicle might be able to squeeze in one more passenger. People crammed into the backs of lorries, climbed aboard milk floats, scrambled on to anything with wheels and hung on. And I knew it would be the same at the end of the day, only then it would be in the blackout.

George came home that evening, suitcase in hand, his gas mask in a box dangling from a string round his neck exactly as it had been the day he went away. He brought a big bag of apples back with him that he had been given by a kindly villager.

Mother cried over him and as I hugged him, he didn't seem like a boy anymore. He was a young man, and he told us he wanted to join the RAF.

I promised I would help him with his application, but there was a more immediate problem. We had to find somewhere else to live.

First thing in the morning, I phoned Mr Nisbett and explained a bomb had dropped nearby and I had a problem. He sounded harassed. He asked no questions, but told me to come back as soon as I could. I learned later that his son, a bomber pilot, had been reported missing over Germany.

Finding somewhere else to live was not easy. So many families had been made homeless that undamaged properties were impossible to find. In the end, we were lucky. George and I spotted an empty three-storied house. The upper floors were blast damaged and tiles were missing from the roof, but the ground floor was reasonable except the windows had been smashed and the front door blown off.

We asked around the remaining neighbours and managed to get a phone number for the owner, who had retreated to the safety of the country. He was only too happy for us to move in. Empty houses were at risk.

The air-raids targeted electricity lines and gas supplies, which meant many homes in the most heavily bombed areas had long spells without either. Families gathered wood from bomb sites to cook or to keep warm. If that was scarce, damaged houses were seen as fair game. Floor boards were prised up and door frames and staircases smashed and carried away.

There was no attempt to repair bomb damage, but council lorries dumped heaps of black plastic and piles of wooden laths on every bomb site so people could help themselves as best they could. George and I nailed black plastic where once there had been glass, wrestled the front door back onto its hinges, and cleaned up the dust, dirt and broken glass.

I worried how Mother would react to our new home. The house was next to a church, and she had always disliked church bells, saying they depressed her, but now she seemed pleased that when the invasion began, she would be the first to know. Also, there was a small garden, and in the middle of it stood an Anderson air-raid shelter.

It's strange, isn't it, how our standards change with circumstances? Until then, I would never have imagined the appeal of a tiny corrugated iron shed, half-buried in a pit in the garden. The roof was covered by a layer of muddy soil and the inside was full of dead leaves, spiders' webs, and wildlife.

We found a carrier to move us, and everything we possessed was dumped in heaps on the floor of the house when dusk fell and the sirens blared out.

We couldn't use the Anderson shelter until we had cleaned the inside, and without proper blackout curtains, we couldn't turn on any lights in the house. With the drone of planes overhead and searchlights probing the sky, we did the only thing possible. We squeezed into the darkness of the cupboard under the stairs, all four of us and the dog we had named Peter.

The catch on the cupboard had been blown off, presumably by the same blast that damaged the front door, so we tied a piece of string to the handle and George sat and held it closed. A piece of string to protect us from the might of the Luftwaffe. It sounds crazy now, doesn't it? But then it was all deadly serious.

The next day we cleaned out the air-raid shelter, made four hammocks out of rope and some old stair carpet, and hung them up. They filled the entire space, but we reasoned that the two middle ones could be let down while we ate a meal, then tied up again when it was time to sleep. Peter would be comfortable on a piece of carpet on the ground beneath us.

Our hammocks worked well enough, except for one night when bombs dropped nearby and the vibrations loosened the knots, depositing Mother on the ground. Then the wails of protest from Peter beneath her were enough to drown out even the sound of the sirens.

Diana and her parents with Peter.

Months passed, and I knew it wouldn't be long before George was called up for the RAF. His headmaster had been proud of his exam results and had already contacted the head office of the Shell Oil Company in the Strand, sending them his school record and references and hoping they might have a position to offer him. It would, he said, be a very good opening for him to come back to once the war was over.

In the meantime, I was grateful to have him home. It was a relief to know he was with our parents during air raids, and with rationing becoming worse, he took over some of the queuing for food. Even gathering basic items, meat, bread, potatoes and the like, meant long queues when deliveries to shops were late or never arrived at all.

Queuing became a way of life but, the worst queues were always for cigarettes. Fortunately, no-one in my family smoked, but if the whisper went round that a delivery was expected, people would queue for hours, just in case. If they were lucky, they might get a packet of ten, but when the queue was very long or the delivery was very small, the packets were opened and each customer was rewarded with two cigarettes. Or sometimes one.

Fish was never rationed, but it was always in short supply. Many familiar types of fish vanished altogether as German submarines menaced our fishing grounds. In their place came a sparse selection of squid, octopus, or whale steaks. To be honest, it wouldn't have mattered what it was. If it was food, were we grateful for it.

The raids grew steadily worse. Usually, the heavy bombs were preceded by a blanketing shower of incendiaries. One evening, I had a particularly long journey home. I had walked for miles and was on the last stretch, along the main road from Clapham Common to Balham.

It was pitch dark, and as the sirens wailed again and again, I dodged air-raid wardens who were shepherding people off the street and into shelters. All I wanted to do was get home.

Then I heard the hum of planes overhead. Searchlights flared across the sky and showers of incendiary bombs fell on the houses on either side of me, lighting the road ahead.

That night, I was genuinely terrified. As I ran, I was numb with the certainty I would never get home alive, and when I stumbled through our gate and dived into the Anderson shelter with my family, many of the neighbouring houses were already ablaze.

Later, when the hum of the bombers and the crashing roar of the anti-aircraft guns died down, George and I crawled out of the shelter. All we could hear was the clang of bells as emergency vehicles raced from fire to fire.

Mother put her head out of the shelter and tugged George's arm.

"I can smell something burning."

George was usually patient with her, but not then.

"Of course, you can," he snapped. "Half the houses in the street are on fire."

"No!" she insisted. "It's closer than that."

Even in the dark, I felt George hesitate. Then he pushed her back into the shelter, caught my hand, and we headed for the house.

She was right. We could smell it as soon as we went inside. George had a torch, and we climbed up into the loft. There was no sign of fire, but there was a hole in the roof, and caught in the angle of charred rafters, was an incendiary bomb. It must have started burning, then gone out.

"We can't leave it." George sounded as uncertain as me, but he tried to take charge. "You stay here. I'll be back in a minute."

It could only have been minutes, but it seemed like hours before he came back with one of Mother's steel knitting needles. There was a small hole on each side of the bomb. We put the knitting needle through them, then very carefully, carried it down the stairs, out into the garden, and as far from the house as possible.

It was probably the most stupid thing either of us would ever do, but there had been no time to think, and if we had thought, we probably wouldn't have come up with a better answer.

The local cinema burned down that night and most of the shops in the High Street.

We were not the only ones who were suffering. Looking across the suburbs, the night sky was stained a vivid scarlet.

"My God!" someone said, "London's getting a pasting tonight."

It wasn't until next morning when I went to work that I realised how bad a pasting it had been.

St. Paul's Cathedral still stood, but around it was nothing but devastation. Buildings were wrecked, fires still burned, and firemen, blackened and singed, fought to get them under control. Tangled hoses draped across the remains of buildings and trailed through a wasteland of mud that was freezing into ice.

Men and women who had struggled to get to work as usual found their workplaces reduced to rubble or burned-out shells.

The raid had been a deadly combination of planning and luck. Six and a half hours of relentless attack starting with a deluge of incendiaries followed by massive, high explosive bombs. A full moon illuminated the city below, making it an easy target and the river Thames was at its lowest ebb, so there was not enough water for the fire hoses. In addition, it was a freezing night in the coldest winter for fifty years.

The Illustrated Newspaper building had been wrecked. After being half-gutted by incendiaries, a heavy bomb had dropped right through the centre of it.

Many of our staff never arrived that morning. Some had been injured, others were rescuing what they could from their own bombed homes.

Mr Nisbett gathered his depleted staff around him. He didn't give orders. He simply asked us to do our best to rescue anything we could from the derelict building, but with the centre of every floor collapsed, we must be very careful, only creeping around the edges, hugging the walls. The weather was freezing and the water, used to fight the fires, had frozen into icicles.

Among the staff was an old man called Podger. His name suited him. He was short, round, apple-cheeked and always topped by an ancient woollen hat. I did not know what his job was, as I had only ever seen him hurrying around, fetching and carrying, and when no-one needed him, polishing the brass handrails up the stairs.

Now he came into his own. Burrowing his way into the wrecked basement, he found a pile of old stone ink jars. Gathering splinters of wood, he made a fire and heated water in any metallic vessel he could find. Then, pouring the water into the ink jars, he scrambled back up from the basement, a gnome-like figure caked in dirt. In the darkness, he negotiated the smashed glass and staircases half hanging off the walls, while still clinging to the hot ink jars cradled in one arm.

Podger presented one to each of the freezing staff, then with a cheerful smile, he returned to the basement and began to boil more water.

God bless him. Without those ink jars to warm them, I think some of the staff, particularly the older ones, might not have made it through the day.

Eventually, everything that could be rescued was removed from the building. A new home had been found for Illustrated Newspapers in Holborn, in a half-finished building, starkly bare, reeking of paint and new cement, alive with cockroaches and bitterly cold.

For days, only the lucky ones had chairs. Most of us sat on the floor, our work on our laps or spread out around us, even Miss Gardner. Typewriters were used on a rota system. For nearly a week, there was only one telephone between all departments, editorial, advertising and the rest. Fortunately, our printing works were in a separate building, and it came through the raids unscathed. Somehow, even that first week, all issues of the various magazines were printed and distributed on time.

Mr Nisbett made a point of thanking every individual personally for their efforts.

CHAPTER 28

George was summoned to an interview at the Shell Oil Company's head office and came back walking on air. He had been invited to join their photographic unit until his call-up.

When he returned from the forces, he would be trained in every aspect of photography, and if he did well, he would be recommended to become a member of the British Institute of Photographers.

I could never be sure how Mother would react to anything, but I need not have worried. She was on top of the world when she heard the news. The idea that her son would one day become a member of an Institute, whatever that was, thrilled her immensely.

A letter from Violet arrived a few days later, and following some premonition, I slipped it into my handbag. It seemed a shame to risk upsetting Mother when she was happy. I would show it to her later.

I read it when I was alone.

Despite all her threats, Edith's husband had joined the Australian army. Hearing the news, she had gone berserk, becoming so aggressive a doctor had been called and she had been put into a secure mental home. Her husband's parents had taken the baby, and Violet had no idea where they had taken it. She only knew they had sold their home and fled east without leaving a forwarding address.

~

At work, everyone struggled to get back to normal. It was impossible to find new office supplies, so second-hand chairs, desks and filing cabinets were brought in and renovated. Some were very tatty, but it was a time for being grateful. Partitions went up, open spaces were divided into offices and soon a sense of normality returned. Of course, we still had air raids, when we hurried down to the basement, and every night two of the male staff took it in turns to be on duty on the roof in case they needed to deal with firebombs.

One morning, I was summoned to Mr Nisbett's office. He explained that the chief cashier of the company had been called up and the assistant cashier, an older man, would be moving up to take his place. The accountant had been impressed by the way I had taken over Miss Gardner's duties when she had been ill and had suggested I be offered a trial for the post of assistant cashier.

I couldn't believe my luck.

It was a position of trust, I was told. Although some of the top executives and heads of departments were paid by cheque, the rest of the staff were paid weekly in cash. I would be expected to calculate the exact amount needed in each type of coin and note, and it would be my responsibility to draw this amount from the bank.

For my safety, a car would be provided to take me to and from the bank, and a policeman would travel with me for protection.

A week later, I met my uniformed police escort. He was elderly, rather over-weight and decidedly heavy-footed.

Mr Nisbett introduced him.

"Don't worry," he said, "Jimmy will look after you. I've known Jimmy since we were boys together."

That was reassuring. What he didn't tell me was that it was Jimmy's first job as an escort, as the regular man had been called up.

And he didn't tell me that Jimmy was not a real policeman. He was a part-time volunteer who could be called upon in an emergency. He had been with Illustrated Newspapers for more than thirty years since the day he and Mr Nisbett started work. In that time, Mr Nisbett had risen to be managing director of the firm, but Jimmy was still an odd-job man at everyone's beck and call. His voluntary police work was his one great pride.

I also wasn't told that, despite his outwardly solid exterior, Jimmy was a bag of nerves. When he sat beside me in the car, his hands clutched tightly round the handle of the empty bag and perspiration ran down his face.

We were heading for Lloyds Bank in The Strand. They had been notified by telephone that we were on our way, but the letter I presented and the list of requirements had to be checked and the cashiers took a long time to fill the bag with the various quantities of coins and notes that were needed.

Jimmy stood close by my side throughout. He never said a word, but I could feel his tension as the cashier came round the counter and handed him the heavy bag.

The car had been waiting in sighting distance and it came immediately and parked at the kerbside. Jimmy grabbed my arm and headed for it at a run. We almost reached it before he tripped and fell. By the time I recovered my balance, the bag had hit the pavement and sprung open, flinging coins and notes everywhere.

The driver jumped out of the car, and two cashiers ran out of the bank to help. Passers-by stared at the sprawl of money as I bent to scoop it back into the bag, but Jimmy didn't move. He sat on the pavement, transfixed.

Mr Nisbett was waiting for us when we got back. The bank had phoned, and he asked me to wait in my office before he led Jimmy away.

Half an hour later, he came back alone. I had been sorting the money and counting it. Some, I knew, had rolled down a drain and possibly some had gone into the pockets of passers-by but, thankfully, very little was missing.

"Jimmy tells me it was his fault, not yours. He said you were calm and level-headed and did your best to put things right. Is that true?"

I had only known Jimmy for a couple of hours, but I was grateful to him for praising me and exonerating me from blame.

"It was an accident," I said. "Mr Meldrum tripped. It could have happened to anyone."

Mr Nisbett stared at me for a long time. Long enough for me to be concerned. I wanted so much to make a success of this job. Then he nodded.

"Jimmy is one of my oldest friends. We started here as runners together in the messenger pool. He's a good man, and he wouldn't willingly let anyone down, but his health is not good. At the moment, he is ashamed and embarrassed. He wants to come and apologise to you."

I told him there was no need to apologise and repeated that it was an accident that could have happened to anyone.

Mr Nisbett shook his head.

"I think he would feel a whole lot better if he did. I'll send him along." He paused at the door. "And thank you for the way you have handled things."

I made two new friends that day. In Jimmy's eyes, I could do no wrong. Nothing I needed was too much trouble. He even asked permission to sit in the corner of my office every

Thursday when I made up the pay packets just to be sure no-one troubled me.

As for Mr Nisbett, he arranged for a car to take us to and from the bank in future, driven by a burly driver who never left my side and who carried half the cash in case it was too heavy for Jimmy.

Two weeks later, Mr Nisbett told me that, if I was agreeable, he would be contacting the Manpower Board.

The publishing trade was classed as an essential service. Illustrated Newspapers had already lost a long list of management staff to the Armed Forces. In view of that, he was applying for certain people in key positions, including me, to be exempted from call-up.

I was amazed to think that I could be considered essential to the war effort, but it was a huge relief to know that when George was called up, I would still be at home to keep an eye on my parents.

George couldn't wait to start work at Shell. All clothes, even socks, ties and handkerchiefs, were on ration, but we managed to save up enough coupons and Auntie Edie, bless her, insisted on putting up the money for a dark suit that transformed him from a schoolboy into a man.

For myself, I was happy in my job. I shared an office with the new chief cashier and enjoyed my responsibilities, but the highlight was the weekly wages run.

With Jimmy, my faithful guard, watching over me, I made up the trays of wage packets each Thursday afternoon. Then, on Friday morning, I began my tour of the staff. Soon everyone knew me. They called me Sunshine and everyone smiled at the sight of me and their pay packet.

I loved Fridays. Despite the gravity of the war, there were always jokes and stories going around the offices. Like the experience of our well-meaning art editor who had been one of the first to join the Home Guard. Not only was he put on guard during the blackout armed only with a cricket bat, but he had the most terrible stutter, which became worse when he was nervous.

Demanding "Halt! Who goes there?" was a major challenge for him and he often had to drop his cricket bat and grab the intruder to force them to listen. Which was embarrassing one night when the intruder proved to be, not a German parachutist, but an escaped bull.

~

One of my tasks, as assistant cashier, was to send comfort parcels to members of the staff who had been called up and were serving abroad. I always carried a collecting box with me on my Friday round. Many of the staff were happy to put the odd coins from their pay packet into it and sometimes I was given items to raffle. The main source of our funds, however, was food parcels.

Our magazines had readers all over the world, some of whom, hearing of the rationing and food shortages in Britain, sent parcels to be distributed to our staff. With Mr Nisbett's permission, I raffled every item individually. Tins of butter, bags of sugar, nuts, sultanas, currants, even tins of fruit. It made the staff happy they had a chance of winning some little extra while helping to raise money to fill the comfort parcels, which, judging from the thank-you notes that came back, were much appreciated.

By then, many food items were rationed, and those that were not were practically unobtainable. People had different needs and bartering became common. A jar of jam for two tins of beans, a quarter of a pound of cooking margarine for a bar of soap.

Fresh fruit from overseas, like oranges and lemons, were

extremely rare, and we never saw bananas. Sometimes American airmen would bring a box of them into England as a gift, and they would be taken straight to a children's hospital to help children with celiac disease.

The meat ration varied, but generally it was one shilling's worth a week for each ration book, which meant those willing to manage on the cheaper cuts of meat got a little more to eat than fussier customers who chose the more expensive cuts.

Argentina made a genuine effort to help us in our hour of need. She sent shiploads of corned beef, a gift that briefly allowed two-penny worth a week to be handed out on every ration book.

Butchers tried to stretch the rations, and to add to their meagre incomes, by making sausages out of every possible left-over scrap, including fat, skin and gristle. There had always been regulations concerning the contents of sausages, but in times of need, such niceties went by the board. There was so little meat and so much bread in wartime sausages the comedians joked no-one knew whether to serve them with mustard or marmalade.

Shopkeepers did their best. Little treats, like a packet of jelly or blancmange powder, were reserved for families with young children. Everyone had a sweet coupon in their ration book, but there was rarely enough to go round and many grown-ups never claimed their ration.

Teabags were a thing of the future, but tea was always in short supply. Every family had its own way of making their meagre ration stretch. Like most people, we always scraped the tea leaves from the bottom of the pot, put them to dry on a clean piece of paper on a window ledge, then, when they were dry, used them again. And sometimes even a third time. Mother had a trick of her own that she rarely confided to anyone. When the tea leaves were wearing out, she would add a senna pod to the pot, just to liven the brew.

At times, I felt sorry for small shopkeepers. They had so little to sell. Customers had to be registered with a shop and supplies were delivered according to the number of registered customers. It was a genuine attempt to make distribution fair, but it didn't always work.

Shops were supplied with just enough bacon to serve their registered customers, but the sides of bacon had to be boned before they could be sliced into wafer-thin rashers. With the bones removed, there was rarely enough to go around the customers, which meant there was nothing left for the shopkeepers' own families.

At one point, when other foods were very short, we were encouraged to eat as many potatoes as we could. A cartoon character, Potato Pete, was on every hoarding and in every newspaper. Then there would be a shortage of potatoes and Potato Pete would suddenly disappear.

There were times when the yearning for a cake to mark a special occasion became too hard to resist. Then relatives and friends would do their best. A few sultanas here, some currants there, a couple of prunes finely chopped, a tiny squeeze of lemon juice. The rest of the ingredients depended on a willingness to make do with whatever was available.

As the war dragged on, flour changed from white to grey. No-one knew what the latest additives were, but the Ministry of Food assured us they were very good for us. Obediently, we combined the discoloured flour with powdered egg, saccharine in place of sugar, and, instead of butter, we had to be content with a good helping of liquid paraffin. A wartime cake was certainly an acquired taste, but it's surprising what people will eat when they are hungry.

CHAPTER 29

The staff in The Illustrated London News editorial office were particularly friendly towards me. One of them, called Harry Hearson, had been a freelance short story writer before the war.

I was still determined to become a writer myself and had finally paid off the last instalment on my typewriter. In a box under my bed were kept the many stories I had begun, discarded, or occasionally finished over the years. There were three that I had sent to various magazines only for them to arrive back, accompanied by printed rejection slips.

I pulled them out and showed them to my new friend. Harry was encouraging, but what I really needed, he said, was an agent to guide me. If I liked, he would show them to his own agent.

If I liked! I could have kissed him on both cheeks, but of course I didn't. I had no intention of letting anyone know how excited I was.

Although daytime raids on London had almost stopped thanks to the efforts of the RAF and the mass of barrage balloons that had sprouted in every park and open space, the sirens still started at around six o'clock most evenings and there was spasmodic bombing until morning.

One evening, just after the sirens sounded, there was a panic. Wardens ran through the streets screaming for the area to be evacuated. Families were hauled from their shelters and loud speakers boomed that the whole district must be cleared at once.

We were in our shelter in the garden and were not allowed to go back into the house. Haste was all that mattered. There was no time to ask questions. We gathered up what we had, a blanket each, the dog, and ran with the rest.

Two schools, many streets away, had been taken over. The crowds jostled into them out of the darkness, men, women, children, dogs, cats, birds in their cages. No-one knew what was happening and no-one stopped to tell us. All we could do was hope that whatever the danger was, the schools were far enough away from it for us to be safe.

We were never given an official explanation of what happened that night, but rumours soon spread.

During the bedlam of the evacuation from Dunkirk, our troops had abandoned huge ammunition dumps, including mines intended to be used against U-boats.

Now we were getting a taste of our own medicine. Parachutes had been attached to the mines, and they were being dropped over London. Three of them had landed in the area that had been evacuated and bomb experts were striving to defuse them. Even as the news was passed round, there was a deafening explosion that rocked the school hall to its foundations. One of the three bombs had gone off. Two more to go.

Unbelievably, there were no casualties. The bomb experts

had not yet started work on the mine that exploded, reducing a whole street to rubble. The other two they managed to defuse.

Next morning, when we went back home, the black plastic had been stripped from the windows by the blast. Pieces of smashed roof tiles were everywhere and the front and back doors had been blown off their hinges.

~

Looking back, it seems strange that the most important thing in my mind at that time was the reaction of the literary agent to my stories. I wanted so much to succeed as a writer. It seemed this was my last hope and the more I thought about it, the more exciting it became. All I needed was advice and guidance.

Perhaps it was a form of selfishness on my part, or perhaps it was simply a way to escape reality. The only news we had was war and hardship. The threat from the Germans waiting across the Channel was as real as ever, and now Germany had invaded Russia. The whole world was in a state of upheaval and disaster.

I presumed the agent would send a message back to me via Harry Hearson, but he didn't. He phoned me at work. Could I drop in and see him?

That was all.

The agent's office was small and cluttered and he was elderly with untidy grey hair that hung over his eyes.

He pulled my stories out of a drawer and spread them across the desk in front of him. Then he frowned.

"Why are you writing stories for men?" he asked.

"I was writing about the war..." I began, but he cut me short.

"Don't bother. No point in writing a story if there's no market for it. People are fed up with death and destruction."

Gathering the stories together, he pushed them back to me.

"Paper's like gold dust. Every magazine's cut to half its size. That's what happens when there's a war."

I can imagine what my expression must have been. He studied me for a moment, then frowned. "The women's magazines. They're your best chance. Can you write about love?"

I didn't know. I had never tried.

From a cupboard behind him, he pulled a pile of women's magazines.

"Here. Take these and read them. If you think you can write what they want, then send me something."

He waited until I was at the door before he smiled, a pleasant, toothy sort of smile.

"Love! Remember, lots of love and passion."

I read every magazine from cover to cover.

It may seem ridiculous, but I had never read a woman's magazine before. It would never have occurred to me to spend hard-earned money on such a luxury.

Father thought the whole idea was hilarious. He was not a man with any real sense of humour. He laughed at what he could ridicule and he flipped the pages of the magazine over, reading out a few passionate lines here and there and laughing disgustedly at such 'mush'.

Mother was different. She never even opened the magazines. She told Father she didn't care what sort of mush I wrote as long as I got paid for it.

For the first time in my life, it didn't matter to me what either of them thought. I was not going to let this opportunity slip by.

I struggled for days to find something to write a story about. It had to be about love, yes, but not just love. I would write about love in a startling setting. Love in unusual circumstances. Perhaps because I was so keen to create something wonderful, I made everything complex and difficult.

In the end, I got a book out of the library about South America. I created a lovely heroine who rode her beautiful horse across the lonely pampas to meet the handsome lover her protective parents had forbidden her to see. And I made it as romantic as I could imagine.

It was two weeks before I heard from the agent. He was friendly, but even over the phone, I could hear the laughter in his voice.

"Write about love. That's what I said. But you don't have to go to the moon or the South American pampas to find love. It's in every home, behind every front door. Write about what you know and make your characters real."

He paused, then added, "I won't send this one back though. You never know. Someone might buy it."

~

Lizzie dropped in to see us when she could. Sid was on Home Guard duty when he wasn't working in the munitions factory, and I think she felt lonely.

"It's like this bloody war is going on forever," she said. "Everybody's fighting everybody and nobody's the better for it. They're filling the hospitals up with wounded. Shiploads of them coming in from North Africa and God knows what good it's doing."

I understood. As the years passed, we had grown used to the war. It was as though, as a nation, we had settled into a kind of timeless resignation.

~

The bombing of Pearl Harbour changed everything. Headlines screamed the news. The Japanese had attacked the

American fleet and America had declared war on Japan. America was with us. We were no longer fighting alone.

Suddenly, American servicemen were everywhere. Confident, perfectly kitted out, they took over London. With money in their pockets, they monopolised the taxis, and with luxuries like chocolate and nylon stockings, they dazzled the girls.

I suppose it was inevitable. They were fresh, boisterous, and excited while we had been at war for years. They were well paid, our servicemen were not. We welcomed the Americans. We needed them, but as with all poor relations, there was an element of envy.

One evening, an elderly gentleman arrived at our door. The air raid sirens had gone, so we invited him into the cramped hospitality of the air-raid shelter.

Andy, as he introduced himself, proved to be a member of the Dramatic Society I had once hoped to join. Many of their members had been called up or moved away from the bombing and the society had closed, but now he was looking for volunteers to form a concert party. Life was grim and cheer of any kind was in short supply. He already had a list of groups who would greatly appreciate an evening's entertainment.

The whole thing would be voluntary. It would probably not even be possible to cover our expenses, but would we be interested? I didn't hesitate. By the end of the week, I had written three sketches.

We rehearsed in an old hall that already had a section of the roof blown off. Our newly-formed group scavenged timbers from wrecked houses and patched enough to keep the weather out. Someone found an old, wood-burning stove and blackout material was nailed over missing windows.

We practised whenever our fire or air-raid duties permitted. Sometimes there was a line-up of elderly men self-consciously pirouetting around as a chorus. Sometimes there were only two or three of us rehearsing sketches that we hoped were hilariously funny.

Our first show was on the outskirts of London. There was no petrol for transport, so we went by Underground, fifteen of us carrying everything we needed, lights, props, changes of costume, even a set of drums. I thanked God a piano was to be provided.

Our venue was an old school. Since the children were evacuated, it had been used to house young conscripts waiting for their first posting, but the old school hall was ours for the night and willing hands packed it with chairs.

Looking back, it was a terrible show. The juggler announced he was juggling with real eggs, then dropped one and it bounced into the audience. A sixty-year-old heart-throb was paired to sing a romantic duet with a nineteen-year-old WAF home on leave, and the large, middle-aged lady singing Danny Boy put so much feeling into it the tears ran down her cheeks and she had to stop and blow her nose half-way through.

I was in two sketches. In one I played a small girl with her front teeth blacked out, her hair screwed into pigtails that stuck out either side of her head and large lace-trimmed drawers, one leg of which continually drooped down and had to be hitched up throughout the act.

I had reservations about the drooping drawers, but to my relief, the young soldiers loved them. Most of all, they loved the puffing, perspiring line-up of middle-aged male ballet dancers with paper roses in their hair and tutus made of old lace curtains, clinging to one another as they high-kicked and gyrated until one fell off the side of the cramped stage.

As I said, it was a terrible show, but the audience cheered at the end and shouted for more.

CHAPTER 30

George's call-up papers arrived a few weeks later. He was going into the RAF as he had hoped and was being sent to Northern Ireland to be trained as a maintenance technician to repair damaged planes.

He wrote every week, telling us the food was good and plentiful, the Irish were friendly and there were dances in the village every weekend with lots of pretty girls.

Mother was not happy. Why had he been sent to Ireland? She didn't trust the Irish. She was already in a dark mood when she found the letter I had hidden, telling us that Edith had been put in a mental asylum.

It was the last straw. She screamed and ranted, threatening to kill herself. When I tried to calm her, the threats only became more violent. In the end, I could think of nothing to do but to call the police. Father begged me not to. He swore if I did, she would never forgive me.

While I was trying to reason with him, Mother began searching for something. She wouldn't tell us what it was, but she turned everything in the house upside down, then exhausted by her efforts, she fell asleep on the kitchen floor.

Next morning, she was white-faced and silent.

It was easy to be grateful for the peace, but as usual, I was wracked with guilt that she needed help and there was no-one but me to provide it.

I had already spoken to our doctor several times about her, but he was overworked and insisted he could not diagnose her problems without seeing her.

I knew she would never agree to see a doctor. There was nothing wrong with her. She was completely sane. Father would verify it, she said, and I knew he would. By now, he was absolutely terrified of her.

With George gone, I hated leaving them alone every day and the fact I was so happy at work made me feel even more guilty.

When I was at home, I tried to concentrate on my writing and think about love stories. I was certain this was my big opportunity, but as I worked, I could feel my parents' restlessness in the next room, and it worried me.

I was grateful that Lizzie dropped in sometimes, mostly, I suspected, because she, too, was lonely, but she even when she complained, she could still lift my spirits.

"Sid? Oh, he's all right. No, that's a lie. He's not really. They've got him out in all weathers guarding the local sewerage works. I know somebody's got to guard it. You can't have that sort of thing blown up and spread all over the place, can you? Oh, and they've taken his broomstick away and given him a gun. It's bloody scary, I can tell you. He hates guns. Dropped it twice while he was showing it to me. I told him. You make sure you keep your mind on what you're doing with that gun or one of these days you're going to end up killing somebody."

George in his RAF uniform.

Three months later, George finished his training. He had expected to have a few days' leave before being posted, but the first we knew was when we received a letter from India. It was a small blue airmail letter that would become familiar in the years ahead, but this one was different. Whole sections had been cut out of it, so much that it was difficult to make any sense of what remained of the message. Obviously,

George had tried to explain his sudden departure to India, but the censors had other ideas.

The shock of finding George was already in India was less important in Mother's mind than the fact the letter had been mutilated. To her, it was ominous and frightening. What were the authorities trying to hide?

She couldn't imagine, but wracked her brains for an explanation. For weeks, she was consumed by the mystery. She sat, staring into space, for hours at a time, and if I'm honest, I was grateful for the peace.

To my surprise, the agent sold my first two love stories to People's Friend, a Scottish woman's magazine. A few weeks later, they bought a third. I was on top of the world. My dreams were coming true. I could finally call myself a writer.

~

It came as a shock when Italy, Germany's ally, changed sides. There had been a revolution and Mussolini was hung. The news brought us a wave of new hope. Perhaps things were beginning to go right at last.

Not that life was any easier on the Home Front. The shortages and deprivation continued, but then, on the 6th June 1944, we heard that Britain and her allies had invaded Europe.

Suddenly, there was something to celebrate. We had made a comeback at last. Behind the joy, we knew it was only the beginning. There was still a long way to go to find peace, but there was a new sense of optimism.

Ten days after we invaded Europe, the first flying bombs dropped on London. They were bigger than anything that had been dropped on us before, more devastating, and more frightening. No-one knew what they were. At first, we didn't know they were pilotless. They would chug overhead, then the buzzing stopped, and they dived to earth.

They dropped everywhere, in cities, in residential areas, in the country. To us, on the receiving end, there seemed to be no pattern to their targets and when they landed, the damage and devastation was worse than anything we had already endured.

My parents were terrified and spent all their time listening for the dreaded buzz overhead, then willing it to keep going, further and further away from them. I hated going to work and leaving them alone.

~

One day, while I was on my wages round, I overheard a conversation in the advertising department. A woman had heard of a house to let. It was a rare opportunity, but she didn't know anyone who was interested.

I was. The house was at Stoneleigh, an outer London suburb close to Epsom. It had been damaged, not by a direct hit but by blast-damage when bombs had dropped behind it. The elderly owner, a builder by trade, had moved his family to live with his sister in Devon. Now he was repairing the house as best he could and wanted to let it.

I did not know what kind of house it was or what state it was in. Nor how much the rent might be. The last thing I wanted to do was to build up my parents' hopes and then let them down, so I lied that I had to go on a fire-training exercise that Sunday and instead went to Stoneleigh on my own.

It had been a nice house once, three bedrooms, dining-room, lounge, and a kitchen looking out across a pleasant garden. The bombing had blown away the fences and torn off part of the roof.

Inside, the owner had replaced the collapsed ceilings, but the walls were still cracked and some of the windows were missing. The floors were covered in smashed plaster and every surface was covered with dust and fragments of glass.

"My family was very happy here," the owner said sadly.

"I'm sure you were. It's lovely."

I meant it. Looking around, I could visualise the home it had been and that it could be again.

My family had never had a proper home. Not one like this one. I paid the owner a month's deposit, and he promised he would have it ready for us to move into in two weeks' time.

It was ridiculous perhaps, but all the way home I built pictures in my mind of how our new home would look. One day soon, I was sure, the war would end and we would be able to buy pretty curtains, perhaps some new furniture and plants for the garden.

When she heard we were moving, Lizzie came to see us. The news from Europe and the Far East was good, and although flying bombs were still causing death and destruction, there was a growing sense that the end of the war was in sight.

"Thank Gawd!" Lizzie said. "Sid's had a right bellyful. What with his work at the factory and all the hush-hush. Hasn't even dared to tell me what they're making in case they shoot him. This war's knocked the stuffing out of him and that's the truth. He's not interested in revolutions any more. D'you know what he wants to do once it's all over?"

We shook our heads.

"He wants to sell the house. We've been lucky, it's not had too much damage. Then we're going to move to the seaside. Perhaps Brighton or Bournemouth. He wants to buy a nice little Bed and Breakfast place and run it, just him and me."

CHAPTER 31

The owner of the house was as good as his word and everything was tidied up and ready on time. I had no doubt my parents would be delighted when they saw their new home. It was further out of London than our existing house and, therefore, a little safer.

I had visions of Father working on the garden while Mother made a home of the bare rooms, but on the day we moved in, Mother stopped in the road and frowned at the lawn.

"It's got no fences," she protested. "Anyone could walk right through it."

I assured her we would soon put a fence around the garden, but she shook her head.

"It's like living in a field. I don't like it."

Inside the house, her reaction was more promising until I opened the door to the sitting room. The floor was swept, and the woodwork was freshly painted, but the centre of the room was occupied by a huge, rusting Morrison shelter.

"The landlord says it's wonderful," I said quickly. "It saved the lives of his family when the bombs hit."

By the time we had emptied the van, carried our

possessions inside, hung the blackout curtains at the windows and made a cup of tea, she had reluctantly accepted the shelter was a necessity.

It was a huge, iron-topped table, walled in with steel mesh like a cage. One side could be removed to allow us to climb in, then pulled back into place once the family was inside. Mattresses had to be packed around it to protect the occupants from flying glass.

To my surprise, Mother warmed to the shelter. Perhaps it made her feel safe. I had expected we would only use it when the air raid sirens sounded, but she insisted we should sleep inside it each night as we had done with the Anderson shelter.

The regular wail of the sirens made it difficult to argue with her, so the shelter became the family bed for my parents, the dog, and me.

Soon, Mother saw the shelter as a place of safety, not only for us, but for everything she valued. That included family heirlooms like the German clock, pieces of special china, even tins of beans, sugar and the dried fruit she was hoarding for George's welcome home cake. As her hoard grew, the sleeping area became increasingly cramped.

There was a ritual that had to be observed each night before we could crawl into bed. It had begun when we were using the previous shelter which was outside, part buried in the earth.

Mother had been terrified that while we were sleeping beetles or earwigs would crawl into our ears and bore into our brains. To protect ourselves, she insisted we block our ears with wads of cotton wool.

It seemed obvious to me that as the Morrison shelter was in the middle of the lounge, we were free from such dangers, but nothing I said convinced Mother. Finally, I gave in and three matchboxes, each carefully labelled and containing two wads of cotton wool, stood on top of the shelter, ready to be screwed into our ears before we settled each night.

Paper was in desperately short supply, and newspapers were reduced to a few closely printed sheets, but times were changing. Now they were filled with news of allied successes as our invading troops pushed back into Europe.

Soon, we were promised, they would reach the launch pads of the flying bombs and the menace would be over. Until then, they buzzed overhead every night and the devastation they caused was heart-breaking. But, with a new sense of hope and ridicule, people referred to them as doodlebugs and we assured ourselves their days were numbered.

The whole of London rejoiced when the launch pads for the doodlebugs were destroyed. But Hitler did not give up easily.

On the 8th of September, another horror began. The first V2 rocket arrived.

V2s were bigger and much more destructive than the flying bombs. They were launched from farther back inside German held territory and they were much quieter and more menacing. We had grown accustomed to the buzz of the doodlebugs and the sound of them passing overhead was sometimes almost reassuring. Now death came silently, with no warning.

Fortunately, the horror of the V2s did not last for long as the retreating Germans were forced to leave the V2 launch pads behind them. The invasion of Europe was going well for us and in the Far East, the Americans attacked the Japanese.

Gradually, life became more normal. There were still shortages and hardships, bomb-damaged homes to be patched up, hospitals full of casualties, but the risk of invasion had passed and the Home Guard was disbanded.

A few months later, the blackout ended too, except for areas around the coast, and on May 6th, 1945 Germany surrendered. The war in Europe was over.

The relief was enormous after so many years of war. A special holiday, V.E. Day was declared and the whole nation celebrated. The church bells rang out and people filled the pews to give thanks, then hurried home to enjoy impromptu street parties.

But the war in the Far East continued, and George was still involved. Father seemed resigned to the situation, but Mother was distraught. While the whole country rejoiced, she was filled with dread. What if George was killed now?

I tried to explain that he was comparatively safe in India, but nothing comforted her.

She had worked hard on the house. The blackout curtains had gone. The bedrooms were bright, the shelter had been taken away and everything was ready to welcome him home.

I, too, had done my best. There was no hope of buying timber to put a fence around the garden, but there was a patch of rough ground nearby where bramble roses grew wild. I had dug up dozens of them and replanted them, so they formed a prickly barrier.

But nothing could improve Mother's mood. She cried constantly, certain that George should have been home by now. I explained there were rules to demobilisation, that those who had been called up first would be released first. She refused to listen and swore I didn't care if my brother came home or not.

Then, on the 6th of August, we heard the Americans had dropped an atomic bomb on Japan. The loss of life and the terrible injuries were appalling. Japan surrendered.

At last, Mother rejoiced. The war in the Far East was over and George would soon be home.

George, Diana and their mother outside the family home.

It was more than a year before George arrived, browned by the Indian sun and wearing an ill-fitting demob suit. Mother made a feast from the oddments of food she had hoarded and we told him all our news.

Slowly, life went back to normal. The staff returned to Illustrated Newspapers, and as I had always known would happen, there was no place for me.

Mr Nisbett was genuinely sorry. We had become good friends, and he offered to find a place for me in one of the other newspaper offices, but I had already decided my future.

I had worked hard to build contacts with editors, and my stories were selling well. Going freelance was a risky business, but I had saved as much money as I could. I believed this was my chance to become a full-time writer, and I was determined to take it.

It was a relief to find George understood how I felt. He, too, had been thinking about the future and planned to go back to the Shell Oil Company, where there was still a place for him in their photographic unit. He would become a photographer, and one day, perhaps he, too, could become freelance.

It was a wonderful thought. Whenever we were alone, we shared our plans and excitement for the future, but we agreed it was best not to mention our dreams to our parents just yet.

At the photographic unit, George became friendly with a likeable young man called Kenneth Brown. He was an experienced photographer, as had been his father before him, and a member of the Royal Institute of Photographers.

But Kenneth had a problem. In addition to his work at Shell, he did freelance sessions at the weekends at sports events. The extra income was very useful, as he had two young children, an expensive wife, and a large mortgage.

Kenneth confided in George that he was indeed a lucky young man. He had everything he could ask for in life, except for one basic necessity. He had no darkroom. He had intended to convert the bathroom in their new house so that it could be used a darkroom on the weekends, but his wife had other ideas. With young children to look after and a host of friends to entertain, she vetoed his plans and refused to surrender her bathroom.

George was quick to see an opportunity and talked his idea over with me. Why shouldn't he and Kenneth form a weekend partnership? Kenneth could provide the knowledge and experience and George could provide the darkroom.

I wasn't sure how Mother would react to his plan, but he begged me to talk to her. This was a big opportunity for him, and after all, the bathroom would only be out of use every

Sunday. On Saturdays, he and Kenneth would be out attending functions.

I did my best, but she didn't fall in love with the idea. I reminded her the downstairs loo would still be available, stressed how much it would mean to George, and eventually, she gave in.

The bathroom was converted, leaflets were printed, handed out to local churches and sports grounds and bookings came in.

Within weeks, George asked if I would like to help on Saturdays. He and Kenneth had decided to expand into wedding photography and felt a female touch would be useful. As for the sports events, he was sure I would like to marshal sweaty footballers and hockey players into groups, combing their hair and wiping the mud from their faces if necessary.

I was delighted. Not only would I be helping George, but it would give me a chance to escape the house. Mother was growing more difficult by the day, complaining that Father was no company. Never had been. As for George. She hardly saw him. He might as well have stayed in India.

She became withdrawn, almost detached, and even the death of little Peter didn't touch her. He had been quite old when we got him from Battersea Dogs' Home and he died one night in his sleep. George buried him in the garden and carved a little cross, but Mother barely noticed.

Since the war ended, building work had begun everywhere to repair the damage. Workmen moved into the empty houses on either side of us and it was obvious we would soon have neighbours.

When they arrived, Mother watched them from behind the curtains in the lounge. A policeman and his wife moved into one house, a young couple with a baby moved into the other.

Mother disliked them all on sight. They were not her class of people.

"Why do we have to have neighbours?" she demanded angrily.

One day, George beckoned me to the end of the garden. He had taken to escape there when the atmosphere in the house became too much for him.

"How would you feel about buying a little cottage in the country?" he asked. "We could make it just the way we wanted it. A study for you. A darkroom for me. A garden for Dad. And no neighbours. Definitely no neighbours."

It came out of the blue, but I could see he was serious.

"I don't mean now," he continued, "but one day, when I can afford to go freelance too. What do you think?"

A cottage in the country. It sounded perfect. I knew it was just a dream, but it was good to have something to conjure up when things became difficult.

"We couldn't do it yet," I agreed. "We'll have to keep saving, but yes… It's a lovely idea."

CHAPTER 32

We rarely heard from Australia. Violet was the only one who wrote to keep us up to date. Her marriage had broken up when her husband walked out, leaving her in a big house overlooking the sea, a few miles from Perth, with three children to bring up.

Mother said she was not surprised. She did not know her brother-in-law, but it was probably for the best. She had never liked Italians.

A few months later, another letter informed us that Trixie's marriage had also broken down and she and her son had moved in with Violet.

Our new neighbours seemed quiet and inoffensive, but everything they did annoyed Mother and whenever she became irritated, she let off steam by cleaning the house from top to bottom. Father would be ordered to move the furniture to the centre of each room and she would polish the woodwork, wash the curtains and scrub the linoleum.

George worked at Shell all week and was busy with

photography every weekend, but I needed peace to write and it was very hard to find.

Now and then, an editor would invite me to lunch and sometimes I dropped in to see Mr Nisbett, but mostly I worked at home, and the more difficult things became, the more I found myself dreaming of a peaceful little cottage in the country.

The next letter from Violet was about Grandfather. He was in his nineties now and the old lady with whom he had been living had died suddenly, leaving him alone. Violet had invited him to move in with her, Trixie, and their children.

Mother was fascinated. All her family were gathering under one roof. She was even more fascinated a few weeks later when she learned that her eldest sister, Mabel, had been widowed for a second time and she too had moved into Violet's house with her daughter, Maybelle.

Mother had never been one to write letters, and she didn't now. Instead, she ordered Father to write while she sat beside him, dictating, then read the letters back to be sure he had written exactly what she wanted.

George and I didn't ask what the letters were about. We were simply grateful for the peace.

One Sunday morning, Father came in from the garden and said he could hear a dog whining nearby. At least he thought it was a dog.

When George went to investigate, he found the sounds were coming from a small coal shed at the back of the house next door. The young couple with the baby were out, and the coal shed door was padlocked.

The policeman who lived on the other side of us had also heard the noises. He phoned the RSPCA and smashed the padlock off the shed door. Inside was a black Aberdeen terrier, covered in blood and squealing with pain.

The RSPCA man arrived at the same moment as the young woman with her baby in a pram. At the sight of the dog, she shrieked and covered her face with her hands.

"I told him not to take it," she cried. "We didn't want a dog, but he wouldn't listen."

The RSPCA man knelt down and examined the dog while the woman explained what had happened. It seemed her husband had agreed to take the terrier from a friend who wanted to get rid of it. He planned to sell it, but had left it with his wife while he went to work.

The woman had given the dog food and water before she locked it in the shed and went shopping. Unfortunately, the food she gave it was an open tin of sardines.

Presumably, the animal had cut itself on the side of the tin as a large piece of its tongue had been sliced off.

The RSPCA man wrapped the shivering creature in a blanket and took him away, but none of us could put the little dog out of our minds.

Father phoned the next day and was told the terrier had lost a lot of blood, but he was expected to pull through. If he did, a new owner would have to be found to nurse him back to health.

Winkie

Three weeks later, he came to live with us. We called him Winkie, and we all loved him.

Mother was especially fond of Winkie. She sat with him curled up on her lap while she dictated letters to various members of her family.

It was a relief to see her so peaceful. Her mind was focused on her correspondence and she beamed with delight every time a reply came back. It never occurred to her to show us the replies, and we never questioned her. It was enough that she had something to occupy her.

But one day, curiosity overcame me. Mother was in the garden and I asked Father, "What on earth does she find to keep writing about?"

He looked at me for a long time before answering.

"She boasts."

I didn't understand.

"What about?"

"Everything. She tells them we live in a great big house in the country with a lovely garden. And we are going to buy a car as soon as they stop rationing petrol so we can go on holidays whenever we feel like it."

I must have looked amazed, because he shrugged apologetically.

"She boasts about you and George, too. He is a successful photographer, and you are a famous writer and earn lots of money. She tells them we're very lucky because you look after us and we have a wonderful life."

George couldn't believe it when I told him, but I knew Father wasn't lying. But what did it matter? She was happy for once, and as far as I was concerned, that was all that was important.

But while Mother was happy, Father seemed more depressed than usual. He was a silent, self-contained man who never discussed anything with anyone if he could help it. I had come to accept that he was what life had made him, but George hadn't.

"I think Dad's worried about something," he confided. "I've tried to get him to talk to me, but he won't. Can you have a try?"

I didn't want to try. All I wanted was for life to go on peacefully so I could concentrate on my writing. I had been asked to submit ideas for a serial that might also be published as a book. It was a big opportunity for me and I didn't want anything to interfere with it.

But I knew George was worried.

I waited until Father was pottering at the bottom of the garden, then asked him as casually as I could whether something was worrying him.

I thought he hadn't heard, so I repeated the question, and after a moment, he turned to me.

"It's your mother," he said. "She wants to go back to Australia."

~

George and I were stunned.

Looking back, I suppose we should have been more curious about the number of letters she was sending and the eagerness with which she waited for each reply. And we should have noticed how her attitude had changed. She still had outbursts when she was aggressive, when she swore that no-one cared about her, but the black moods had been much less frequent of late.

"It's ridiculous," George said. "You know what she's like. It's a passing fancy. She'll get over it."

But Father shook his head.

"She won't. Please believe me. She won't."

He was earnest, his face white and drawn.

"She's been planning it for months," he went on. "When we're alone, it's all she talks about. She wants to go back to her family. She wants to spend the rest of her life with them."

He looked piteously from one to the other of us.

"Please. You have to talk to her."

We tried, but as far as she was concerned, there was nothing to discuss. She had made up her mind.

She had already sent a letter to her sisters saying she was

coming, and Violet had replied that she would be most welcome.

Every attempt to talk her out of her decision was ridiculed. She was doing no harm by going back to her own family. We had no cause to be upset. All we had to do was to buy her a ticket and send money each month for her to live on. Arguing, reasoning, and pleading with her made no difference.

Eventually, George gave up in frustration. He had spent a lot of his life away from her, first evacuated, then sent for training in Ireland, and finally posted to India for years. He had lived among other people, normal people.

I was different. My mother had always been my responsibility, and I felt she still was.

There were times when I don't think she even liked me. In her anger, she would abuse me and swear that I hated her. I didn't hate her. She was my mother, and I always clung to a hope that one day, if she was happy enough, she would change, but I did worry what the future held for her.

"Mother," I said carefully, "George and I can't just pack up and move back to Australia. We have our work. We've made our lives here."

She brushed my words aside.

"I'm not talking about you and George. You'll up and leave us as soon as you find someone to marry, anyway. No, it's just going to be your father and me."

It never occurred to her that Father would not go with her, and she was right. He had lived in her shadow for over thirty years, suffering the violence of her temper and the overpowering force of her moods. He had married her and he would never leave her. He knew nothing else.

He summed it up himself when we were alone.

"She could never manage on her own. Somebody's got to look after her and it had better be me. I've got nothing else to do with my life."

George and I practically lived at the bottom of the garden during the next few weeks, anxiously discussing how best to deal with the situation. It was obvious that no amount of persuasion was going to make Mother change her mind. She had already written to all her relatives, telling them she would soon be coming to live with them.

She was like an excited child, wildly happy as long as no-one crossed her. She spent hours sorting through her meagre wardrobe and making lists of what she would need, ignoring the fact that all clothing was still rationed.

Father didn't help. He was resigned to the inevitable and wanted us to accept Mother's decision.

After all, we only had to book the passages, help them pack a trunk and arrange for money to be sent regularly to an Australian bank so they could live. That was all. Then we could be free and live our lives as we pleased.

Only it wasn't as simple as that. All my adult life, I had been responsible for them, supported them, and warded off my mother's unpredictable bursts of anger. I couldn't just shrug my shoulders and wave them goodbye, although if I am honest, there were moments when the idea was very tempting.

In the end, I wrote to Violet. It wasn't an easy letter to write. I didn't want to sound as though I was checking up on my mother, but I needed to know she hadn't misinterpreted her sister's intentions.

Violet wrote straight back. Yes, she had agreed that my parents could come and live with her. She had plenty of room and they would be very welcome.

It wasn't the reply I had expected, but it was reassuring. Perhaps I was worrying too much. It was clear Mother was missing her family and perhaps she really would be happy with them.

George's reaction was one of pure relief. They were welcome to live with Violet. That was enough.

I understood. He was thinking of a peaceful little cottage in the country with no sense of guilt. Our parents were choosing their own future, and they were going to be happy.

"Of course, Winkie will miss you."

It was the simplest of remarks, but Mother's mood changed in an instant. Picking up the little dog, she cuddled him in her arms.

"I'm not leaving Winkie behind," she cried. "Poor little thing. We're taking him with us."

~

"She meant it."

"I know."

George and I were at the bottom of the garden again.

"But can you take dogs to Australia? I mean, do they let them on liners?" I asked.

Neither of us knew.

We went to Australia House and spoke to a clerk.

"Yes, it is possible to take a dog to Australia, but it is complicated and rather expensive," the clerk explained. "Dogs are not allowed on passenger ships, so they have to travel on a cargo boat. A large cage has to be provided which is lashed to an upper deck and a ship's officer has to be paid to care for the dog during the journey. Then, when it reaches Australia, it will have to go into quarantine for six weeks."

When we explained this to Mother, she burst into a flood of tears.

"I don't care how much it costs," she sobbed. "I won't leave him behind. Not after all he's been through."

~

A few days later, it was Auntie Edie's birthday. We usually sent her cards and a present through the post, but this time we went to visit her. George and I had never talked to anyone about our private lives or our parents, and we felt she was the only person we could confide in.

She was living in an orderly, ground-floor flat and was delighted to see us. She made us tea and sat, hands folded in her lap, as she listened to our problem.

"Let me make sure I have everything correctly," she said at last. "She wants to go back to Australia and live with her family?"

We nodded.

"And you know she will be welcome. You believe she would be happy, and your father wants to go with her?"

We nodded again.

"Then surely that's the best thing for everyone. They will be happy, and you two will have the freedom to live your own lives."

"But we can't just wave them off across the world on their own," I objected. "Father couldn't cope if she had a really bad turn and there was no-one to help him."

I turned to George.

"You know what she's like. She'd end up in a mental home."

Auntie Edie looked from one to the other of us.

"It seems to me there is only one solution. You two should take your parents to Australia, see that they are settled and happy, then come back and start your own lives. Doesn't that make sense?"

It did. It sounded so simple.

"It would cost a lot though," George said, "and we don't have much saved yet."

Auntie smiled.

"But everyone would be happy, wouldn't they? I'm glad you came to see me. I'm all alone, you know, and I lead a quiet life. As it happens, I have some money saved. If you need it, then you are welcome to it now. No point in waiting until I'm dead."

Of course, we had no intention of taking advantage of her generosity, but it was so like her to offer. I was amazed, yet again, that my mother could dislike her so much.

CHAPTER 33

It was a big step, and there was so much to plan. The first thing was to book passages, four outward and two return. There were no scheduled airline services to Australia in those days, so the only route was by sea.

But we were in for a shock.

There were no passages available because all liners had all been converted during the war to carry troops. Only a few had yet been refurbished for passengers, and there were long waiting lists.

We decided not to tell Mother, but instead we wracked our brains to think of someone who could help us. The only person I could think of was Mr Nisbett. He knew a surprising range of people and when I went to see him, he promised to do his best for me.

A week later, he phoned. He had called in favours and had managed to get our names to the top of the list at the Orient Shipping Line. We had been allocated four outward bound passages in a month's time and two return passages, the date to be arranged when we reached Australia.

We called into the shipping offices the next day, and our tickets were waiting for us. They were all first class. It was the last thing we had expected, and the price was breath-taking.

~

George had to arrange leave from Shell. He told them a family emergency had occurred, and he had to take his parents back to Australia. He needed three months' leave, and to our relief, he got it.

As a freelancer, I was my own master, but I contacted my agent and various editors who were interested in my work. I was pleased to find they were all understanding and one told me I was bound to come back with a wealth of ideas for new stories.

It hadn't occurred to me that I could work on the trip, but it seemed a great idea. I could take my portable typewriter and George decided to take his camera and photographic equipment. Just in case.

Back at Australia House, we were told that Spratt's, the dog food people, had a department that dealt solely with the transportation of animals.

Spratt's were wonderful. They found a cargo ship leaving from Southampton that would take Winkie, and arranged for a suitable cage to be made.

The house was more of a problem and George and I talked it over anxiously. Should we close the front door and walk away for three months, putting our trust in neighbours we hardly knew to keep an eye on it? Or should we give it up, save the three months' rent and sell the contents, to help our dwindling savings?

Mother wasn't interested. She wouldn't need the house again.

George and I sorted out our personal treasures, toys we still loved, books that had been school prizes, and favourite pictures. These we packed into a trunk and placed in a storage warehouse until we returned. The rest we sent to an auction.

George seemed happy. He clung to the dreams we had woven, and he carried me along with him, but when I was alone, there were black times. I felt I was destroying the only real home I had known.

"Cheer up," he told me. "We're doing the right thing. When we get back, we'll find a nice little flat until we can afford our cottage."

It is impossible to explain how grateful I was to have George. Ever since he had been evacuated as a schoolboy, I had battled alone. Now, when I needed him most, he was with me.

Mother drifted around the house singing to herself. She was embarking on a great adventure with a fairytale ending that would transport her back to her family. Even Father seemed content. I knew the last thing he wanted was to go back to Australia. There were too many bad memories buried in the past, but he had assured us he would never leave Mother alone and now that we were going to travel with them, he was almost cheerful.

When we went to say goodbye, Auntie Edie hugged us and gave us her blessing.

"You are doing the right thing," she said. "Enjoy yourselves. I shall be thinking of you until you get back."

We sailed from Southampton on the S.S. Orontes. It was the third time I had travelled on a liner, but this trip was different. Most of the passengers were Australian. Some had served with the Allied Forces in Europe and were now demobbed. Some had been on holiday and had been trapped by the sudden declaration of war. They had waited years for the chance of a passage home.

We were warned by the purser that, although the liner had been refurbished and redecorated, it had not yet been restored to its former luxury.

There were no recreational activities or entertainment provided. No shows, no deck tennis, no organised games or competitions. Only a daily lottery based on how far we had travelled in the last twenty-four hours.

To my surprise, my parents made some friends of their own age. I was grateful. They seemed content to sit and chat and signal to the deck stewards for endless drinks and dishes of ice-cream. Then, when the afternoon tea bell rang, they trooped down to the dining room where tea and cream-filled cakes awaited them.

Mother was in her element. I had never seen her so happy before and even Father looked relaxed.

Every passenger was allotted a particular seat in the dining room, and as the days passed, it was easy to strike up conversations with fellow diners.

A flamboyant woman sat next to us in the dining room. She was a ballet mistress who had been working in the West End of London and was excited to be going home to New South Wales.

She was an energetic type, and I suspect she was easily bored. Soon she complained that if there was no entertainment provided to help pass the hours, then someone ought to do something about it.

She told the purser she intended to arrange an evening's entertainment. Among the multitude of first-class passengers, there must be some with suitable talents. Would he kindly put up notices asking for volunteers who would like to be involved?

He did, and the result was amazing. Soon musicians, singers, even a ventriloquist and an amateur magician were attending morning rehearsals and George and I had written a one-act comedy play which was hastily cast and included in the program.

Sensing the level of enthusiasm for the project, the purser put two sailors at our disposal to assist with anything we needed. One was large and round, the other thin and tiny. They introduced themselves as Stan and Ollie and turned out to be real treasures.

The ballet mistress had set her heart on a chorus line, but to her disappointment, she managed to find only two dancers. At her request, the purser put up another notice, asking for volunteers to form a chorus. Anyone interested was asked to report to the show committee in the main lounge.

When the ballet mistress arrived the next morning, she was speechless. A group of elderly gentlemen had taken to meet in one of the bars and ended each evening with a singsong. Egged on, one by another, they had come to volunteer.

Their expressions changed when they were told they had volunteered, not for a choir, but for a ballet chorus. Some headed for the door, but our ballet mistress was too quick for them. With the help of the two professional dancers, she soon had them puffing and blowing as they struggled to learn a few dainty steps.

Perhaps it was because the passengers were starved of entertainment, or perhaps word had leaked out that the show was going to be lighthearted. Whatever the reason, on the night of the show, the audience, including the Captain and a crowd of officers, were packed in jam-tight.

The full cast of volunteer performers with Diana second from the left..

It was a fitting beginning that Stan and Ollie, immaculately dressed, were standing to attention on either side of the closed curtains. As the introductory music came to an end, they both bowed, then tugged heartily on the ropes that controlled the curtains.

But little Stan was no match for big Ollie. The two halves of the curtains both shot across to the same side. Stan, flushed with embarrassment, pulled violently at his rope and both halves of the curtains immediately shot across to the other side.

The audience exploded into a gale of laughter. Ollie responded with another violent tug, and the curtains flew back across to him. But Stan had had enough. With a black look at Ollie, he made an exaggerated bow and retired to loud applause from the audience, and the curtains remained where they had settled for the rest of the performance.

It was a good evening, and when I climbed into my berth, I was still smiling to myself.

CHAPTER 34

Three days later, we docked at Fremantle and found, to Mother's delight, Winkie's ship was already there.

I was glad to see her in such a good humour. She had enjoyed the voyage, revelling in the luxury, and on the rare occasions when her temper had flared, Father had managed to calm her in the privacy of their cabin.

I knew he was making a big effort to prove he could care for her, and I was grateful.

The family was waiting amid the crowd on the quayside. Not all of them. Grandfather was too old to make the trip to Fremantle and no-one mentioned Edith.

There were some new faces, cousins I had only seen long ago as young children, but I recognised the rest instantly. It came as a shock to realise it was fifteen years since I had last seen them. They had grown older, and they all spoke with strong Australian accents, but to me, the tanned faces hadn't changed. Only the character lines had grown deeper.

They seemed pleased to welcome us, and as Mother threw her arms round them, I tried not to remember that fifteen years before not one of them had come to wave us off, to wish us luck, or even to press an extra coin into our hands to help cushion the bleakness of our future.

But that was all in the past, brushed aside with so many other unpleasant memories. We were starting a new life now. Or rather, my parents were.

Mother chattered excitedly as the luggage was brought ashore and I dropped back and stood beside George.

"Taxis?" he asked quietly. "Has anyone said anything to you about taxis?"

I shook my head, and he frowned.

"Apparently they came in three taxis," he said. "They're standing outside waiting to take us all back. The taxi driver just asked if I will settle the bill."

He pulled out his wallet. "I hope they don't think we're made of money."

Violet lived in Cottesloe, a beach resort close to Perth, where her house stood alone, aloof from the cluster of hotels and holiday shacks, facing out to sea. The view from the veranda was spectacular, a panorama of sparkling blue water and endless golden sands, but the house itself was not so impressive. It was big and had once been attractive, but now there was an air of dilapidation about it. The paintwork was flaking, a broken window had been boarded over, and three rumpled beds surrounded by odd possessions filled the front veranda.

At the back, another veranda with two newly made-up beds faced a derelict vineyard. The soil stretched away dry and sandy and dead vines clung to wires clustered with bunches of rotting grapes.

This was the view from the room that had been prepared for my parents, and the two made-up beds on the veranda were for George and me for as long as we wanted to stay.

Grandfather was bedridden, but he had been propped up with pillows to greet us. His thin, wrinkled face lit up at the sight of us, but he looked very old, much older than I had expected.

"He's been looking forward to seeing you again," Violet whispered. "I don't think he'll last much longer."

Violet prepared a meal for the whole family that evening. Cold meat and salad were followed by little cupcakes. She had never been an enthusiastic cook, but she had done her best and we were grateful.

Mabel was not. After the first effusive kisses at the docks, we had seen little of her. Now she wrinkled her nose.

"Not bloody salad again," she muttered. "I thought you were cooking something special."

Violet sighed.

"We usually cook our meals separately, but I thought it might be nice to have a family meal tonight."

Later, she came to my parent's room as we helped them unpack.

"Sorry about Mabel," she apologised. "She can be a bad-tempered bitch sometimes. Ignore her. She'll get over it."

I nodded and smiled, but somewhere in the house angry voices were raised and a door slammed noisily.

Violet had come to sort out the 'pennies and pounds' as she put it.

She had written everything down. The rent of the room, the electricity, the use of the two veranda beds, the cost of installing a cooker so Father and Mother could prepare their own meals in their room, china, cutlery, saucepans and a frying pan...

It was a long list, and I saw George wince as he glanced at the total. We agreed we would settle the bill, and in future, my parents could draw a monthly sum from a bank in Perth to cover their expenses.

"A bank in Perth?" Violet nodded as she added an item to

the list. "Once a month? Well, that will be all right. I'll just add a bit on to cover the petrol."

George was anxious to go into the shipping offices in Perth and arrange our passages home.

"There will probably be waiting lists," he said. "The sooner we get our names on them, the better."

But Mother's mind was on Winkie. She was desperate to visit him in quarantine, so we gave in and contacted the port authorities.

"He's been really well cared for," she told me when she returned, "and he hasn't forgotten me. One of the keepers takes him for a walk every day. I hated leaving him. He barked and howled when I walked away, but it won't be long until we can bring him home."

She disappeared into Grandfather's room to tell him about her visit to see Winkie, and I was carrying teacups into the kitchen when I overheard them.

Clearly, no-one had noticed I was there, and judging by Trixie's tone, she wouldn't have cared if they had.

"Why the hell did the silly bitch bring a dog with her?"

Violet had her back to me.

"Because I said she could."

"Well, we're not having it in the house. I hate bloody dogs."

"Calm down," Violet snapped. "It can sleep in the shed. It'll be all right."

The conversation worried me, but at that moment, Mother reappeared and announced she was going to visit Edith.

"You'll regret it," Mabel said bluntly, but Mother was not going to be put off.

There had never been any insanity in the family, she

insisted. Edith had a temper, certainly, but was she insane? No. She suspected there was a plot to shut her sister away so that her husband could be free and take their son with him.

Trixie and Mabel stalked out of the room, but Violet agreed, reluctantly, to go with us to the asylum. She admitted the family rarely visited Edith as they found it too upsetting. Only two visitors were allowed at a time, so Mother and I could go in while she waited outside.

Violet phoned and made an appointment for our visit, but it was an appointment we were not to keep. That night, Grandfather died in his sleep. I suppose it should not have been a shock, and looking back, I think he only held on long enough to see us.

I always loved Grandfather and in my childhood, there were times when he was the only person I could turn to for comfort and advice. He taught me about faith, self-control, loyalty, and so much more. Through him, I learned that God was my friend and no matter how dark the days, he would always be beside me.

More than anything at that moment, I wanted to creep away somewhere quiet and grieve for him.

But it was not like that. There was no quiet corner.

In Australia, as in any hot climate, burials are swift. It had been obvious Grandfather was nearing his end, yet the family was totally unprepared. There was so much to do and there were arguments as to who should do what.

Mabel was adamant we must all wear black to the funeral and busied herself sorting through everyone's wardrobe.

I had a dark grey suit which was approved as being nearly black, but Mother loved colour. Nothing in her luggage was black, so Trixie offered to take her into Perth to buy a suitable outfit.

George was volunteered to go with Violet and make the funeral arrangements, and I agreed to order wreaths and gather a long shopping list of food to feed the family and friends who would gather at Violet's house after the funeral.

It was a long time before Trixie and Mother returned clutching a host of parcels. Trixie had chosen an expensive black dress with a jacket and an enormous black straw hat for Mother. She had also bought a colourful silk dress for us to give Edith.

~

The day after the funeral, Violet called a family meeting. She had a list of the expenses which she added up and divided by four, between Trixie, Mabel, George and me, and herself.

"Anyway, that's what it cost, so I hope you're all agreeable."

She glanced round at the reluctant faces. Grandfather had been duly buried in the plot beside Grandmother that had been waiting for him since she died. I had a feeling I knew what was coming.

"There is one more thing. We always said when the two of them were gone, we'd put up a nice headstone, so I'll find out how much it would cost."

George, Father and I nodded, but Mother wasn't listening. She was lost in her own thoughts, frowning and plucking at her handkerchief.

I decided it wasn't the moment to raise any concerns I had about the proposed headstone. I didn't want to upset Mother any more. She had cried throughout the funeral and now she had only one thing on her mind. She wanted to see Edith.

We went a few days later, and the atmosphere inside the square, prison-like institution was horrible.

We walked through long, grey passages and metal doors that clanged shut behind us, until we were taken into a small, white-walled room, bare save for a table and two chairs. A grim-faced warden brought Edith to us, locked the door, and stood with his back against it.

Edith had barely changed, except for the deep wrinkles in her face and the whiteness of her hair. She wore a shapeless cotton dress and shabby sandals.

"Don't rile her," the man warned. "It's not one of her good days."

"Remember me? I'm your sister, Hilda," Mother began pleasantly, but Edith's eyes were on the parcel in her hands. She snatched it and ripped away the wrapping paper. Reaching the brightly coloured dress, she held it up against herself.

"It's for you," Mother said. "I thought you'd like it…"

But Edith glared at her. Screwing the dress into a ball, she threw it across the room.

"One of your bloody left-offs, is it? Well, you can keep it, whoever you are."

Darting across to the dress, Edith scooped it from the floor and threw it straight at Mother.

"I don't need your charity," she screamed. "Keep your bloody old rags. Wait 'til I get out of here. I'll buy what I like and sod the lot of you!"

Violet nodded when I told her what had happened.

"The doctors explained it," she said. "Edith's a schizophrenic with a violent temper. She has better days, but you can never be sure. They say there's nothing they can do for her, so it's best to let her be."

~

"Well?" George asked when we got back to the house. I waited until we were alone before describing the visit.

"It was such a shock to Mother. She cried all the way back."

George shook his head sadly.

"It sounds awful."

We sat in silence on our beds, listening to flies droning in the warm air.

"But we must go to the shipping offices tomorrow," he said at last. "Time's passing and we're spending a lot more money than we expected."

I nodded reluctantly, and I suspect he read my thoughts.

"We've done everything we promised," he reminded me. "We've given them a lovely trip. We've brought Mum halfway across the world to her family. It's what she wanted. We can't do any more."

He put his arm around my shoulders.

"She had a dream and we've tried to make it come true. Now it's time for us to go. You haven't forgotten that little cottage in the country, have you? And all the wonderful things you're going to write? And all the beautiful photographs I'm going to take?"

We went to the shipping offices the next day. I told Father where we were going, but I didn't mention it to Mother. I told myself she needed time to settle down after the shock of her visit to Edith.

~

At the shipping offices in Perth, the clerk was polite but regretful. Their office in London had given us the wrong impression. It was practically impossible to get a passage from Fremantle to England while berths were so scarce. All available spaces were filled at the eastern ports.

"If you are really anxious to get back to England, then take my tip," he confided. "Go over to the East and get your names on a waiting list there."

We didn't go straight back to Cottesloe. Instead, we found a bench in a park overlooking the Swan River. We needed to think. How long would it take for our names to reach the top of a waiting list in the East? And what would we do in the meantime? We had no answers.

"Don't say anything to Mum and Dad yet," George insisted. "Not until we decide what we're going to do."

As we approached Violet's house, a blazing row was in progress and Mother's voice screeched in the middle of it.

She had discovered Trixie and Mabel throwing out Grandfather's possessions and had let fly at them. The old man had kept his treasures in a box under his bed, an old pipe, a tin of sweets, a little picture of an unknown ship, a woman's hair slide, two brightly coloured texts and assorted odds and ends.

"It's just a load of junk." Trixie had said as she emptied the suitcase on to the bed in front of Mother. "Don't bother yourself. There's nothing worth keeping."

"That's when your mother flew at them." Violet told us. "She said they had no right to throw Grandfather's stuff away without everybody having a chance to see it."

She shook her head sadly.

"You can imagine the reaction. Trixie always gives as good as she gets. She told Hilda to mind her own bloody business. I heard them from the kitchen, but by the time I got in here they were going at it hammer and tongs. Who the hell did Hilda think she was? Throwing her weight about, when she hadn't lifted a finger to help the old man in fifteen years. Well, she could go back where she came from. They didn't need her money or her bloody dog. They had one lunatic in the family. They didn't need another one."

Violet looked miserable, and I found myself pitying her. She was the only one in the family who had ever tried to be a peacemaker.

"It isn't going to work, is it?" she asked, looking from George to me. "I'm sorry. It's my fault. I encouraged them to come, but in their letters, they sounded so eager to be here with us."

"To tell you the truth…" She looked ashamed. "I thought they were a gift from Heaven. I've been trying to let that room for years, but now…. You'd best go and see her. She's very upset."

Mother was in her room, sobbing.

"They all hate me! They called me a lunatic. I can't stay here. They'll put me in a madhouse like Edith. I want to go home."

Later, when she had fallen asleep and Father was keeping watch over her, George and I walked down to the sea. It was peaceful as we watched the waves rolling in.

"What do we do now?" I asked.

George stared out to the horizon.

"God only knows," he said.

CHAPTER 35

The next day we went into Perth, taking our parents with us. It was clear we couldn't leave them at the house. No-one had spoken to us except Violet and it seemed we had become the enemy, unwelcome intruders who had spoiled the pattern of their lives.

George was upset and bewildered by the sudden change.

I wasn't. There was an awful familiarity about it. I could remember my childhood in Swan Street and the raving arguments that came from nowhere. From Violet's letters, I believed the family had changed over the years, but they hadn't. I couldn't believe I had been foolish enough to imagine they would have.

By morning, Mother's mood had changed entirely. The anger and disgust of the previous day had been replaced by the pathos of a terrified child. She begged us not to leave her.

All she wanted to do was to go home and Father, white and trembling, nodded his head in agreement.

We took them to the gardens that bordered the Swan River, bought them drinks, sweets and a newspaper, then settled them on a seat in the shade of a tree. We told them they must stay there until we came back, and like nervous children, they promised.

George and I needed time to think. Much as we might want to walk away, return to England and chase our dreams, we knew we would not. They were still our parents. All they wanted now was to go home, and so did we.

But it wasn't as easy as that.

If money had been no object, we would have taken a train over to the East and booked into a hotel in Sydney until we could get passages back to England.

But money was an object. George and I had budgeted our trip before we left England and had each left some money in our bank accounts. It wasn't a large amount, but we had seen it as our 'starting again' fund for when we returned.

Now everything had gone wrong, and we had no idea how much money we would need to get us all home again.

We spent that afternoon gathering costs. How much was the rail fare to Adelaide? How much was the passage from Adelaide back to London? How much would the cheapest hotel rooms in Adelaide cost?

We went back to the gardens with a notebook full of information and heavy hearts. We simply didn't have enough money left to cover the costs. But we couldn't give up. We had to find answers.

"Why don't we buy a caravan?" George suggested suddenly. "We'd have to buy a car as well, of course, but then we could drive across to the East and save the train fares."

"And we wouldn't have to pay to stay in a hotel," I agreed.

"We would have to get the bank to send the rest of our money over," George went on. "But we would get it back when we sold the car and caravan before we sailed."

It was a brilliant idea, and I felt my spirits lift as we headed to the nearest bank.

The bank manager was friendly and arranged for the rest

of our money to be transferred to us in Perth, but he seemed doubtful about our plans.

Did we really intend to travel overland to the east coast? He had never met anyone who had tried it. Was there actually a road across Australia?

Our faces must have shown our surprise because he leaned across the desk and patted George's arm.

"Look, I'm not trying to worry you, but I think you need to get more information before you make a decision. If you do decide to buy a car and a caravan, make sure you get advice from someone reliable. I'd hate for you to break down in the middle of nowhere."

It was a sobering thought. The manager's words undermined our confidence in our plan. Surely there must be a road across to the East. But what if there was not? As for the car and caravan, where could we go to get advice from someone reliable?

~

A letter arrived telling us Winkie's quarantine was over, and he had passed all his tests. It was good news, but added another problem to our list, as we didn't feel we could take him to the house in Cottesloe.

A sour silence had fallen over the place and we slipped in and out, avoiding all contact if possible. We felt sure Winkie's presence would spark another confrontation, so we phoned the quarantine station and arranged to pick him up and settle his bill in a few days.

But what could we do in a few days?

"The bank manager was right," George admitted miserably. "I know nothing about cars. I drove trucks for the RAF in India. I can put water and petrol in, and pump up the tyres, but beyond that..."

He shook his head helplessly, and I understood. I knew nothing at all about cars. Or caravans.

I wracked my brain to think of someone who could help us. It was fifteen years since I left Perth, a schoolgirl whose parents, ashamed of their poverty, had never encouraged her to make friends with anyone. I had known no-one outside the walls of the convent.

"What about Sister Mary Emmanuel?" I asked hesitantly.

He stared at me as though the sun had addled my brains.

"Sister Mary Emmanuel?" he echoed. "How much do you think a nun would know about cars and caravans?"

"Not much, I suppose, but she might be able to suggest someone who does."

George shook his head.

"She's probably dead by now," he said flatly, but I clung to my idea. I had no others.

"Why don't we go to the convent and ask for her? What harm could it do?"

Even after fifteen years, everything looked the same. The arched entrance set into the long grey stone wall, the polished brass sign announcing The Convent of the Sisters of Mercy, and beside it, the bell.

We had rehearsed what we were going to say if Sister Mary Emmanuel was alive and available. Certainly not the truth. George was insistent about that. He realised our problems were all of our own making, since we had allowed Mother's moods to lead us into our present predicament. We had been fools. There was no denying that, but now we had to find a way out, and if possible, hang on to our dignity.

We rang the bell and after a long time, the door was opened by a white-veiled nun. I recited the words we had practised.

"Sister Mary Emmanuel?" she repeated blankly.

"Yes. My name is Hilda Spear. I used to be one of her pupils at the college."

"I'll ask. Please wait."

She closed the door, and we waited outside.

"She's dead," George whispered. "That nun looked as though she'd never heard of her."

"She's heard of her all right," I said confidently.

"How do you know?"

"Because she was in my class at school. Nora Something-or-other she was called then."

A few minutes later, she came back and opened the door wide.

She led us into a familiar white-walled room. Nothing had changed. The same picture of the bleeding heart on the wall. The same little table waiting for the same round tea tray. It arrived a few minutes later, carried by a beaming novice. The same plain white china, the same plate of neatly-arranged biscuits. I could have been eleven years old once again.

Then the door was flung open and Sister Mary Emmanuel burst in. She stared at us and shook her head as though she could not believe her eyes, then she flung out her arms and I was enveloped in a mass of black and hugged until I could barely breathe.

She hugged George, too, although I saw him wince when she called him Cecil.

Sister Mary Emmanuel was exactly as I remembered her, only older and thinner.

"A lot thinner," she beamed and delved among the black folds to show us the huge safety pin that skewered her skirt into place.

We told her the story George and I had agreed, that we were travelling around Australia gathering material for articles and stories. I was a writer, George was a photographer, and we had brought our parents and our little dog with us to turn the trip into a happy family adventure.

She was delighted.

"I've often wondered how you fared, but obviously you have done well."

I felt a twinge of guilt as I continued. I didn't want to lie to Sister Mary Emmanuel, but I couldn't bear to tell her the truth.

I explained that we had run into problems and needed a car and caravan so that we could travel wherever we pleased in comfort and work at the same time.

The problem was that we were out of our depth. The bank manager had warned us to be careful, as Australia was not an easy country in which to travel. We needed expert advice before we bought our vehicles, but we knew no-one to turn to for advice.

Her old head wagged.

"That bank manager is right. The car trade is full of shysters," she agreed. "You need someone you can rely on, and I know the very man. He's called Matthew. Just tell him Sister Mary Emmanuel sent you."

We left an hour later, and I felt a huge weight had been lifted from me. Chatting with Sister Mary Emmanuel after so many years had been wonderful. She had not questioned why we were in Australia, but had simply been delighted that one of her girls had come back to visit her. As we left, she assured me she would do anything in her power to help us.

~

Matthew was a cheerful, middle-aged man with very little hair and a lopsided grin that widened as we mentioned Sister Mary Emmanuel.

"If you're friends of hers, then you're friends of mine," he said heartily. "Bless her. A real card she is, with a heart of gold. But she gets things done. I often think she would have made a damned good Prime Minister."

I laughed, but I think he was right. Matthew owned a repair garage and a car hire service on the outskirts of Perth. When the nuns at the convent needed transport, he was the man who hired a car and drove them wherever they needed to go.

We told him our problems.

"A caravan for four and a dog and a car to pull it?" He screwed his face up. "You'll have to give me a day or two."

~

We spent as little time as possible at the house. We had told Violet we were making arrangements to go back to England, and she seemed relieved. No one else spoke to us.

The fact that Winkie would soon be with us kept Mother happy, and both she and Father were fascinated by the prospect of living in a caravan.

We couldn't tell them how long we would need to live in the caravan or where exactly we would be heading, but they didn't seem concerned. It was almost as though we were planning a holiday.

George and I went back to the shipping offices and asked how long we would have to wait for passages from East Australia back to England.

The clerk recognised us and did his best to help. He phoned Adelaide, then Sydney, and came back shaking his head. The wait was likely to be at least three months, and we should put our names down on the list before it got any longer. We did.

We went back to see Sister Mary Emmanuel two days later, and she told us she had a message from Matthew. He thought he had found something that might interest us.

We would have hurried straight to see him, but she too had a lot to tell us. She had been talking to people.

"You need all the publicity you can get, don't you?" she said. "Everywhere you go, you will want to meet people who can help you, show you round and tell you the local history and all the interesting facts."

One glance at George's face told me that was the last thing he wanted. I felt the same, but Sister Mary Emmanuel plunged on.

She had told everyone she thought would be useful that we were a brother and sister team come to photograph and write articles on the South West of Australia.

"I did mention that you were connected to The Illustrated London News." She chuckled. "That impressed them. And that your brother was a photographer from The Shell Oil Company. Oh, and that you are going to write a book. You are, aren't you?"

George found his voice. "Who did you tell?"

She beamed. "The Secretary of the Roads Board at Harvey, the Mayor of Bunbury. The Editor of the newspaper at Manjimup. They all promised to introduce you to anyone else they think could help you. Oh.. and I've spoken to the radio. They were very interested. They'd like you to make an appointment so they can meet you as soon as possible. They thought it might be good to have an introductory interview before you actually took to the road, then others along the way."

I thanked her over and over again. What else could I do? George was speechless.

CHAPTER 36

We hoped Matthew might have found us a car, but when we saw him, he explained we couldn't decide on a car until we knew the size and weight of the caravan it had to tow.

He had found a caravan. Not just any old caravan, this one was truly unique. It had been designed and built by an elderly businessman who wanted his wife and family to enjoy his retirement with him. They planned to travel the country, wandering wherever they pleased, but sadly, he had suffered a heart attack months after he retired and the caravan had been relegated to the back of the garage.

It certainly was different. It wasn't particularly attractive, but it was spacious and solidly built, and contained an impressive amount of fittings.

Fifteen feet long, the front section was a kitchen, complete with safety racks for travelling. It had a breadbin, cutlery drawer and plenty of cupboard room, but no oven or means of cooking.

When we queried this, Matthew was dismissive. Of course not. This was Australia, land of wide-open spaces.

Wherever we went, there would be plenty of wood for campfires.

At the back of the caravan was an array of drawers and there were four beds, two-tiered along either side when in use, then strapped back to the walls during the day, leaving plenty of space for a folding table and chairs.

"It's got every convenience you could wish for," Matthew assured us. "And it's cheap because the old lady wants to get rid of it. Myself, I think it's a damned good buy."

The caravan seemed ideal to me, but I could tell George was baulking, so I suggested we went for a walk to consider our decision.

Once we were alone, George admitted he felt we were being swept along by circumstances. Were we about to make another mistake?

We both agreed on two things. First, we couldn't stay at Cottesloe any longer. Second, we had to collect Winkie as soon as possible. His quarantine bill was growing every day.

Perhaps it was only because he couldn't think of any alternative, but as we talked, George warmed to our original ideas.

We had three months before we could get tickets on a liner. Why shouldn't we buy the caravan and potter through the South West? We could take advantage of Sister Mary Emmanuel's introductions and produce articles and photographs of what we saw? I felt sure, if we made them good enough, my agent in London would be interested. And why not gather notes for a book? We really were innocents abroad. Perhaps a publisher might be interested in our story.

Suddenly, George saw the caravan from a different perspective. The windows were small and high-up. With a set of black curtains and a tank full of water, he could transform it into a functioning darkroom.

I was relieved to see his enthusiasm return.

"Shall we tell Matthew we want the caravan, then?" I asked.

George nodded, and I smiled.

Our decision was made.

The Buick and caravan ready to ford a small river.

Two days later, Matthew found us a car, a big American Buick. To me, it looked enormous, but he assured us that once we had packed provisions, water, spare petrol and our own possessions into the caravan, we would need a car as big as the Buick to tow it.

We believed him and trusted his assurance that the car was in good order. Petrol was still on ration, but George went with him to the local Fuel Office, where Matthew was well known, and came back beaming with a generous petrol allowance.

Now that we had a car and a caravan, our outfit was almost ready for the road.

But what would we do with it? Obviously, we couldn't take it to Cottesloe, but we couldn't leave it standing in the middle of the garage forecourt either.

Then it dawned on us that we couldn't take it anywhere

at all. We had no driver. Despite the fact he had driven in India, George had never held a driving license. He had never even taken a test.

When we told Matthew, he stared blankly at us, then doubled up with laughter.

It was a long time before he stopped chuckling. The idea of a family crossing the world, buying an outsize car and caravan and planning routes to tour the country, then suddenly remembering that none of them could drive, was the most hilarious thing he had ever heard.

After a while, even George saw the funny side.

Again, Matthew was our saviour. He contacted the driving test centre and got George pushed in when another driver cancelled their test a few days later. In the meantime, he arranged for one of his staff at the garage to help George prepare for his test.

George passed, and the relief was enormous.

We thanked Matthew again, but he only laughed. Apart from the fact we were friends of Sister Mary Emmanuel, he liked us, he said. He had never met anyone quite like us before. We took it as a compliment.

George was going to be our driver, and he insisted, in return, that I should be the one to be interviewed on the radio.

I was not at all comfortable about the idea, but the people at the Australian Broadcasting Commission were reassuring. They asked me to chat about my family, making it as lively and interesting as I could, then finish with a promise that I would keep listeners up to date with news of our travels and adventures.

When they played the recording back to me, I sounded like a timid ten-year-old, but the interviewer was happy and I was grateful it was over.

To my amazement, we were paid for the interview.

We went to see Sister Mary Emmanuel when we were ready to leave, and she was excited for us.

"As soon as you come back to Perth, come straight in and tell me all about it," she insisted. "I might have a surprise for you. I know some people at Government House. I might be able to get you an interview with the Governor."

She shrugged happily.

"He's old and not very bright these days. I don't think he would be any real help to you, but it would be a feather in your cap for the book, wouldn't it?"

~

At last, we were ready. All we had to do was pick up our luggage from Cottesloe and Winkie from quarantine.

We all hugged Violet, but there was no-one else about. She looked sad, and I felt sorry for her. None of it had been her fault.

Winkie was a trembling bundle of joy when he was reunited with us. He licked our hands and cowered close to us every time anyone else came near, until finally, he jumped up into my mother's arms and knocked her over. Fortunately, she laughed.

We passed the garage on our way out of Perth. We had already said our goodbyes, but Matthew signalled for us to stop.

He had a little parting present for us. It was the last thing we were expecting, and it made us all feel decidedly stupid. It was a toilet.

Grinning at our embarrassment, he presented us with a little tent, still wrapped in its packaging, with a sheet of instructions and a square kerosene tin. He had cut the top off the tin, thoughtfully rolled over the cut edges, then added a wire handle.

"You can pick up a seat somewhere if you need more

comfort," he said. "It's basic, I know, but it will do. Oh, and you'll need this shovel."

Once again, we thanked him. Looking back, we had a lot to thank him for.

Once outside the city, George drove slowly and carefully up into the foothills of the Darling Mountain Range.

He was a new driver, and it was asking a lot to expect him to handle, not just a huge car, but a huge car dragging a heavy caravan loaded with all our possessions.

He made no secret of being nervous and admitted he needed to get used to turning and backing. Ideally, he wanted to find a quiet spot where we could stay for a few days while he practiced and built up his confidence.

Since no-one had a better idea, I suggested Kalamunda. I remembered it fondly from my schooldays. It was a beautiful spot where birds of every kind fluttered among the trees and wild flowers bloomed undisturbed.

Each year, our botany excursions had visited the reserve and notebooks had been filled with flower sketches under Sister Mary Emmanuel's stern gaze. Then, when she called an end to work, we had stripped off our shoes and stockings and paddled in the cool water of the stream that ran down the hill-side.

The reserve was watched over by a caretaker and when we arrived, his weatherboard house looked exactly as I remembered it.

He came to greet us as we stopped and we told him our story. To my surprise, he had heard me on the radio and was delighted to welcome us. He suggested a sheltered spot where we could park and told us we could stay as long as we chose.

When we were settled, he came back with his wife. They

led a quiet life, he said, with no neighbours and few visitors. They would be thrilled if we would have a meal with them.

From the outside, his sprawling veranda-encircled house looked just the same as so many other houses we had passed, but inside, it was a wonderland. He laughed at our surprise to find books everywhere. The walls were lined with bookshelves from floor to ceiling. Piles of books encroached from the corners of the rooms, and even the kitchen floor and the stairs were piled with books on either side, so there was barely room to step between them.

"I love books," he explained unnecessarily. "Can't resist them. I've got books on every subject you can imagine. I've even got an up-to-date set of London County Council regulations for parks and open spaces used by the public."

His wife smiled.

"It's his bible," she said. "He knows it from cover to cover."

The caretaker nodded.

"I pride myself that I run this place as strictly as they run the Royal Parks in London."

~

We stayed at Kalamunda for three days until George told us he felt he was as ready as he ever would be.

It was a beautiful morning when we left. Sage-green slopes towered above us, and the valley below was a patchwork of farms and orchards.

We had spent hours discussing the trip and George believed it was the chance of a lifetime. Armed with Sister Mary Emmanuel's introductions, we should be able to produce some excellent work.

We had stocked up with notebooks, pens, film and chemicals for developing photos. We even had a special filter for the darkroom light.

In the late afternoon, we reached the little township of

Armadale and bought oil, petrol and more food. As we pulled out of the petrol station, the most amazing contraption blocked our path.

An ancient car, battered and sagging low to the road, was held together by pieces of wire and rope, but it was so crammed full of luggage, the wire and rope appeared in danger of giving way at any moment.

Behind it, dragged a dilapidated, two-wheeled trailer on which was mounted a startling assembly of machinery, all painted bright red, and crowned by a large chimney.

From somewhere among the luggage in the car, two men clambered out. The older of the two stopped and stared at our car and caravan, then strode across to us.

He announced that he and his partner were on their way back to Carnavon, where they were prospecting for gold. He asked about our outfit, and flattered by his interest, George offered to show him inside the caravan.

It must have impressed him, because, to our amazement, he fished in his pocket, brought out a bulging wallet, and asked if we would accept a thousand pounds, on the spot, for the outfit?

Misinterpreting our stunned silence, he smiled, showing a row of discoloured teeth and assured us that, in addition to the thousand pounds, he would throw in the car, trailer and tent, for our convenience, so we could continue our journey.

One thousand pounds was far more than we had paid for the outfit, but we refused his offer. I had a vision of my parents perched on top of the rusting trailer as we arrived outside the Roads' Board office in Harvey and announced ourselves as friends of Sister Mary Emmanuel.

~

As we drove further, orchards and small-holdings gave way to vast paddocks and finally uncleared bush spread out either side of us. We bumped and jolted off the road and found a spot to park for the night.

Father gathered wood, and George took out the kerosene tin and the tent. Tomorrow, in Harvey, we would buy a wooden seat, but in the meantime, erecting the privacy of the little tent was our priority.

George unwrapped the canvas, spread it out on the ground, then realised there were no poles. The instruction sheet explained no poles were needed for this convenient little tent. It was designed to be hung from the branches of a tree and the bottom edge pegged to the ground.

But there were no trees in sight. Only bush. We chose the biggest clump of bush we could find and took it in turns to hide behind it while the others stood around guarding our privacy.

There was not a soul in sight, not even a sign of habitation, but I had a vision of Matthew, bent double with laughter. After all, he had explained to us that in the timber areas of the South West, trees grew over two hundred feet high, usually without a branch for the first hundred feet. Perhaps we should have listened more carefully.

It was our first night in the bush and silence enveloped us, broken only by the crackling of the fire as we cooked sausages and boiled a billy of tea before retreating inside the caravan.

As we ate, we talked of England and the house and garden we had left behind. We weren't sad, but a little homesick perhaps.

Mother wiped her eyes, and we hastily changed the subject, reminding ourselves we had taken the first step on our long journey home.

It was also our first time sleeping in the caravan, and it was much more involved than we had imagined.

Once the beds were let down from the walls, there was

only room for one person to pass along the middle of the caravan.

A curtain screened off the front section as a changing room, but the space was only big enough for one person at a time. Mother went first. She always put curling pins in her hair at night and rubbed cream into her face. It was a slow ritual, and we were grateful when at last she was hoisted up into her bunk.

Father went next, but he was afraid of heights and was sure he would roll over in the night and end up on the floor. I took pity on him and swapped places so he could have the lower bunk. George was the last in and it became his duty to lock the door and turn off the light.

Habits are strange things. We had always bolted the door at home and it never occurred to us not to do so now. Not even in the remote, uninhabited loneliness of the bush.

CHAPTER 37

Harvey was our first main stop, and we approached the town in high spirits. Western Australia was divided, not into councils and boroughs, but into Roads Boards. Sister Mary Emmanuel had given us a letter of introduction to the secretary of the Harvey Roads Board, who, I guessed, was similar to an English mayor.

The secretary proved to be a friendly little man. Having read the letter of introduction, he welcomed us effusively, whisked us into an impressive boardroom and regaled us with iced beer.

He told us Harvey was an important town, and he was sure it would yield plenty of material for the books, articles, and picture stories we were preparing.

I shrank back into my seat at once. Whatever Sister Mary Emmanuel had written, it was clear she had given the impression we were established journalists.

I felt we had cheated, albeit unintentionally, and tried to put the record straight, but my protests were met with understanding smiles. The secretary had met modest celebrities before. He only hoped we would not carry our modesty so far as to refuse to sign the town's Visitors Book.

After all, we would be in good company. The Duke and Duchess of Gloucester had already signed, and so had Anthony Eden.

We signed. It is surprisingly difficult to persuade someone you are not important when they have convinced themselves you are.

We explained that, while we would have liked to have seen everything and met everyone, we only planned to stay for a few days. The thing that particularly interested us, we told him, was the great forest surrounding Harvey.

The secretary was disappointed we could not stay longer, but promised to arrange a visit to the biggest sawmill in the district. In the meantime, he would arrange somewhere for us to park our outfit. How did we feel about Myalup Beach? Or beside the Little Weir?

The beach sounded inviting. The secretary provided us with a guide, and we were soon on our way to the coast. The road deteriorated quickly, and it wasn't long before it was little more than a track winding its way between enormous jarrah and red gum trees.

After some miles, the forest dropped behind us, and ahead, beyond a ridge of sand hills topped by straggling growth, lay the sea.

Myalup Beach was fifty miles long and was certainly not a beach resort in the English sense. The vast expanse of sand stretched out, unbroken, into the distance. There was no sign of a human or any form of habitation. There was not even a bird.

George and I looked at our parents. Their blank, disappointed expressions said it all.

"I'm sorry," George smiled apologetically at our guide. "We've changed our minds. I think we would prefer the Little Weir, after all."

It was the right decision. The Little Weir was a beautiful spot where huge wattle trees covered with golden blossom grew close to the river's edge, their branches drooping down to touch the sparkling water.

Mother and Father were delighted with it, which was a relief to George and me as we planned to spend the next three days at the saw-mill. Every evening, we brought back food, cooked it over the campfire, and kept them entertained with an account of what we had been doing.

My notebook was filling up, and George had taken innumerable photos. We had been out in the forest watching huge logs being felled and had visited the sheds, where screaming saws reduced the giants of the forest to flat, uninteresting planks and soft red sawdust.

We were not journalists. George was a photographer, and I wrote stories for women's magazines, but we did our best and I was hopeful our articles would sell.

On our last morning, the weather changed. The sun disappeared, and rain came down in sheets, churning the ground to a sea of mud. By mid-day, the caravan began to leak. In our ignorance, it had not occurred to us to check that it was weatherproof.

There was nothing for it but to inspect the roof and try to effect repairs. We gathered all the waterproof clothing we could find and looked at George. He was the tallest of us and we hoped that, by standing the portable caravan steps on top of one of the upended drawers from the caravan, he might be able to locate the leak.

We were right. He climbed down, gloomy and dripping, explaining that a seam in the roof had come apart. It was not a big fault and could easily be sealed… if we had anything to seal it with.

After much thought, we found a tube of waterproof glue among George's photographic kit. Unfortunately, the glue would only work on a dry surface, and the caravan was running with water as though it was under a waterfall.

Armed with a big towel, the toilet tent, and the tube of

glue, George climbed up on the roof. Muttering beneath his breath, he dried the damaged spot, effect the repair, then stayed perched on the roof, the toilet tent draped over him, while he waited for it to dry.

The roof was mended, but George snuffled reproachfully all night.

~

Our next stop was Bunbury. We had a letter of introduction to the mayor, but by the time we arrived, it was too late to present it that day. We needed to find somewhere to spend the night and were relieved to see an area of rough ground on which was erected a notice announcing, 'Forest Park'.

There was a track leading in, but beyond that, it was too dark to see. George reconnoitred and returned to tell us the track led into a belt of trees under which we could park until morning.

It was cold and damp under the trees and smelt like a swamp. It was also alive with mosquitoes, but we didn't know that at the time because the tiny insects were horribly cunning.

There was no sign of them as we picked our way between the trees, and they kept well out of sight while we parked.

It was only when we were settled and nothing could have persuaded George to move again that they came out in their millions. By morning, we looked as though we had all succumbed to a horrible, disfiguring disease.

Fortunately, Forest Park was not nearly so forbidding by the bright light of day. We moved the caravan as far as possible from the mosquitoes, then George and I headed into town to buy stores and to present our letter of introduction.

Again, we were made welcome, but while he poured our iced beer, the mayor apologised. Unfortunately, he was busy that day, but as soon as he had an opportunity, he would take great pleasure in showing us his town.

For once, we felt we could relax. The next morning, the sun shone, and we decided to enjoy a lie-in.

We stretched and grunted, dangling our feet over the end of our bunks and bemoaned our innumerable mosquito bites. Then, at nine o'clock, we sat bolt upright as a loud hammering on the side of the caravan was followed by the mayor's voice enquiring whether anyone was at home.

There is something embarrassing about being caught in bed by an unexpected visitor, but in a caravan, it is ten times worse. The front door opens straight into the bedroom.

When we eventually opened the door, we found the mayor was accompanied by a small, white-haired man with a pleasant but business-like manner.

"Our local historian," the mayor explained. Then he pointed upwards. "What in God's name made you park under that? One high wind and you'd all have been pulped."

We looked up to see an enormous tree branch stretched out above our caravan. It was dead and already sagged ominously.

We felt even worse when the mayor and his companion rolled up their shirtsleeves and helped us manhandle the caravan out from under the tree.

Bunbury was a busy town with impressive docks, huge municipal buildings and even an embryonic art gallery, featuring some stunning paintings by Aboriginal artists. Yet the mayor flaunted none of these. Bunbury, it seemed, was only proud of its history. In fact, the social structure of the town appeared to be based solely on a person's descent from an early pioneer.

As George commented later, it was just as well we were not thinking of settling there. Unless we could produce a pioneer grandfather, we would never have been accepted.

Our next stop was Busselton, thirty-two miles away. According to a tourist guidebook, it was one of the most popular holiday resorts in the state.

As we approached, dark clouds masked the sky, and raindrops splashed against the windscreen. Puddles filled the hollows in the road, and as we entered town, great sheets of water sprayed up from either side of the car.

We knew we were visiting out of season, but the town was far from the popular holiday resort we had expected. There was an air of sleepy gloom about it that made me think of the Wild West.

On the journey from Perth we had seen billboards encouraging travellers to visit 'The Playground of the South West,' a camping resort south of Busselton. We decided to sample its attractions rather than stay in the town itself.

We were greeted by a grizzled caretaker who seemed surprised to see us. Following his instructions, George guided the car along a track towards the sea and parked in a deserted clearing.

The rain had stopped, so we walked back to the entrance where the caretaker was repairing a damaged gate.

Laying down his hammer, he grinned widely and held out a hand. We were his only customers. Later, during the season, there would be a rush of visitors, but, for the moment, every amenity was available for our comfort.

He showed us around proudly. In a tin shed, there was a bath, and outside there were three pipes sticking up out of the ground with a shower rose attached to the top of each. He explained that a piece of canvas would be rigged around each pipe during the holiday season so that visitors could enjoy a shower in private.

But, like a true showman, the caretaker saved the highlight of his tour for last.

Flinging open the door of a small, square building, he demanded our admiration. Before us was the latest in sanitation….. a septic tank.

"Now, there are no flies," he confided proudly. "Well, almost none..."

That night we went through our maps to check the next stage of our journey, which would take us out of the forests and into apple-growing country.

As we talked, the wind rose and the grumble of the surf a few yards away became an ominous roar.

At first, we ignored it, hoping the wind would die away, but as the caravan rocked, we felt as though it was in the sea rather than beside it. Solid and heavy though it was, it reeled drunkenly under every onslaught while the whipped-up spray from the surf slashed across the windows. As though to complete the effect, great tongues of lightning ripped across the sky and thunder boomed.

I would be lying if I said we weren't afraid. The ferocity of the storm made our caravan feel small and vulnerable. Mother was certain we would be swept out to sea, and for a fleeting moment we were tempted to hitch up the car and make a dash for a more sheltered spot, but hitching up the car and caravan was a major operation at any time, and even if we succeeded, where would we go?

We stayed. We sat in a tight-lipped row, leaning our weight against the windward side of the caravan, and hoped for the best. At three o'clock in the morning, the storm ended abruptly, as though someone had turned off a tap. No one was ever more grateful to crawl into bed than us.

The relief on the caretaker's face when he saw us the next morning was comical. For hundreds of miles in each direction, trees had been uprooted, roofs stripped from houses and telephone lines torn down. He had expected us to be washed away. Ours must indeed be a very sturdy caravan.

We agreed it had been 'a little rough' and went on our way, feeling proud of ourselves. Even Mother was smiling.

~

We drove north for about seventy miles and suddenly we were in apple country. Apple trees were everywhere and between them were rambling clumps of blackberry.

When settlers first arrived from England, a gentleman yearned for a pot of blackberry jam. He arranged for a root of blackberry to be sent all the way from England and nursed and protected it until it was safely acclimatised.

Over the years, the innocent little root flourished and spread. Now, its descendants are so rampant blackberry has been damned as a noxious weed, and a continual war is waged to stop valuable agricultural land being overrun.

When we reached Bridgetown, we bought our supplies, and Mother announced she wanted an apple. To our surprise, the shopkeeper shook his head. There were no apples.

We didn't understand. Apple trees were everywhere.

"Why can't we buy an apple?" George asked.

The shopkeeper frowned.

"Because I don't stock them."

"But why not?"

"Because…" His patience snapped. "Because everyone around here is sick of the sight of bloody apples. Understand?"

We understood.

We found a quiet spot for the night and headed for Manjimup the next morning. Soon we were in timber country again, rich with beautiful Karri trees.

Arriving in town, we located the newspaper office and presented our introduction. The editor, we were told, was away for a couple of days, but he had heard the radio broadcast about an English family touring the South West and he hoped Manjimup would be included in our schedule. There was so much to see, but of course, if time was pressing and we couldn't wait for a day or two, he would understand.

We assured him we were happy to wait. In the meantime, we would find a pleasant spot out of the town where we could camp.

CHAPTER 38

Mother was tired, but, to our relief, she wasn't angry or aggressive. In fact, she was unusually interested in what was going on around her and the fact we would soon be going home. All we had to do first was to drive across a continent.

We had plenty of time, so we decided we would rest for a few days and take it easy. George and I could sort out the notes we had taken and label the growing pile of films waiting to be developed.

We spent two happy, lazy days and had just unhitched the caravan from the car, ready to go into Manjimup for more supplies, when Mother realised Winkie was missing.

From the moment we collected him from the quarantine centre, we had been careful to keep an eye on him. Whenever we were busy, or there had been the slightest chance he might wander away unnoticed, we had tied him to the side of the caravan. Now the rope was there, and so was his collar, but it had snapped in two.

We called, we whistled, and we searched, but there was no sign of Winkie. As the hours passed, our fears grew, but we told each other he would turn up soon and went on searching.

George took the car and drove for miles in each direction. At the only house he passed, he asked for help, but no-one had seen a lost dog.

We were still searching when night fell. We knew we had to find Winkie because Mother would never agree to leave without him.

That night, we took it in turns to stand outside the caravan and listen. Looking back, it seems pointless, but we prayed one of us would hear a bark or a whine in the darkness.

We found him the next afternoon, stuck down a hole half a mile from our camp. It seemed he must have chased something, probably a rabbit, down the hole, then the ground had collapsed, leaving him trapped in a tangle of roots. One paw was bleeding, and so was his nose, where he had struggled to dig himself out.

Mother burst into a flood of tears at the sight of him, and it was impossible to see which of them was shaking the most. We had intended to return to Manjimup, but the anxiety of losing Winkie cast a gloom over us all.

I wrote a polite note to the editor saying we were sorry, but we had to return to Perth unexpectedly. We hoped we would be able to return soon and take up his kind offer.

Feeling like cheats, we slipped it into the letterbox at the newspaper offices and headed back.

When we reached Kalamunda, we popped in on the caretaker and his wife, and they greeted us like old friends.

They had been lucky, they said. While we had been gone, there had been rain. A few miles north, there had been a drought for over a year, the rivers had dried up and the cattle were dying in their paddocks, but at Kalamunda there had been so much rain we were welcome to have a day's use of the copper and the luxury of a hot bath.

We were grateful for their offer, but we had a favour to ask. Could they spare enough water for us to develop our films?

Much to our delight, they agreed.

We put the black curtains across the caravan windows and went to work. It wasn't easy in the cramped darkness, but there was a peacefulness about the caravan and a sense of achievement as row after row of developed films were hung up to dry and we could admire the results of our weeks of work.

"We've still got a long way to go," George said at last, "but if we keep on like this, we're going to have some really great material."

George and I had promised to go back to see Sister Mary Emmanuel, and now we did.

True to her word, she had arranged for us to see the Governor and had thought of other places we ought to visit.

The first was Boystown at Bindoon, a settlement for orphans. It would be a crime if we didn't go to New Norcia and we really ought not to miss Sister Kate's School. Of course, we would go to the goldfields. You couldn't visit Western Australia and not go to the goldfields.

I felt a deep sadness when it was time to leave. I could not have imagined, when I first arrived at the convent, what a huge influence Sister Mary Emmanuel would be in my life.

As we said goodbye, she kissed us both on the cheek, gave us her blessing and made us promise to write to her.

Before we could leave Perth, there were still problems to overcome, including the fact we would need a huge allowance of petrol if we were to travel across the arid wilderness of central Australia.

We decided the first thing to do was to keep our

appointment with the Governor. Perhaps if we made a good impression on him, he might put in a word for us at the Fuel Office.

I had expected Government House to be imposing. It was, after all, the centre of government for Western Australia, but the relaxed elegance of the building surprised me. Light and airy, it lacked the fussiness of so much Victorian architecture.

Huge windows looked out across splendid gardens, and wide staircases led from one level to another. A woman carrying a sheaf of files walked along a corridor and we asked her for directions.

The Governor's secretary was expecting us when we arrived. He was polite, but suspicious.

"Why do you want to see the Governor?"

For a moment that stumped us. We couldn't say, "Because Sister Mary Emmanuel thought it would help us sell our book."

As we hesitated, the secretary's expression darkened.

"You haven't come to make trouble, have you?" he demanded.

"No… of course, not… we, err…"

George was lost for words, so I cut across him.

"We've been gathering material for books to write when we get back to England. Everyone's been so helpful to us, we thought it would be a nice gesture if we could thank the Governor himself before we head east."

I must have sounded sufficiently innocent because the frown lifted.

"I'm sorry," the secretary said. "I don't want anybody hassling him, that's all."

He went on to explain the Governor's health was failing and he preferred not to worry him with day-to-day problems. If there was anything we needed, he would try to help us himself.

George mentioned our need for petrol and the secretary agreed that a letter from the Governor to the Fuel Office recommending we be granted whatever petrol we needed would help us on our way.

We waited while he dictated the letter and were invited to accompany him when he took it to be signed.

The Governor sat behind an enormous desk, doodling on a pad. He shook hands with us, then went back to doodling. I am sure he had no idea who we were or why his secretary wished us the best of luck.

In the corridor outside, the secretary hesitated. I guessed he was trying to decide whether he could trust us, after all, we had introduced ourselves as journalists.

"What are you going to write?" he asked.

I smiled reassuringly.

"I was thinking of something along the lines, We met the Governor and he was very pleasant. He wished us the best on our travels and we promised him a copy of our book when it is published. Would that be all right?"

"Honestly? That's all?"

We both nodded. "Honestly."

Suddenly, he was our friend.

"Thank you," he said. "Thank you very much. The governor is a good man, but he does have his bad days."

~

The letter from the Governor did the trick and the clerk at the Fuel Office was most co-operative. Petrol was still rationed, he reminded us, but obviously we were a special case.

Even in normal times, few people took the overland route across Australia, and with petrol so scarce, hardly anyone was attempting it now.

We couldn't carry enough fuel to cover us for the whole

distance, so we needed to collect supplies at intervals throughout the journey.

Drums of petrol would be waiting for us at each depot until we reached Norseman. That would be our last pickup point and from there we would have to carry enough to take us the 1,726 miles across the Nullarbor.

The clerk was friendly and eager to help, but he looked at us doubtfully. When he said goodbye, he shook George's hand.

"Be careful, won't you? It's a long way. You do know that 1,726 miles is farther than it is from London to Moscow?"

To be honest, it had not dawned on me until that moment quite what we were undertaking.

The clerk went on, impressing upon us how important our supply of water would be when crossing the desert.

It was, he told us, dry, merciless country. There had been many tragedies over the years involving people dying of thirst under the blazing sun.

There were a few water catchment points along the road, round corrugated iron tanks with a couple of iron sheets to collect the run-off, but they were hundreds of miles apart, and with no rainfall at all for most of the year, we could not rely on them.

Disturbed by his words, we did our best to take precautions. Matthew made us a second water tank, as big as we could accommodate, and fixed it under the caravan.

He also gathered a collection of spare parts he felt we might need. Seeing George's blank expression at the sight of them, he took him aside for a quick course in emergency repairs.

There was one last thing with which we needed help. When we set out, we would be carrying our first issue of petrol, which came in a row of forty-four-gallon drums.

With four of us and Winkie, there was no room for the drums in the car. They would have to be stored in the caravan while we were on the road, then stood outside for the night to make enough room to put down the bunks.

We could chain the drums to the caravan to stop them being stolen during the night, but we couldn't drive hundreds of miles over rough country with forty-four-gallon drums of petrol rolling loose in the caravan.

Matthew performed his last good deed for us. He produced a coil of rope, tied all the drums together, then bored holes in the base of the caravan so they could be secured to the floor.

He was confident the drums would travel safely, but we would have to manhandle them in and out of the caravan every night and morning.

There were times, I admit, when I wondered if we really were crazy. I was sure there must have been an easier way to get back to England, but we were committed now and there was no turning back.

Before we left, we tried to tell Matthew how grateful we were, but he grinned and brushed our thanks aside.

"Just drop me a line sometime," he said. "Maybe one day I'll come over to England and see you."

CHAPTER 39

We were ready. Everything was packed, strapped down, and this time we would not be coming back.

It sounds ridiculous, but after all the preparation, I felt that somebody, anybody, ought to notice our departure, but there was no-one.

We had said our farewells to Matthew the previous day, and he was away working on the other side of Perth when George revved up the Buick's engine and we rolled out onto the road.

Above us, the sky was blue from horizon to horizon, and it was not long before we left the city behind and moved into the bush.

We passed a sign that pointed to Mundaring Weir. From there, we had been told, a pipeline set off on its three hundred and sixty mile journey inland to bring water to the goldfields. Without it, towns like Kalgoorlie could not exist.

We headed north towards Bindoon and I noticed the sun was already high in the sky. It had taken longer than expected to manhandle the petrol drums into the caravan and secure them to the floor. Perhaps we should have had a practice run, but it didn't really matter. We had no deadlines to meet.

As the miles passed, the land became drier and more barren. There was no grass, only a scatter of sprawling bushes now and then, and in a dust-filled hollow that might once have been a river bed, a dead cow lay in a crumpled heap.

Hours later, George swung the car onto a sideroad and after a few miles we spotted a rough piece of wood propped against an outcrop of rock. On it was scrawled BOYSTOWN.

We had been told Boystown was a settlement built by immigrant boys, mostly orphans, under the supervision of monks. We knew nothing more and were astounded when we topped a ridge by the sight that lay before us. The stone and brick buildings would have been a pride to any city.

A black-clad figure hurried towards us as our outfit pulled up. Sister Mary Emmanuelle had phoned ahead, and they were expecting us. We had driven all the way from Perth, hadn't we? Perhaps we would like to have a meal with the boys?

There were about fifty of them, ranging from chubby toddlers to lanky teenagers, all brown as berries from the sun. They spoke only in whispers, but their gaze never left us, and when it was announced we were visitors from England, a boisterous cheer went up.

"Tomorrow," they were told, "we will show our visitors around Boystown, and you will be able to show them all the things we are doing here."

We parked our outfit and a team of older boys arrived to help us unload the petrol drums from the caravan. We promised them we would be up early the next morning to make sure we saw everything.

The following day, the boys waited for us, eager to show

us around, but even more eager to question us about England.

One of the monks had been appointed as our guide and he explained that all general chores like window-cleaning, washing dishes, etc, were shared on a rota system.

Each age group had their own responsibilities. The youngest grew vegetables and fruit and helped in the kitchen as well as looking after the chickens. As they grew older, they graduated to looking after the cows, producing milk, making butter and cheese, and caring for the beehives.

They also learned how to make their own rope and nails, as well as repairing fences and the basics of electricity.

It was the oldest boys who actually constructed the buildings. Not only did they lay the bricks, they had to make the bricks by hand, and bake them first. Some were also taught to carve stone, cut glass to size and glaze the windows.

Two young apprentices hard at work.

Once the boys became adults, most of them left to start their own lives, except a few who stayed on as teachers.

We had never seen anything like Boystown. It was part of an ambitious scheme devised by the Government and we were told there were similar settlements scattered across Australia. Some accepted girls, but most only took young boys.

Our guide explained the rationale behind the scheme.

He was sure we understood that Australia was a vast

country and needed to be populated, but finding suitable immigrants was difficult. Some years before, the government had decided the country needed an army of young people who would grow up to see Australia as their home. They had contacted other countries and actively sought out orphans, unwanted children, youngsters of any age as long as they were healthy and white.

The boys in front of us were the result of that campaign. Children who had been sent away from their homeland, and any surviving relatives, so they could help establish a country on the far side of the world.

I thought about the three small children, two uncles I and Aunt Annie, Grandmother had sent on a similar scheme in the belief that when they were grown up and earning, they would help her achieve her dream of coming to live in Australia.

Was this the life that awaited them?

I never knew my uncles, but I thought of Annie and her loveless marriage, and as I looked around the young faces in front of me, I felt a profound sadness.

We travelled on to New Norcia, knowing only that the monastery we were to visit was founded long ago by a band of Spanish missionaries and had been funded by Queen Isabella of Spain herself.

We hoped there would be a shop where we could buy bread and a few supplies, but we were disappointed. There was no shop, no garage, no pub, nothing but a tiny church nestling beside a huge monastery, topped by a large cross, and a few rambling sheds.

Monseigneur himself came out to greet us. He, too, had received a phone call from Sister Mary Emmanuel, and we were very welcome.

But first he had to apologise. He had not realised there would be females in our party. The strict rules of the order did not allow women to set foot inside the monastery itself, which, he admitted, was a pity because the monastery library contained many interesting books and manuscripts.

Naturally, the men were welcome to take a tour of the monastery while Mother and I enjoyed some refreshments. I would have loved to have seen the library, but I nodded politely and watched as Father and George walked away.

Freshly baked cakes and wine made with grapes from the monastery's own vineyards soon arrived, and despite my disappointment at missing the library, it was undeniably enjoyable to sit in the shade and watch sweating novices unload the petrol drums from the caravan.

Later that afternoon, Monseigneur introduced us to Brother Francis, a portly monk with a broad smile and ancient sandals that were tied to his feet with string.

Brother Francis, would look after us, we were told. He would show us around the church, then, as some of our party could not enter the monastery itself, he would see that an evening meal was served to us in our caravan.

We thanked Monseigneur for his kindness, and once he left us, I asked Brother Francis if he could explain something that had intrigued me since we arrived.

The monastery church was quite small, but it was encircled by a row of large white stones about two metres from the walls.

Brother Francis smiled as he explained. The white stones represented the outline of the beautiful cathedral that would one day replace the church. They had been put there many decades ago when the detailed architectural plans in the monastery library had first been drawn up, but time had passed. The cathedral was still just a dream, and the white stones sank slowly into the dust.

The church itself was bright and unadorned.

"It was only meant to be temporary," Brother Francis said as we stepped inside. "A place to gather and pray until the cathedral was built. But there was never any money. And, anyway, no-one ever comes here." He sighed. "I think they might if they knew what we could show them."

Mother listened intently, and sensing her interest, he directed his remarks to her. I was grateful. I had been afraid New Norcia might bore her, but she was fascinated.

She stared as Brother Francis opened drawers behind the altar and pulled out the most exquisite pieces of embroidery.

"These were brought over from Spain by the first missionaries. There is everything needed to furnish the cathedral when it is finally built."

He opened a cupboard door, and to my amazement, it was crammed with gold and silver dishes and a beautiful gold wine chalice.

"But these things must be priceless," George gasped.

Brother Francis nodded and ferreted through another drawer. "Somewhere in here, there's an altar cloth embroidered by Queen Isabella herself. The settlement here was her idea. She raised the money to fund it and her ladies worked on the cloths and draperies that were needed."

He broke off as a novice put his head round the church door. There was a whispered conversation, then Brother Francis came back to us.

"I'm sorry," he said. "I am needed."

George had laid out a collection of gold and silver pieces ready to be photographed. We began gathering them up, but Brother Francis waved at us.

"Don't stop. You're welcome to photograph anything you like. Perhaps you could put everything back in the cupboards when you're finished."

I gazed at him in disbelief, but he only smiled.

"And please be sure to shut the church door after you."

The next morning, Brother Francis tapped on our caravan door. The sun had risen and there was a sense of excitement in the air as black-clad figures bustled between the monastery and the church.

"Come on," he cried. "We've got something special for you today."

New Norcia was going to pray for rain. There would be a procession led by Monseigneur himself and behind him, all the monks would walk in order of their importance. The novices would follow at the back.

Once the parade had circled the church, it would pause at the door for silent prayers, then it would circle the church again, this time outside the white stones, before everyone filed inside.

George had his camera ready and strode around, selecting the best positions from which to take his pictures.

He chose a spot where the parade was assembling, and one where it would circle the church, but he wanted another, perhaps at the church door as the monks entered for prayer.

It was Brother Francis who made the suggestion. A ladder inside the church led up to the bell tower. From such a high vantage point, George would be able to get the perfect shot.

George agreed. He would have to move swiftly from one location to the next, but it would be worth it.

Father, Mother, and I stood back as the procession assembled. George took his first photo and darted away to his next vantage point. I heard the shutter click as the parade circled the church and saw George disappear inside. Looking up, I saw him peer down from the little tower, camera to his eye, as Monseigneur reached the church door and bowed his head.

It was then the bell rang out, a loud clanging peel that

reverberated through the wooden church and George disappeared from sight.

Brother Francis helped him down the ladder and practically carried him out of the church. As I reached him, George's face was scarlet, his eyes bulging.

"Are you alright?" I cried, but he didn't seem able to hear me.

We helped George to the caravan while Brother Francis apologised profusely. He had forgotten to warn the bell-ringer of George's presence.

I said I hoped the commotion hadn't marred the seriousness of the occasion, but Brother Francis only shook his head and stared out of the window at the cloudless blue sky.

"I don't think it was the right day to pray for rain, anyway," he said resignedly. "Perhaps we'll try again next week. Or the week after."

We stayed on for an extra day to allow George to recover from his headache and to make sure his hearing was back to normal. He was our only driver, after all. He had made a few attempts to teach me to drive in case of an emergency, but it was obvious he didn't have any confidence in my ability. I can't say I blamed him. The Buick was so big, I could barely see over the bonnet.

Our next destination was Sister Kate's School. Sister Mary Emmanuelle had told us little about it, except that it would be our first contact with Aboriginal children.

The school was a sprawling, weatherboard building with large windows and wide verandas. A row of pegs ran around the entire outside of the building, each peg covered by a round cotton hat, and below each hat stood a pair of sandals.

The woman who greeted us introduced herself as Matron

and explained that she had taken over running the school when Sister Kate retired due to ill-health.

She led us into a little room, and once we had sat down, she took a breath.

"I don't know how much Sister Mary Emmanuelle told you about us," she said, "but I think I should explain how our children come to us. It is the law in this state that any children born to Aboriginal mothers who are deemed to have pale skin are not allowed to stay with their families."

She hesitated, waiting for our reaction, but we were too surprised to say anything.

"It's been that way for generations," she went on. "If there is any suspicion a child has white blood, law officers are sent out to take it away from its parents. Most come to us when they are still very small, sometimes only babies, but we do occasionally have much older children."

I couldn't believe what I was hearing.

"Do they still see their families?" I asked.

"No."

Beside me, Mother flinched. For all her problems, she valued family above everything. I knew how much she had struggled when George was evacuated.

"That's terrible…" I said without thinking.

Matron nodded.

"Please remember, we didn't make the laws. In the past, no-one seemed to care much what happened to the children after they had been removed. That is why Sister Kate opened this school over forty years ago. She was a remarkable woman, and she devoted her life to these children. I merely carry on her work."

She stood up abruptly.

"Now I expect you would like to look around."

She took us upstairs to see the dormitories, one for boys and one for girls. The sheets were fresh, but the rooms were small and the beds were pushed closely together. At the end of the girl's dormitory, there were four cots with sleeping babies.

Next, she took us to the dining room, and then to the classroom where children stood up politely from their desks when we entered.

Young pupils at Sister Kate's School.

The children were of every age, from the tiniest right up to teenagers, and all their feet were bare.

Matron introduced us, and every eye turned in our direction. I tried to smile, but I wanted to cry.

George asked them their names and what lessons they liked best. The younger ones hung their heads shyly, but the older ones were eager to talk to us.

"They rarely see anyone new," Matron explained when we returned to her office. "Most of them are very intelligent."

"How long do they stay here?"

"Until they are old enough to work. We teach them and care for them and give them as good an education as we can.

Many of them are excellent pupils. They learn quickly and have sharp minds, but by the time they are teenagers, it is much harder."

"What do you mean?" I asked.

"They lack motivation," Matron said simply. "They see there is nothing ahead for them. What is the point of studying for exams when they know there is no chance of going to university or having a career?"

"So, what happens to them?"

"When they are old enough, we try to find them work."

"What kind of work?" George asked.

"Mostly menial." Matron admitted. "But many of them are capable of a lot more."

George took a great many photographs, and we promised to send the children copies as soon as we could.

I felt dejected as we left Sister Kate's School, and the glaring mist of distance swallowed up the building and the children waving us off. I wracked my brain for something I could do to help, but I could think of nothing, save to keep our promise and send the children their photographs.

CHAPTER 40

Then we were on our own.

The easy acceptance that sprang from Sister Mary Emmanuelle's phone calls was over, and we had to fend for ourselves.

We headed towards Southern Cross. It was easy to pinpoint our destination on the map, but finding a road that led across the two hundred miles of open country appeared impossible. In the end, we decided our best hope was to head east into the wheat belt, then try to pick up a road leading north to Southern Cross. Our supplies were running low, and we hoped to pass a siding with a store where we could replenish our stock.

The arid, semi-desert landscape dropped behind us and we passed a few wheat paddocks stretching away to the horizon interspersed with broad swathes of golden sand, looking for all the world like huge beaches without a sea. Swarms of parrots and pink and white galahs flew up as we passed.

Our progress slowed as the road surface became rough and uneven. We had already emptied some of the petrol drums, but our outfit was heavy and George was anxious to avoid any problems.

He pulled off the road earlier than usual and Mother began preparing a meal, but to make a campfire, we needed wood. Looking around, we realised there was nothing more substantial than a few leathery grasses.

George and I scoured the area, but it was a long time before we gathered enough twiggy bushes to get a fire going.

Our next task was to haul out the petrol drums and clear the caravan ready to put the table up. We had moved three and were preparing to shift the fourth when Mother let out a bloodcurdling scream.

The biggest spider I had ever seen was crawling across the floor. It was the size of a dinner plate, like an enormous, hairy crab. No-one hesitated. We scrambled out of the door.

To be honest, for a few minutes we were speechless. Then Father peeped inside the caravan. The spider was still there, motionless now, as though waiting for us to make the next move.

"Be careful!" Mother called. She was still retreating, and so, I must confess, was I. "It may be poisonous. Some Australian spiders are. I read it in a book."

There was a shovel in the boot of the car, and Mother squealed as she saw Father return to the caravan with it.

"No! You mustn't kill it. It's unlucky."

Father didn't listen. Stepping hesitantly into the caravan, he held the shovel ready to attack. A moment later, he stumbled out, the giant spider clinging to the shovel blade, two legs waving indignantly in the air. He flung it as far as away as he could, then sat down in the dust, complaining he didn't feel well.

None of us did. It was ridiculous, and we knew it. We were in the Australian bush and we would have to get used to spiders.

But it was easier said than done. It didn't help that

Mother insisted every inch of the caravan must be searched. She was convinced spiders came in pairs and she wouldn't hear of going to bed until we found its mate.

Father searched the caravan from end to end, but it was well after midnight before Mother gave in and let us pull down the bunk beds.

From then on, every morning and evening, the car and caravan had to be thoroughly searched for spiders.

A day later we reached Merriden, and it was wonderful to see a real little town with a store, a baker and a garage. There was even a school, but the most heartening thing was the sight of the great silver pipeline that ran past on its way from the coast up to the goldfields.

The thought of running out of water had been at the back of our minds ever since we left Perth. At Boystown, New Norcia and even Sister Kate's School, there had been big corrugated iron tanks that stored the rainwater from the roofs of the buildings.

Our hosts had been generous in allowing us to top up our tanks, but once we were out on the open road with no idea when we would next find a water supply, we had been careful about every drop we used.

Now we had reached the pipeline, and once we had restocked our cupboards at the store, we had no hesitation in asking if we could top up our water tanks.

Our next stop was Southern Cross, and as we set out, we felt confident. We had plenty of stores, enough water for the immediate future, and we would soon pick up our next supply of petrol. Even the lizards that waddled across the road didn't dampen Mother's spirits, although some of them were nearly a metre long.

The day became hotter, and the car began to misbehave,

spitting and spluttering. George pulled off the road to give the engine a chance to cool down, when suddenly a black cloud gathered above us, blocking the sun.

Next minute we were engulfed by a swarm of grasshoppers.

"For God's sake, shut the windows!" George yelled.

We did, and in the sweltering heat of the car, we watched the invaders swoop down on us. Massed insects covered the car and caravan, their yellow bellies pushing against the glass, blocking the light from windows, crawling into every crack and crevice.

George turned on the windscreen wipers, but the blades smeared the insects to a paste. Through the smears, we could see the road ahead was black with grasshoppers and George had only one thought. Escape.

He revved the engine, and we skated on the crawling mass for almost a mile before the road ahead was clear and we dared to open the windows. The last survivors flew off, but some had found their way under the bonnet to the engine and the smell of burning bodies was sickening.

~

I had read a lot about Southern Cross, the first of the Australian gold towns. Before Coolgardie or Kalgoorlie became known, people across the world had heard of Southern Cross. It was the place where a man could become a millionaire overnight.

Or it had been once, during the height of the Australian goldrush. Now, it was a well-preserved shadow of the past, with its wide verandas and wooden balconies.

Once its rich seams of gold had been mined, its magnetism faded. There was still gold to be found, but only tiny scraps and flakes, although some prospectors still clung stubbornly to their dreams.

At the Shell garage, they were expecting us. They unloaded our empty petrol drums, replaced them with full ones, topped up our water tanks and wished us a safe journey.

~

Our next destination was Coolgardie, eighty miles away across barren, waterless scrub. From a distance, the land appeared to be covered by an unbroken mantle of dark green vegetation, but at close quarters, there was nothing but parched earth and a scattering of dwarf eucalyptus.

We had driven about twenty miles when we topped a rise and found ourselves staring at a vast salt lake.

There was something awe-inspiring, almost frightening, about the scene. Glaring, white salt stretched away into the distance, like a huge shroud, broken only by the occasional remains of dead trees, frozen in time, like mourners at the last rite of some gigantic primeval soul.

I don't know what the others thought, but I saw George shudder. Ahead of us, the dark strip of road beckoned us on and he put his foot down, not stopping until we reached the other side.

It was a relief to leave the dazzling whiteness of the salt lake, but after a few miles, the car began to splutter and finally stopped altogether.

George opened the bonnet. It was the carburettor, he announced. If Father would help him, he was sure he could fix it.

Mother and I crowded close to watch, impressed by George's confidence. In fact, we were so impressed it took a few minutes before I realised there were not four, but five of us around the car.

A large emu had appeared beside us and was staring into the engine with interest.

When it realised it had been seen, it took a couple of steps backwards, then calmly circled the car, pausing for a moment on the other side to stare back at us. Then, wings outstretched, it scuttled away.

Suddenly, Father came to life. "Oi! It's nicked my watch!"

Father was a meticulous man. Whenever he had to do anything 'dirty', he always took off his watch. This time he had left it on the mudguard of the Buick.

George chased after the emu, but it was too late. It had disappeared with its prize.

~

Coolgardie was a dusty, half-deserted oasis in the middle of the bush. Its wide streets had once been lined with busy shops and its pavements thronged with prospectors, but it was eclipsed when massive seams of gold were discovered at Kalgoorlie and its own reserves were exhausted.

We intended to carry on to Kalgoorlie to visit the gold mines, but Mother had been following our route on the map in the car and decided we could save time by turning south.

We remind her we were gathering material for a book and needed to visit the goldfields, but she was only interested in reaching the East as soon as possible. She wanted to escape from the heat and dust. She had no patience with diversions.

We had come this far and we couldn't give in. We needed to visit Kalgoorlie.

We spent hours reasoning with her, but she was beyond listening, beyond understanding what we were trying to explain. In the middle of the bush, there was no river to throw herself in, but she ranted and raved while we took it in turns, to watch her.

Gradually, the anger passed. She cried for a day and a night, then fell into a deep sleep. George carried her out and settled her, still sleeping, in the car and we headed for Kalgoorlie.

As we neared our destination, the red earth was scarred with gaping holes and mounds of white quartz. There were thousands of them, where the land had been churned up in the feverish search for gold, right to the outskirts of the city itself.

We passed a few iron shacks, then clusters of weatherboard houses, until the road widened into a broad avenue that led into Hannan Street, the main thoroughfare of the city.

At the edge of the pavement, outside the Town Hall, was a statue. It was a life-sized figure of a grizzled prospector, perfect even to his battered hat. Seated on a boulder, he leaned forward, holding in his hands a tilted water bag from which gushed a stream of water to quench the thirst of any passer-by.

This was a statue of Paddy Hannan, the man who had first stumbled across the legendary wealth of Kalgoorlie. To him, and thousands like him, his water bag had been even more precious than the incredible bonanza he discovered.

In the unforgiving vastness of the outback, water without gold meant life, but gold without water meant death. Paddy Hannan had been lucky, which was why he was famous. He not only found gold, but his water supply lasted long enough to make it back to town. No one knows how many others were unlucky.

Kalgoorlie was bustling when we arrived. The shops were bright and well-stocked and cars were parked along both sides of the road. We drove the length of Hannan Street without finding a parking space big enough to take our outfit.

George pulled into a layby, and a frowning policeman appeared beside us.

George nudged me, so I climbed out of the car and smiled. We were English journalists from Fleet Street, I explained. While we were in Perth, the Governor had suggested we visit Kalgoorlie before heading overland to the East. Perhaps he could help us.

His frown vanished before I finished speaking and was replaced by a broad smile. Of course, he would help us, but if we wanted to know about gold, we should go to the Chamber of Mines. It was no distance. He would show us the way himself.

The Chamber of Mines building was large and impressive. A clerk came forward as we entered and the policeman pounced on him. There was a whispered conversation, surprised glances in our direction, then the policeman shook our hands, wished us luck, and left.

We followed the clerk up a wide staircase and waited while he tapped on an office door. A middle-aged man looked up from his work as the clerk spoke to him. Then he rose and held out his hand in welcome.

He introduced himself as Stephen Burrows and told us he would be delighted to help us in any way he could.

It was as simple as that.

There had been no letter of introduction, no pre-arranged telephone call, but we had found a new friend.

When we explained that our first priority was to find a place to park our car and caravan, Stephen picked up his phone.

We waited while he rang number after number, but his smile faded after each one. I began to wonder if we would have to spend the night in the bush surrounded by holes and mounds when Stephen had a brainwave. He made another phone call and told us everything was settled. We could camp on the racecourse.

A racecourse? I had a momentary vision of being surrounded by galloping horses and cheering crowds, but Stephen quickly reassured us. We would have the place to ourselves, as the site was no longer used for racing. What was more, Stephen lived nearby, and he intended to escort us safely to our destination.

He left us at the gate of the racecourse. We could camp wherever we chose, he assured us, and we would soon find our way round. Tomorrow, he would make arrangements for us to be shown over one of the larger mines and would put us in touch with some of the remaining prospectors.

As he left, Stephen locked the gates behind him and the city, with its lights and people, was lost to us. We were left in a silent world of shadows where small buildings crouched beside twisting paths, and the silhouettes of deserted stands loomed against the sky.

"I don't like it," Mother wailed, and as though following her lead, Winkie growled.

CHAPTER 41

In the morning, everything looked different.

It could not have been long since the racecourse was in use, because, although the grounds were overgrown, the lawns were green and vibrant. Hedges of purple bougainvillea surrounded us and there was a peaceful sense of being cut off from the dust and heat of the world outside.

It was not until we had enjoyed a lazy breakfast under the shade of a wattle tree that George noticed he had run over a stone kerb in the darkness and badly dented the car's exhaust pipe.

Our parents seemed content, so George and I set off in search of a garage. Luckily, we found one close by and a mechanic in grimy overalls assured us he could do the repair while we waited. He was called Joe, and he chatted as he worked. Needless to say, the subject was gold.

"Oh, yes, I've got my own hole. Most everyone has one." he said. "My brother and I get out there most weekends and work it. Sometimes the wife comes, too. Then we take a picnic, make a day of it."

"Have you ever had any luck?" George asked.

"Not really. I've found a couple of little nuggets, but nothing to get excited about. It's just a hobby, really. We all do it."

He finished the repair and crawled out from under the car.

"I'll bet there's something you don't know. This is the one place in the world where the streets really are paved with gold."

Grinning at my doubtful expression, he went on.

"A lot of the roads around here were made with the slag from the first mines. In those days, they could only extract a percentage of the gold, but now, with modern methods, they can get practically everything out. Take the road outside, for instance, they reckon, if it was dug up and put through again, they'd get around twenty thousand pounds worth from it."

Relieved the repair had been done so quickly, we returned to the caravan and found Father tying a length of rope between two trees.

"Mother wants to air our clothes," he explained. "She's worried about moths."

We decided to leave them to it. George and I had an appointment at one of the largest mines in the area, so after a quick cup of tea, we set off.

The freshness of morning had given way to shimmering heat by the time we left the racecourse. On our right lay the city, on our left rose a shallow ridge, known as the Mile. It was bare of vegetation and broken at intervals by the towering poppet heads of mines and clusters of dusty buildings protected by high wire fences.

At first, there was little sound, only a pulsing vibration that hinted at some distant activity, but gradually the sound increased until the air was filled with a clattering roar as we approached the State Crushing Battery.

It was a tall, corrugated iron structure, coated in white dust and looking, for all the world, like a tumbledown flour mill. This was the mecca of the independent miners. Here they brought their hard-won 'dirt' and watched eagerly as it was crushed and processed.

We drove on until we came to the Perseverance Mine. We peered through the high fence at the sprawl of buildings, but they gave no clue to the wealth they housed. If we were to see gold, we would have to go inside.

After presenting ourselves at the gate, we waited to be cleared, before being taken to the manager's office.

We had been warned at the Chamber of Mines we would not be able to go underground, and I had tried to look disappointed at the news. All we really wanted was some good photos of gold.

The manager was friendly as he took us on a tour of the stone crushers that pounded the ore, reducing it to dust. We passed massive electro-magnets, huge drums of cyanide solution used to remove gold dust from the ore, and mercury tables that looked, to our ignorant eyes, like old-fashioned washing boards.

Everywhere we went, the machinery made an appalling din, and it was barely possible to understand what the manager was telling us. It was only when we heard the words 'the Gold Room' that our ears pricked up.

We had come all this way to see gold, and now, at last, we would be able to take our photos.

But our guide shook his head. There was a strict company rule that visitors were never allowed in the Gold Room.

Our feet ached, our heads throbbed, and our throats were raw from the fumes. I had scribbled down pages of notes and I was sure I could write an excellent article, but it would be useless without photos.

We pleaded. We pointed out that we were not casual sightseers. We were journalists, attempting to capture the spirit of Australia. We didn't actually say the Governor would be disappointed, but we certainly implied it.

In the end, the manager agreed to make some enquiries. A long time later, he came back with two burly guards. He told us he had spoken to the directors of the mining company and they had agreed that under the circumstances, he could show us inside the Gold Room.

I tried to control my excitement, but I couldn't help grinning.

The manager unlocked the door, signalled to the guards to stay outside, then locked the door behind us. The Gold Room was a single, cell-like space and two elderly men looked up in surprise at the sight of us.

The manager spoke to them, then turned back to us. As we watched, a table was cleared, a safe in the wall opened, and with considerable effort, gold bars were carried out and piled in a heap.

Here, at last, was real gold.

"There you are," the manager said proudly. "Will that do?"

Our parents were waiting for us back at the racecourse. It had been a beautiful day, but as evening approached, the air became sultry and lightning flicked across the sky.

We were halfway through our evening meal when a sudden wind blew up, bringing with it a choking dust. Black clouds massed overhead, and the lightning became vivid and frequent. George drove the car to the windward side of the caravan and jammed an empty petrol drum under each corner.

The wind grew wilder, but there was no rain, and dust crept in through every crevice. We packed our food away and closed the cupboards and drawers as tightly as we could. Then we could do nothing but sit and wait, as the caravan rocked, and the wind howled around us.

It was hours before the storm eased and we crawled into our dust-covered beds.

Next morning the dust storm had passed. All was still, and the sun beat down from a flawless sky.

But it took hours to clean up. Mother insisted we carried everything moveable out of the caravan and swept it from end to end. George shook the bedding, and I wiped dust from ledges and sills, but while we were busy, Father slipped away.

It was only when the outfit was ready to leave that he appeared with a small branch in his hand.

When Mother asked what he had been doing, he looked apologetic.

"It was something Matthew said," he explained. "Nullarbor means 'no trees'. Once we get to the desert, there will be nothing for poor little Winkie when he needs to go. I thought if we carried a little tree with us, I could stand it in the ground for him. I thought it would keep him happy."

~

Once we were packed and ready to leave, we headed into Kalgoorlie. We stocked up on provisions, then took it in turns to drink from Paddy Hannan's water bag. We had been told it would bring us luck.

George had been studying our maps and saw that halfway across the Nullarbor Plain was a place called Eucla.

It had once been a relay station for the telegraph line, which had long been abandoned, and now appeared on the map as Hotel Eucla.

What a hotel was doing in the middle of the desert, we

could not imagine, but if it was there, we wanted to take advantage of it for a meal and perhaps a bath.

We tried to phone, but although the man at the Post Office assured us there was a direct line, Hotel Eucla did not answer. No doubt the storm the night before had brought down the lines. It might be days, or possibly weeks, before the line was repaired.

We only had one more call to make before we left. Joe, the mechanic, had invited us to see his hole.

We had been given exact directions, and we looked carefully for our first landmark, an extra-large pot-hole in the middle of the road, with the burned stump of a fallen tree a few yards further on. Sure enough, there were faint wheel marks on our right leading away into the bush.

It could hardly have been called a road. It was merely a track that had been forced through the scrub, avoiding the bigger sprawls of bushes and the occasional outcrops of rock.

After about a mile, the track ended abruptly in front of a patchwork shanty of corrugated iron and hessian bags. On the ground in front of it was an amazing collection of old tins, picks, shovels and empty boxes while to one side was a fireplace built of piled stones with the billy still dangling over the dead embers.

We hardly had time to climb out of the car when Joe and his brother, Charlie, came hurrying out of the bush. They were obviously surprised at the sight of my parents and Winkie, but their manners were perfect. They both took off their hats, held out their dirt-grimed hands and said how pleased they were to see us.

Joe told Charlie to brew some tea while he showed us round the mine. Leaving his brother on his hands and knees before the fireplace, Joe led us across the clearing to a gaping hole which looked for all the world like an ancient well. A primitive windlass of bush timber was rigged over the top with a battered petrol drum as a bucket. Mounds of red earth and broken white quartz surrounded it.

"Well, there she is." Joe stood aside to give us a clear view. "The best hole we've worked in years."

Peering down into the hole with its rickety wooden ladder, George asked why they had chosen this particular spot.

Joe scratched his head.

"Dunno, really. You have to get a nose for it. It's kind of an instinct."

Charley's voice shrilled across to us. "Billy's boiling. Come and get it."

Joe brought a couple of rickety chairs from the shanty and offered them to Mother and me. The others sat on empty boxes and one, covered with newspaper, served as a table.

Arranged on top were a plate of biscuits, a tin of condensed milk, a tin of sugar with a teaspoon stuck in the top, and three assorted cups supplemented by three cleaned-out baked bean tins.

It was our first taste of outback hospitality. The tea was thick and black and spiced with the smell of eucalyptus smoke. No doubt the billy itself added to the flavour, for it had been tanned to a rich maturity by innumerable brews.

Joe and Charlie beamed at us and insisted on a second cup all around. Inevitably, the talk veered to the next most precious thing after gold. Water.

Joe and Charlie's grandfather had been a prospector during the gold rush and his experiences had been passed down through the family.

"One and sixpence for a gallon bag, water was," Joe explained, "and they had to queue up half the night at the condensers to get it."

We were eager to know more about the condensers and

Joe dipped his finger into his tea and drew an illustration on the newspaper tablecloth.

"Condensers are big iron tanks set up over roaring fires. It was done at night, of course. It'd be too hot by day. They filled them up with salt water from the lakes and condensed the steam that came off."

Joe shook his head.

"Water sure was scarce back then, for drinking, let alone washing. They used to charge two and six for a wash and seven and six for a shower."

Charlie grinned. "Real high-class, it was. Grandpa said the shower was a bit of sacking draped around four poles with a tin hung over the top. You soaped yourself all over, then pulled a string, so the tin tipped and poured the water over you."

"Of course, they didn't waste the water," Joe grinned. "You had to stand in a tin. They let it settle for a bit, then put it back, ready for the next customer."

It was a memorable afternoon, and it did us good. By the time we left, Father was smiling and Mother told Joe she hoped he would find a hole full of gold one day.

"Suppose you did?" George asked. "What would you do?"

Joe thought for a moment, then shrugged.

"Not bloody likely, is it?"

Charlie grinned. "I reckon we'd just drink ourselves to death celebrating."

"You're probably right." Joe nodded. "And I can't think of a better way to go. Can you?"

CHAPTER 42

I left Kalgoorlie with mixed feelings. It is said that anyone who visits a gold town can't help being touched by its influence. You arrive looking up at the stars and leave looking down at the dirt.

But our stay was over and the next destination was Norseman, where we would begin our overland trip. It was time to leave the bitumen behind and venture onto the dirt roads we were to follow for more than a thousand miles.

As the day wore on, the road surface became rougher. There were deep corrugations, pot-holes, jutting outcrops of rock, loose slippery quartz and patches of soft sand.

After grinding and jolting our way over a particularly bad stretch, an ominous sound came from the caravan. Pulling up, we found one of the stays on a water tank had come adrift.

There was nothing for it but to wire it back as best we could and hope we could get it repaired in Norseman.

The heat was intense and Father looked ill, so I volunteered to take his place as George's assistant. I crawled under the car and was struggling to push the tank back into position when a commotion broke out. Mother sounded frightened.

Hurriedly, George crawled out to see what was wrong, leaving me to hold the tank up on my own.

It was ages before he returned.

"Nothing to worry about," he said cheerfully. "There was a whole bunch of kangaroos. Dozens of them. They came right up and circled around us. But it's all right. They've gone now."

I didn't say a word. Looking back, I am proud of my restraint. I had travelled hundreds of miles across Australia and the thing I had wanted to see most was kangaroos.

By the time we had wired the stay into place, it was late afternoon and we decided to camp for the night.

The next morning, we were up and off very early, having agreed we would travel as much as possible in the mornings and evenings and rest during the stifling heat of the day.

We passed Lake Lefroy on our left and crossed over Lake Cowan, two great salt lakes that glistened dazzling white, and soon we saw the poppet-heads of mines ahead of us.

Norseman was a town of nearly three thousand people, living entirely by gold-mining. The buildings were constructed of corrugated iron, mostly small, makeshift shanties. The only stone building was the hotel.

Our petrol supply waited for us at the garage, and they agreed to give the car a quick check-over and to improve our temporary repairs.

There was no sign of other customers.

"Petrol rationing," the mechanic explained sadly. "We used to be busy. Sometimes two or three cars a week going over to the East, but the rationing changed that. Now everyone goes by train."

"By the way," he added. "You will be sure to tell them at the police station you're leaving, won't you?"

We had no need to visit the station, as Norseman's policeman arrived in person at our caravan that afternoon.

He explained the police used the old telegraph line to notify the homesteads along the overland route whenever a party set out. In that way, it was possible to check how travellers were progressing.

"And you will remember to call at the post office to pick up mail, won't you?" he said.

We were not expecting any mail, but he we agreed we would. In any case, we wanted to make another attempt to contact Hotel Eucla.

The line was still down and the woman at the post office was apologetic. Would we like her to give them a message when the line was repaired? We thanked her and George asked her to tell them we would like a meal, baths and a place to park the caravan when we got there.

He pulled out his wallet and asked how much the call would cost.

"It will be twopence."

"But it's nearly five hundred miles!" George was open-mouthed.

The woman nodded.

"Yes, but it's still a local call. There's only one line all the way to South Australia. If anybody rings, everyone along the way answers it."

She ferreted under the counter and brought out a bundle of letters.

"And this is the post for the homesteads on the way over. I hope you don't mind. We have to rely on the kindness of travellers to deliver it."

We had given a lot of thought to what provisions we would carry. Obviously, we couldn't take too much because of the weight, but neither could we risk running out of food.

We bought what we thought best, filled our water-tanks,

then George sat down with a pencil and paper to do some calculations. He was shocked to discover our total weight, including petrol, was close to four and a half tons.

~

We left Norseman next morning and passed a signpost that announced Adelaide 1,276 miles.

How far that sounded.

Since leaving Perth, we had studied our maps intently, and had learned it was wrong to assume that on an Australian map, a dot with a name beside it indicated a town. Sometimes a dot marked only a homestead or even something less than that. Sometimes it marked a water tank. Or a dried-up water hole.

There were various names marked on the route between Norseman and Penong, but in over seven hundred miles, less than half a dozen indicated human habitation.

The few outback settlements of Western Australia were spread over a million square miles of barren country. We had often heard the expression "the dead heart of Australia" and now we appreciated what it meant.

This huge barrier between east and west, stretching from the North to the South of the continent, was crossed by three routes. In the extreme north lay a track that linked with Darwin. It was often impassable and, in places, non-existent.

In the centre, the Transcontinental Railway Line, leaving Kalgoorlie, headed on the longest straight stretch of line in the world, across the Nullarbor Plain to Port Augusta in South Australia.

And in the south, some eighty to a hundred miles from the railway, was the road we planned to take.

A few miles south of the road, the central plain ended with sheer, unbroken cliffs that dropped one hundred metres down to the treacherous waters of the Great Australian Bight.

The sun was blisteringly hot and now and then the strangest lizards, like tiny prehistoric monsters, with spikes all over their backs, scuttled off the road, their heads perked up as though in resentment as we passed.

It is difficult to describe the loneliness that descended the moment we left Norseman. For hours, there was nothing but the road and endless blue sky. Then, after about sixty miles, a gate blocked our way. It was set across an iron grid over a trench in the road.

We had reached the Fraser Range sheep station. We opened the gate, clattered over the grid, and closed the gate behind us. There was no sign of sheep, or a building, although we strained our eyes at the heat haze in the distance. No people came out to greet us, but we were not surprised. We had been warned that at the Fraser Range, visitors were not welcome.

A few miles further on, Winkie became restless and Father decided he needed to go 'walkies'. Mother was certain he would disappear if we let him out on his own, so I clipped on his lead and Father brought the 'tree' from the boot.

But suddenly Winkie pulled the lead out of my hand, raced back to the car and cowered on the back seat. I was struggling to pull him out when I heard the crack of a breaking branch and a heavy padding behind me.

Instinctively, I scrambled into the car and slammed the door.

Outside, George burst out laughing. Three camels had appeared behind us, stared at our outfit, and lumbered away.

Camels in the middle of Australia? It was the last thing I had expected.

The country changed with every mile, becoming ever more scorched, baked and desolate. We only drove in the early morning and late afternoon, but during the heat of the day, there was no shade, no respite, and both the car and caravan became airless ovens.

At last, we saw a massive outcrop of rock looming ahead, and beside it huddled a house, Balladonia, the next homestead.

With more than four hundred thousand acres of land, Balladonia was an enormous property. We pulled up at the fenced area surrounding the house where, in stark contrast to the scene around it, a great peppermint tree drooped its branches to the ground beside a small, rock-bottomed lake.

A woman and a boy came out of the house to meet us. The woman wore a large, shady hat and smiled as she brushed aside the trailing branches of the peppermint tree.

The action was so gentle, I could have been watching a scene from a delightful rural film, if it were not for the bleached skeleton of a dead cow at the woman's feet. Stepping over the remains, she held out her hand to welcome us.

She was the station owner's wife with their eight-year-old son. The police had phoned ahead, as promised, and we were expected. To our surprise, the woman invited us to share a meal, and we gladly accepted.

Remembering our job as postmen, we brought out the mail, and while his mother glanced through it, I couldn't help noticing the gravity of the little boy. He seemed less like a child than a miniature man.

He took charge of us, guiding George to the best spot for parking, and helping to unload the petrol from the caravan.

He chatted freely, and it was fascinating to listen to him. He had never known the company of another child, only the company of adults, including the station workers, and so, from birth, he had learned an adult's outlook on life. Although he was only eight years old, he could drive a truck, or ride a horse, with the next man. He went out for days at a time droving, and he could bait a dingo trap, or follow a track, as well as anyone.

To us, it was pathetic. He was a little boy, yet he had never been young.

When he saw Winkie, he told me he too had a dog. A puppy had been born to one of the drovers' dogs some months before and he had been allowed to keep it.

I asked if I could see it, and the boy ran to the house, returning with a lean, sandy-coloured creature.

I held out my hand, and the dog sniffed curiously, its ears flat back against its skull.

"I won't be able to keep him much longer," the boy said matter-of-factly. "When the dry season comes, Dad will shoot him. There's no water to spare for pets here."

That evening we were welcomed to the house and introduced to the station owner, a quiet, friendly man with tanned skin and pale blue eyes. He surprised us by asking if we had seen any of his wife's paintings.

She showed us her studio, and I was amazed. It would have been the envy of any artist. The whole of one wall was glass from floor to ceiling and a canvas stood half-finished on an easel.

The other walls were covered by hundreds of paintings, some in water colours, some in oils, but all beautifully detailed and brilliantly coloured. They were drawn from nature, images of spiders, lizards, beetles, ants, birds and all the myriad small creatures of the surrounding bush.

There were also other, larger paintings that expressed more clearly than any words, the way of life on the Nullarbor. A magnificent pair of oils showed a dingo pack attacking a group of cattle in the bush. In one, the fear-crazed animals were at bay from the snarling dogs, and in the other was shown the agony of the creature the dingoes had dragged down for the kill.

It was horribly realistic, and I was grateful to turn to another canvas showing seventeen camels harnessed to a great loaded wool wagon. I was intrigued. Our hostess explained the overland route had only been made passable by the army during the last years of the war. Before that, supplies arrived once every six months on wagons pulled by camel teams.

However, once the roads improved, the camels were no longer needed, and many were left to roam by themselves. The camels we had seen on the road were no longer a mystery.

We returned to the kitchen and enjoyed an appetising meal, for which we were most grateful. To finish, our hostess produced attractive little cakes topped with pink icing and coconut.

Father confessed he had a great weakness for cake and was rewarded with another coconut-covered delicacy.

Our hostess then shared her own favourite food. She said she liked bardis, but we had to admit we had never heard of them.

Bardis, she explained, are large grubs, some of them twenty centimetres long and as round as a man's thumb. They live under the bark of trees and are a great delicacy. Her son loved them too, and like his mother, he preferred them raw, enjoying them most when they were nearly full grown and the faint outline of head and wings was discernible.

Then she told us how they preferred their white ants. The insects must be at the right stage, they said. When they first hatch out, the whole nest is dug up, shaken through a coarse sieve to remove the soil and dust, then blown until only the ants remain.

There was an awkward silence, and to cover it, Mother asked how the ants were cooked.

Our hostess looked surprised.

They didn't need to be cooked, she assured us. It would only spoil them. Shaking the ants killed them, and they were best eaten raw when they looked and tasted just like coconut.

We didn't stay long after that.

CHAPTER 43

We did not take on any more water. It was a priceless commodity in the outback, and having been offered none, we were reluctant to ask, especially as we had used very little and our maps showed water catchment tanks only eighty miles ahead.

The dirt road was rough and littered with potholes that slowed us to a crawl. We had only gone about twenty miles when there was a loud crack and the car bucked violently, slewing across the road.

It was a blow-out. The tyre and inner tube were ripped to pieces and with the weight of the caravan pushing from behind, it was as much as George could do to keep the car under control as he brought it to a halt.

George examining the remains of the burst tyre.

The sun was already blazing and as I looked around, there was no shelter, no shade, nothing but stunted saltbush straggling away to the horizon.

Worried we might face more such emergencies, George decided to put on the new tube and tyre we were carrying rather than use the spare wheel, which was already pumped up. I am sure it was a sensible decision, but the effort involved was unbelievable.

George and I wrestled to fit the tube into the tyre as the sun beat down on us, then took it in turns with a foot pump.

Suddenly Mother screamed.

In the back seat of the car, Father's face was scarlet as he gasped for breath. I fetched a cup of water and Mother dabbed at his forehead to cool him. Moments later, he sagged back against the seat, his eyes closed.

"He's dead!" Mother squealed.

Father's eyes fluttered open, but Mother screamed

relentlessly. George tried to calm her while I tended to Father.

"How is he?" George asked.

I tried to sound confident.

"I think it's only the heat affecting him, but the sooner we get moving, the better."

It was after mid-day when we reached the tanks. They consisted of a few corrugated iron sheets, supported by bush poles, which sloped down towards a pair of round water tanks.

We couldn't see how much water the tanks contained, but the shade they cast was welcome. George drove up close so he could stand on the car bonnet and look inside. Then he climbed down, shaking his head. There was a drain of water at the bottom of each tank, but it was difficult to see because of the layer of dead creatures floating on top.

We stayed in the shade of the tanks until the sun went down. The chill of evening revived Father and quietened Mother. George and I put on cheerful faces, but we were worried. Tomorrow would be another day of fierce heat. We decided to drive on through the evening and as far into the night as possible.

The next sign of habitation marked on our map was Cocklebiddy. We had been told it was deserted, but we hoped there might be buildings and some blessed shade.

We were right. Our headlights picked out a track leading off the road, then, about a mile later, the remains of a building that had once been a dwelling. We parked beside it and settled down to sleep for the rest of the night.

We woke to glaring sunshine and were grateful for the meagre shade of the derelict house. Millions of tiny white seashells scattered the red-brown earth, reminders that once, long ago, this vast plain was part of the ocean bed.

The silence was absolute. Nothing moved, nothing lived. I think we were all relieved when we were on our way.

There was, we knew, a pass to be negotiated. We had been travelling on the edge of the Nullarbor itself, but soon the road would dip down three hundred feet to the coastal plain.

How steep or rough that dip would be, we did not know, but there would be no turning back.

The pass, when we reached it, was certainly steep and horribly rough, but George kept us moving forward, sometimes at barely a walking pace, as he searched for the best route through the ruts and potholes.

It took a long time, but there was a consolation. As we crept down the pass, the heat became less intense and once or twice, a faint breeze stirred the air.

At last, the ground levelled out and the road veered around until it was heading east. We were on the coastal plain, heading for Hotel Eucla, and somewhere away to our right was the sea.

But there was a new concern. Glancing at the dashboard, George noticed the battery was not recharging.

Stopping the car, he disappeared under the bonnet and reappeared frowning. He didn't know what was wrong, but we were only twelve miles from Eucla. Rather than risk pulling things to pieces and perhaps ending up stranded, he thought we should take a chance on the battery holding out long enough to get us to the hotel.

I agreed, and we drove on until we noticed something ahead that looked like plumes of white smoke on the skyline. Our first thought was that it could be a bush fire. Then we thought of something even worse. Perhaps Hotel Eucla was going up in smoke.

In our agitation, we forgot about the battery and our attention focused on the spiralling columns ahead. Then we understood. The clouds billowing on the skyline were not smoke. They were clouds of pure white sand blown before a gentle wind.

We had reached the sea.

Hotel Eucla must have been the strangest and loneliest hotel in the world.

The settlement at Eucla was built in 1870 as a relay station for the overland telegraph line between Western and South Australia. It comprised a group of stone buildings with timber ceilings and floors.

However, when the telegraph station closed, it fell into disuse and the fine white sea sand drifted into great dunes that overwhelmed the buildings, one by one, until only three could be seen.

Hotel Eucla

The largest of these, still battling the encroaching sand, had become Hotel Eucla. There was an air of resigned desolation about it. At the windows, ragged curtains had faded to a mustard colour and above the rotting boards of the veranda, a lantern swung on a string. It was only lit, we were told later, when travellers were expected up or down the pass.

No-one came out to greet us but we rapped loudly on the woodwork and at last a woman appeared. She was not expecting us, but she told us we were welcome. The breakdown in the telephone line had been in South Australia and had only just been repaired.

Mrs Gurney was the hotel-keeper and lived there with her five children and two Aboriginal servants. Her husband lived at Koonalda homestead at the other end of their property, a mere sixty-four miles away. He ran the sheep station while she ran the hotel.

As soon as one of the children came in, they would make us a cup of tea, Mrs Gurney said, but in the meantime, she had an important job to do.

We watched as she hurried across to a white box set on a post. Opening a door in it, she produced a pad and pencil and began making notes. Finally, she stared up at the sky for a moment, wrote down something else, then hurried back inside the building.

Intrigued, we followed her and found her standing in a little alcove off the hall where two old-fashioned telephones faced each other on opposite walls. She was giving a detailed weather report.

Eucla, we learned, was a weather recording station and every four hours Mrs Gurney phoned Ceduna with the latest readings and information.

Her husband, Roy, brought her supplies once a month, which he collected from the tiny settlement of Cook, a maintenance outpost on the Transcontinental Railway line.

Cook was only a hundred and sixty-five miles away, but there was no road, only a track made by his ancient car.

When Mrs Gurney's children burst into the hotel, Mother was fascinated. Five children growing up in the middle of nowhere. She couldn't contain her curiosity.

"What if one of them's taken ill?" she asked.

Mrs Gurney was unconcerned. The nearest doctor was at Ceduna, but, of course, if it was something really serious, she could always call the Flying Doctor.

"And education?"

Mrs Gurney smiled round at her brood.

"We don't go in much for education round here, but they send us a parcel of lessons for each of them. They're supposed to do them and send them back, but with petrol rationing and no cars going through…" She lifted her hands helplessly. "What can you do?"

When our tea was finished, Mrs Gurney told us she could spare enough water for a bath. Later, we realised she meant just that. One bath between the four of us.

She took us along the hall to the kitchen, where two Aboriginal girls were working before the wood range, and giggled at the sight of us.

Topsy and Sheelah, looked about sixteen and wore simple print dresses. They had been brought up at a mission station where they had been taught English and learned to cook and sew.

Outside, one end of the veranda had been walled off to form a bathroom. Mrs Gurney threw open the door, revealing a battered tub with less than ten centimetres of water in the bottom. "There," she said proudly, "all ready for you."

When the sun had set, we had our evening meal by the dull light of an oil lamp. It was rabbit.

Mrs Gurney was candid.

"We're running low on supplies right now. Hope you

don't mind rabbit. The children have a lot of fun catching them. Usually, we feed them to the dogs."

Bright and early next morning, George set to work on the car to find out why the battery was not recharging. To my surprise, it didn't take him long to identify the problem. The brushes in the generator had burned out, and needless to say, we had no spares.

Mrs Gurney came to our rescue. Her eldest boy, a wiry thirteen-year-old, took George across to a small building which housed a collection of broken, burned-out or discarded odds and ends left behind by other overlanders. It was an impressive heap and bore witness to the toll the road took on vehicles that ventured across it.

Luckily for us, some other unfortunate had burned out a starter motor and had added it to the heap. Inevitably, the brushes were too big, but George set to work with a will, wearing them down with an old file. It was slow work, and it was nearly mid-day by the time he had fitted them and replaced the generator.

Our exit from Eucla was more spectacular than our entry. At the last minute, George's faith in his repair deserted him. His finger quivered above the starter button, but then he changed his mind. He didn't have the courage to use the last charge in the battery, only to find his handiwork was no good and the generator still wasn't charging.

The alternative was simple. I had to get out and push. As I headed to the back of the car, the five children sat dangling their feet over the edge of the veranda and Topsy and Sheelah's shiny, black faces were pressed against the kitchen window.

Mrs Gurney watched, arms crossed, but when I bent to start pushing, her voice rose in a bellow.

Next moment, everyone, including a beaming Topsy and Sheelah, joined in. Even three mangy dogs appeared from nowhere, barking furiously, and followed us long after the others had dropped, waving and cheering, behind.

We felt like cheering too. The battery was recharging. Good old George!

CHAPTER 44

We headed inland across a vast plain until we saw before us a towering wall of limestone cliffs with a road cut into it, leading up once again to the inland plateau.

As we got closer, the road appeared much steeper than we had expected. George stopped the car, and we looked ahead apprehensively. I knew the Buick was powerful, but could it really drag our heavily laden outfit up such an incline?

I could see from his expression that George shared my fears, but he kept his voice level as he announced he was going to take a run at it. Our parents fell silent in the back and I found myself clutching my seat as he put his foot down and the car roared forward.

At first, we climbed steadily, bouncing over the uneven surface, but our rush petered out a third of the way up when George dropped back into bottom gear and couldn't make the change in time.

I tumbled out of the car and heaved rocks under the rear wheels to stop it running backwards. George roared the engine, the wheels spun for an instant, then gripped, and the whole outfit shuddered violently before creeping forward.

I stayed out as an emergency brakeman. There were rocks and stones everywhere, but in my eagerness, I staggered all the way up the slope carrying the same two heavy rocks, ready at any moment to rush to the rescue. At the top, I was speechless as I climbed back into the car.

The next few miles were treacherous as we dodged small trees and knotted roots, but the stunted bush petered out until we were back among the familiar mix of saltbush, spinifex and bare earth.

We had become used to a few minor rattles in the car but now a new sound intruded, an intermittent knocking that came from somewhere under the floor. We stopped and looked underneath but could see nothing, so we decided to ignore it.

Then, as we rounded a bend, a yellow notice board announced we were crossing the border. Western Australia lay behind us. Ahead was South Australia.

For some reason, crossing the border was too much for Mother. She broke into a torrent of tears, and then anger took over. Why couldn't we have boarded a ship at Fremantle and sailed straight back to England like anyone else? Why had she been subjected to the misery of crossing this terrible country? Nothing was her fault, yet she was always the one to suffer.

We parked beside the yellow notice board for two days, until she tired enough to sleep, then we headed on.

Since we left Eucla, the weather had changed. It was still unbearably hot during the day, but after sunset, the nights were bitterly cold.

The road was full of pot-holes and occasional deep depressions filled with soft, red dust. Hitting them was like plunging into a flour sack, and by now the grinding knock beneath us was continuous.

It was a relief when we saw the turnoff to Koonalda homestead. We crawled along a track for about half a mile until we reached a bare patch on which were built four shacks, two of corrugated iron and two of wood.

A man came hurrying out of one of them and waved. George let in the clutch and we were rolling towards him when the noise from underneath ended in a grating crunch. We stopped abruptly.

The man was Roy Gurney, husband of Mrs Gurney of Eucla, who lived at Koonalda with his brother, Cyril, his sister-in-law, Audrey, and their two young children. Mrs Gurney had phoned to say we were on our way, and after two days, they were becoming concerned.

Roy was short and stocky, his clothes worn, his feet hidden by a pair of outsize boots, and his head topped by a battered hat that sat squarely on his ears.

George explained our problem and as Roy listened, he lifted his hat to scratch his head. George faltered, and we all stared. The leathery darkness of Roy's face ended with knife-edged abruptness at the hairline. Everything above was white, soft white skin and pure white hair. We learned later he never took his hat off. Not even inside the house. Never.

We waited while Roy crawled under the car, still wearing his hat, then climbed out again and circled it. His verdict was summed up in a single question.

"How are you off for food?"

He frowned when we admitted our stores were low.

"Well… it could be clutch, universal, diff… We won't know until we pull her down. Probably means new parts anyway. Still, a few days isn't going to hurt, is it? Give you a chance to see our caves."

George brought up the delicate matter of water and Roy assured us we could help ourselves, providing we were sparing with it.

He led us behind one of the shacks to a square water-tank. Old Bob was having a drink from it. Old Bob was a horse. Big, shaggy and gentle-looking, but definitely a horse.

Roy shooed him off with a grin. "Don't mind him. He won't hurt you. Best be a bit careful with the cows, though."

~

Next morning, Roy and George set to work on the car. A couple of hours later, they announced the worst. The universal joint had collapsed. Our only hope, we were told, was to phone for the part to be sent to us from the nearest garage. Roy phoned Ceduna, three hundred and sixty miles east, and Norseman, five hundred miles west. Each promised to get the part as quickly as possible and put it on the first overland car on its way through. Then there was nothing we could do but wait.

~

Father was busy putting up our toilet tent when Roy asked what he was doing. Father explained, but Roy assured him there was no need for the tent. Koonalda had a perfectly good loo.

He took us to a three-sided construction with a tin squat in the middle. There was no door. There was no need for one, Roy told us. No-one could intrude on our privacy. The open side faced north and there was nothing in that direction for at least five hundred miles.

~

The prospect of being stuck on a remote sheep farm in the middle of a desert for an unknown length of time did nothing to improve Mother's mood. As the day grew hotter, I persuaded her to settle down for a rest in the caravan while I sat on the steps looking out across the wilderness.

Idly, I picked up a stick and dragged it across the dirt.

Grains of sand sparkled in the sunlight, and as I twisted the stick in my fingers, I noticed a tiny black circle on the ground.

Looking more closely, I spotted another circle, and another. They were everywhere, and I was curious what they could be.

I prodded the nearest circle with the end of the stick and it sank down into the dirt, but, to my amazement, a moment later, it popped back up to the level of the ground around it.

I prodded the circle down again, and again it popped back up. I tried another circle, and the same thing happened.

I was so intrigued I didn't hear Roy walk up behind me.

"Best not to do that," he said. "Trap-door spiders, those are. Nasty little buggers. Really aggressive if you upset them."

~

That afternoon, there was a tap on the side of the caravan. When we looked out, a round, black face grinned at us. Roy had told us there were four Aboriginal workers on the station, an old couple, Jimmy and his wife, Judaby, and a young couple, Tommy and Molly.

We guessed our visitor was Jimmy, as his frizzy hair and stubbly beard were both almost white. He had come to ask if he could see Winkie. Apparently, he had seen him from a distance and was fascinated by his stubby body and short legs, a shape so different from Australian dogs.

When we took Winkie out, perky in his tartan harness, Jimmy hurried to find Judaby, Tommy and Molly. They arrived moments later and broke into peals of laughter at the sight.

Over the next days we would make friends with them all, but it was Judaby who fascinated me the most. In her own words, she was "coming up a hundred," and she looked it. There was not a tooth left in her head, but there was a healthy alertness about her, and although her legs seemed little thicker than matchsticks, she stood perfectly upright. Her eyes were bright with a proud independence, and everywhere she went, she was followed by her little half-dingo dog.

Late that afternoon, Roy came across. He had decided to take us down to see his caves, which, we were left in no doubt, were his pride and joy.

Koonalda, like the whole of the Nullarbor, is riddled with caves and blowholes. Blowholes are openings in the ground, sometimes only a few centimetres across, sometimes big enough for a car to drop down, and from them comes a strong blast of cool air. If the temperature ever drops enough, the blowhole sucks in instead of blowing out. These holes often drop further down than the light from a torch can pierce, then lead off into a maze of underground tunnels.

George gathered his photographic gear together and bemoaned his shortage of flashbulbs, but Mother and Father politely declined Roy's invitation, saying they felt they should stay with Winkie.

It was almost six o'clock when Roy brought his car across. Even now, I find it hard to describe that car. It was not so much that it was old, it was more that it had an air of being completely exhausted. Everything about it sagged.

And it stank.

The reason was obvious. The floor and seats were littered with wool and feathers, and stained from carrying a procession of sick sheep, dead dingoes and shot bush turkeys.

George and I, laden with photographic gear and a torch each, climbed into it. After a few hundred yards, we came to the Aboriginal camp. It consisted of two 'wurlies,' low round structures made of hessian bags, supported on a framework of bush wood.

As the car pulled up in front of the wurlies, a racket broke out and we were surrounded by a pack of barking dogs.

"Still want to come down the caves with us, Molly?" Roy bellowed.

Tommy and Molly

Molly certainly did, but not before she had changed into a clean dress. She was determined to look good, not for us, but to impress any evil spirits that might inhabit the caves.

As soon as Molly was ready, Roy turned the car and followed a barely discernible track across the plain. The light was fading, and it was almost dark when we drew up beside a huge, sheer-sided hole in the ground.

It was about seventy-five metres long, twenty-five metres wide, and twenty-five metres deep. A wire ladder dangled down into the gloom and one by one, we clambered over the edge and began the descent. It was not a pleasant experience. The ladder twisted and shook and we were all burdened with something to make the climb more awkward, torches, a lamp, a camera and so on.

At last, we reached the bottom and set off behind Roy along a rock-strewn ledge until we reached the entrance to the caves. Inside was black and forbidding.

Roy stopped to light his hurricane lamp, then we entered a narrow tunnel in single file. After a few metres, the roof arched abruptly into the blackness above our heads and the floor fell away below us.

We were standing on the edge of a vast black void, angling steeply down as though into the bowels of the earth. The light from the lamp died before it reached the walls and our torches showed them only dimly in the distance.

Without hesitation, Roy strode into the darkness and next moment we were all slipping and sliding after him down a slope of boulders and loose scree, broken here and there by patches of wet clay.

Behind me, I heard George slip. He managed to save himself but let go of his torch. It hurtled down, the light flickering as it fell, crashing and tinkling, on and on, as we crouched in the silence, listening.

Finally, the sound stopped.

"Want to be careful," Roy growled. "There's another two hundred feet of this before it levels out."

We kept going down and all I could think about was how we would ever get up again. How Molly managed on her bare feet, I shall never know. Stones slid away from under us, and in places, to avoid tipping forward into the blackness below, there was no choice but to sit and slide down.

Roy told us the great cavern around us was an antechamber from which two tunnels led off, the Western and the North Western.

He was anxious to show us the main caverns, so, in single file, we set off again down more loose scree. This time, it was not far. Within a few minutes, we were standing on a smooth clay floor more than one hundred metres below the surface.

The size of the chamber was unbelievable. Our lights barely reached the huge domed roof above our heads and the walls, far away on either side, showed only faint outlines of our huge shadows as we moved. These fascinated Molly and she laughed as she waved her arms and went into all sorts of amused contortions.

Here we took our first photograph, and Molly's amusement died. The flash of the camera startled her, and she became genuinely frightened.

I was far from happy myself. There was an uncomfortable starkness about the caves. There were no stalactites or stalagmites, no shawls or attractive little grottoes. In the darkness, I could see no beauty in the rock formations, only the terrifying vastness of the endless tunnels and gigantic caverns.

I held Molly's arm as we went on and felt her shiver.

The clay beneath our feet gave way to sand, and we stood on a gently shelving beach with inky black water that reached ahead of us into yet another tunnel. The water stretched from wall to wall, so, without a boat, it was impossible to go on.

Instead, we turned down another huge tunnel, at the entrance to which an enormous white rock towered above us.

Roy had christened it the Iceberg, and high in the roof, we could make out the gaping hole from which this massive lump of rock had come hurtling down.

I felt sick. We were miles from anywhere, deep in caves that were practically unexplored, with a man we barely knew and a frightened Aboriginal girl. And who could tell when another great mass might choose to come crashing down?

I wanted to leave, but Roy was eager to show us one last feature, a lake he had christened the Swimming Pool. Reluctantly, I agreed, and we turned into the North West Tunnel, scrambling over the rocky floor until we stood in another cavern.

There, its surface mirror-perfect as though unruffled for a thousand years, lay a great oval pool of water. It had sheer sides and an overhanging rock that might have been a diving board. I understood at once why it reminded Roy of a swimming pool.

The scale of the caverns was extraordinary, and I was grateful to have had such an unexpected experience, but I was exhausted and bitterly cold. Beside me, Molly shivered so much I wrapped my arms around her and tried to keep her warm.

I yearned to return to the surface, but George had one flash-bulb left and wanted to take a final photograph of the cavern.

Climbing onto a pile of rocks, he perching his camera on a ledge and shouted down to me to let off the flash.

I did.

Nothing.

The bulb was a dud.

Muttering loudly, George retrieved his camera. We had done our best. It was time to go.

Diana in the caves at Koonalda.

The climb up was far worse than the climb down. The flame in the hurricane lamp had burned low and my torch was fading.

Roy held the lamp high as he picked his way upwards, and the rest of us scrambled hopefully where he led.

Once he trod on a rock that broke under his feet. How he saved himself, I don't know, but the broken pieces went crashing down and down.

At last, we smelt the night air. Gasping with relief, I stumbled along the narrow entrance tunnel and saw the stars above us.

We were out of the cave system, but the climb up from the sink-hole was the worst part of all. The night was pitch black and the battery in my torch finally gave out.

Roy said it would be safer if we climbed separately, so he went first, carrying the lamp, then held it out over the edge of the precipice once he reached the top. The rest of us climbed up the twenty-five metres by its distant glow while the flimsy rope ladder twisted in the darkness.

As I stood at the bottom, waiting my turn to climb, my

imagination ran riot thinking of all the snakes, spiders, and creepy-crawlies that might have made the great hole its home.

~

It was after midnight when Roy dropped us back at the caravan. We had been away for over six hours and the relief on Father's face when he saw us would have been comical at any other time.

We had had nothing to eat since the morning, but, like me, George had only one desire. We crawled into bed and slept.

CHAPTER 45

Roy came round early the next morning. He was going to see his wife, and he promised, if possible, to bring some food back from Eucla.

George and I were clearing the campfire from the previous night and saw him walk away, then stop suddenly, staring at the ground. A moment later, he was off like a bloodhound on a scent. Darting into the house, he came out carrying a rifle and waved to us to keep our distance.

"A snake," he said, advancing cautiously towards a pile of discarded rubbish.

We watched as Roy moved a little this way, a little that, then froze.

"Anyone got a mirror?" he called.

I was back with one in a flash and handed it to George.

"There! By that four-gallon drum," Roy hissed.

Edging forward, George held the mirror and tilted it until the reflected beam of light fell upon the drum.

"A bit to the left. That's it! That's him." Roy eased himself sideways. "Good! I can see his head now!"

Without hesitation, he swung the rifle up and fired.

George recoiled, but Roy picked up a pole and hooked the body of a large black snake from among the rubbish.

"Got him," he said happily. "He was a bad 'un."

Roy Gurney with his rifle.

Turning, Roy caught sight of our unhappy faces and gave us a short lecture on the various routes to the grave that were all around us.

Obviously, we must be careful of the red-backs, small black spiders with a vivid streak down their back. For their size, they were one of the deadliest species on the planet. Scorpions were common and came in various shapes and sizes.

"They pack a punch and hurt like hell, but they don't often kill anyone," Roy reassured us. "Giant centipedes are nasty little buggers, too, but you should be alright unless the bite festers."

He pushed his hat back and scratched his forehead.

"What you really want to watch out for are the brown snakes. If you get bit by one of them out here, the chances are you're a gonner."

When Roy left, I gave a quiet prayer of thanks Mother had not overheard our conversation.

Later, Roy rounded up Old Bob, slung his rifle across his shoulder and rode off. Jimmy had found the remains of a sheep killed by dingoes. There had been a number of such attacks recently and Roy wanted to round up as many sheep as he could find and bring them close to the homestead for safety.

Before he left, he came across to the caravan. One of Koonalda's cows had calved, which meant fresh milk was available. The Gurneys, including the children, were so used to condensed milk they wouldn't drink fresh so we could have as much as we liked.

This would have been a joy, except the cows grazed on saltbush and the milk tasted strongly of onions.

We still had one loaf of bread left, but after nine days on the road, it was harder than the proverbial brick, so when Audrey, Roy's sister-in-law, told me she was about to make bread and asked if we would like a loaf, I offered to help.

My first job was to unearth a sack of flour from a shack and heave it into Audrey's kitchen.

She seemed happy to have my company and said my next job was to sieve the flour. That seemed reasonable enough until she explained the flour needed to be sieved because there was a rat problem.

In the past, if rats got into a sack, the whole thing would

have been tossed out, but times were hard. If the body of a dead rat was found in a sack, then it would probably still be thrown away, she told me, but if there were only rat dirts, the sieving would get rid of them.

Later, I took two loaves of fresh bread back to the caravan and said nothing about rats to the others.

Our sixth day at Koonalda, began well. We were enjoying breakfast, fresh bread and our last half tin of beans, when Roy appeared. The garage at Ceduna had phoned to say our part was on its way to them. They would have it in a few hours and would put it on the first overland car.

It was wonderful news. We would soon be on our way again. In our excitement, we cleaned the car inside and out, checked the tyre pressures, and filled the radiator.

But in the afternoon, Audrey appeared at the caravan door. We took one look at her face and our hearts sank. The garage had phoned again to say our part had arrived, but it was the wrong type and they were sending it back to Adelaide.

We tried not to be downhearted. A few more days at Koonalda wouldn't make any difference. The Gurneys wouldn't let us starve and there was no-one waiting for us, no-one to worry over us.

We had to be patient, but that wasn't easy for Mother. She was sick of the heat, the dust, the poisonous spiders under her feet, the onion-flavoured milk, sharing the water tank with Old Bob and the cows, and above all, the restless flock of sheep that had been brought in to save them from the dingoes and now milled continually round the caravan.

It wasn't easy for us either when she flew into rages, and we had to explain to Roy that she was exhausted and needed to rest.

If our parents were stressed, then so were George and I. We had got ourselves into this situation and we knew it. There was no one else to blame. All we could do was pray the days passed quickly and we would soon be able to head for home.

At first, we had clung to our dream of a peaceful cottage in the countryside. It had kept us going, even if it would have to be a cottage large enough for four and a little black dog.

But as the relentlessly sunny days passed, the dream faded into a bitter unreality. We didn't talk about it anymore. I tried not to think about it.

It was four more days before Roy pushed his way through the sheep round the caravan. The garage at Norseman had been on the telephone to him.

Our spirits rose at once. Our part! It must have arrived and be waiting for an overland car to bring it to us.

But Roy shook his head. There was no sign of the part yet, but something else was on its way.

A circus was coming through.

CHAPTER 46

A circus was coming. We could hardly believe it, but it was true.

The show, based in Sydney, usually toured Western Australia every three years, travelling by a specially adapted train on the cross-continental railway, but now, with the West Australian tour finished, they had been forced to change their arrangements.

They had a sick animal and vets had warned them it wouldn't survive the constant rocking and jolting of a train for over a thousand miles. The only hope for the animal was to take the overland road back to Sydney. Then they could pull off and rest whenever necessary.

At first, they had planned to send a single truck containing the invalid on the long journey, but the show people had objected. If the invalid had to go overland, then the whole circus would face the journey together.

For the next few days, Koonalda churned with excitement. A circus was coming, and Roy was determined to make it welcome.

The sheep were herded back on to the plain, the dingoes temporarily forgotten. Holes were dug, and piles of rubbish disappeared into them. Audrey tidied her shack and baked bread and Jimmy and Judaby begged us to tell them exactly what a circus was.

Even Mother brightened, and she explained about clowns and performing animals, acrobats and stilt-walkers until her audience stared with amazement.

It was five days before Roy told us the circus had passed Eucla and was heading towards the pass. It should be with us the following day.

We were up early. A circus was coming. We knew it was not bringing our part, and we had heard nothing from Ceduna, but we were full of curiosity. The idea of a circus in the middle of the Nullarbor seemed incredible.

By mid-day there were faint smudges of dust on the skyline. They grew through the afternoon and as we watched, they became individual balls of dust, each wrapped around a tiny truck and caravan.

The hours passed, and the distant vehicles grew. When the sun dipped towards the horizon, I made a meal from the remnants of a loaf soaked in water, mixed with a few sultanas, and fried in the fat from a tin of sausages.

As we ate, the first of the vehicles rolled to a halt in front of the shacks. They were huge red and yellow trucks. The words Silvers Circus painted across the sides were almost indecipherable under the dust, and each truck hauled behind it a caravan or a tightly shuttered animal cage.

Roy shook hands with the driver of the lead truck as he climbed out, and soon they were deep in conversation. We watched from a distance as the rest of the fleet trundled to a halt and lined themselves up in a row.

To my surprise, Roy brought the truck driver across to us.

He was a youngish-looking man and possibly quite presentable when shaved and scrubbed, but at that moment he was dirty and dishevelled. Lines of sweat streaked his face, stubbly growth covered his chin, his hands were black with grime, and he looked exhausted.

Roy introduced him as David Hardie, one of the owners of the circus. He had been telling him about our plight.

"I'll help if I can," David promised, then turned to Roy. "If you have no objection, I'd like the show to rest up and take a breath tomorrow before we press on. If so, I can take a look at your problem in the morning. Right now, I need to get the animals fed and watered and everyone settled."

Seeing the circus set up camp was like watching a transformation scene from an elaborate pantomime.

The empty plain had vanished, and in its place was a vibrant pageant of vehicles. Caravans, their open doors spilling out light, unshuttered cages, with pacing lions roaring for food, restless horses walked by grooms, and the kitchen wagon sending out a glorious smell of cooking food, beside a blazing campfire.

News of our plight spread quickly, and the circus folk were friendly. Their stores were low, but if we were in need, they would rustle something up between them. In the meantime, they crowded round the fire with us, chattering strangers bonded by shared experiences.

A girl touched my arm as I stood watching.

"Hallo, I'm Leila," she said. "I've heard about your breakdown. Don't worry. I'll bet David can fix it. He's a genius. If anything goes wrong around the show, everyone yells for David."

She was interrupted by Audrey, who hurried across from the house and thrust a jug of milk into my hand. "This is for Johnny. Do you mind taking it? I'm trying to put the children to bed."

I had no idea who Johnny was, but before I could object, Leila joined in.

"Here. I'll show you," she said and led me along the row of trucks to one that stood a little apart. She tapped on the side, then climbed up into it and beckoned me to follow.

David was sitting on the floor, but I barely noticed him. Snuggled up to him was a baby elephant. It held David's hand in its trunk and sucked at his fingers like a hungry baby.

Leila smiled at me as I handed over the milk. "This is Johnny, our little invalid," she said. "Isn't he lovely?"

She ran her finger gently up the elephant's trunk, then turned away. "You'll have to excuse me. They'll be looking for me."

David watched her go. "That's Leila. She's married to the Shipway Twins, our acrobats."

He must have seen my surprise because he hastily added, "No, I mean, she's married to one of them, but she looks after them both."

Johnny had found the milk in the jug and we watched as his little trunk plunged into it.

"What's wrong with him?" I asked.

Suddenly, David was serious.

"His mother was shot by poachers. He was found by her body and an animal agent brought him to Perth. I'm sure he thought he would get a good price for him, but anyone who knew about elephants could see he didn't have much chance without his mother. It was unlikely he'd live for long, so no-one wanted him."

Johnny finished his milk, and I watched David wipe his trunk clean and give him a quick cuddle.

"And you?" I asked.

He shrugged. "Everyone thought I was mad. Especially travelling constantly as we do." He took a banana from a bag, peeled it and held it out. "But somebody had to give him a chance. He deserved that, at least."

We were silent as we watched Johnny munch his banana.

"I'm sorry," David said at last. "I don't always look such a mess. It hasn't been an easy trip. I've been up nearly every night repairing the trucks and…" He looked down at himself. "I haven't had a bath for weeks."

Suddenly, I had a vision of what I must look like myself. Grimy face, greasy hair, not a sign of make-up. I smiled.

"Don't worry. Neither have I."

David Hardie after a wash and shave.

David knocked on our caravan door early the next morning, but not before a dish of hot griddle cakes, dripping with honey, had been delivered to us by the circus cook.

"Breakfast," he had announced. "Boss's orders."

I thanked David, but he brushed my thanks aside. Now that he had shaved and changed into a clean shirt, he looked years younger, but still drawn and tired. He said he was ready to have a look at our car, and I watched as he and George disappeared among the circus vehicles.

~

When I first heard the circus was on its way, I had been concerned my parents might find the atmosphere overpowering and shut themselves away.

Father in particular, was a strange man. He was an onlooker who was rarely comfortable around other people, but I could not have been more wrong. While taking Winkie for his morning walk, he spotted the clowns practicing some new gags and promptly settled himself on a nearby props box to watch them.

Mother was different. She loved being important, and when a young girl came to the caravan looking for Leila because her costume needed to be repaired, Mother was in her element. Why bother Leila when she could help?

Left alone, I went to see how the repair work was progressing. David was by himself, having despatched George to the spares wagon to get more tools.

"How are we doing?" he echoed. "Quite well. Your husband told me he didn't know much about cars, but…"

"My husband?" I said blankly. "George isn't my husband. He's my brother."

"Oh?" David grinned as George reappeared. "Your brother, is he? Well, he's been very helpful."

Leila was in her caravan and beamed at the sight of me. "Want a cuppa? I've just made a pot."

I told her the repairs on our car were going well and she didn't seem surprised. David was brilliant, she said. He had designed and built the circus himself, even the caravans and animal cages. His father, a Sydney businessman, had put up the finance and David, helped by his younger brother, Les, and an animal trainer named Merv King, had built it into a huge success.

"His father doesn't travel with the show." Leila sounded bitter. "He visits sometimes and takes the surplus money back to Sydney. And he raises hell if the takings aren't high enough."

She sighed. "I'm sorry. Don't take any notice of me. It's just that David is such a lovely person. I hate to see him wearing himself out. He gets terrible headaches, sometimes for days at a time. But at least he's trained a good team. We all think the world of him and no-one would let him down."

David was waiting for me back at the caravan. He seemed happy and said he had managed some emergency repairs. The circus would move on tomorrow, ready to show in Penong. Why didn't we travel with them? Then, if we fancied staying on for another night, it would give us a chance to see the show.

I could hear the pride in his voice, and he waited for my reply. I said I was sure the family would love to see the show.

Later, he called across to me when he brought Johnny out to play. I was with Leila, and she cocked an amused eyebrow at me.

"What have you done to David?" she whispered. "He usually keeps his distance from females. Some jokers even say he's a woman hater."

I watched as David produced a big ball and tossed it to Johnny. For a while, they played, kicking the ball to and fro, but David frowned when the little elephant stumbled.

"That's the trouble." He frowned. "That's why I want to get him to Adelaide. His bones aren't strengthening properly. He was parted from his mother far too soon, but I'm hoping the vets at the zoo might be able to help him."

"Poor little, Johnny," Leila sighed. "We do the best we can

for him. He's never left alone. He trumpets if he is, and he's terrified of dogs."

"And he has to have bedsocks," David added, "because his feet get cold at night. Fortunately, we have plenty of volunteers to knit them."

CHAPTER 47

In the afternoon, the show prepared for the next day's move.

Costumes were hung in the sun to remove creases, horses were groomed, leather polished, shoes cleaned. Acrobats and gymnasts practised their tricks, and around the trucks, a team of hands checked the loads and tightened straps and ropes.

But in the evening, David collapsed with one of his headaches and Whitey, a grizzled old hand who cared for the animals, helped him to his caravan.

I was passing when Whitey called to me from the caravan door.

"Could you keep an eye on him, Miss? Just while I go and find Leila."

"Leila?" I asked in surprise. "Hasn't he got anyone to look after him?"

Whitey shook his head.

"He's got a sister, but she lives with their father in Sydney. And Les, his younger brother, didn't come overland with us."

"He's not married then?"

Whitey chuckled.

"Not him. He works too hard to notice girls."

In the caravan, David lay on his bunk, his face screwed with pain. Without thinking, I picked up his hand, and as he turned towards me, he managed a faint smile.

The circus didn't go to Penong the next day. David was still too ill to drive.

By sundown he appeared, pale, apologetic, but anxious to get back to work. I watched from a distance as he went from vehicle to vehicle, checking everything was prepared and the show was ready to leave.

Later, he called at the caravan to remind us the show would leave early the following morning. Hopefully, they could make up time and still reach Penong to keep the show date.

"In this business, you can't let people down," he said. "Once the word is out, an audience will come in, sometimes a hundred miles or more, to see a show."

When he left, we packed and were off with the rest in the morning. It was strange, but in a way, I was sorry to leave Koonalda. The Gurneys had been good to us. They had shared what little they had, and I knew I would never forget Koonalda caves.

Roy planted a hearty kiss on my cheek as we said goodbye.

"Don't be afraid to come back," he said. "Come for a holiday, if you like. Stay for a few weeks. You'll always be welcome. But don't leave it too long. One day, the world will realise what wonderful caves we've got here and you might get killed in the rush of visitors."

~

The road to Penong was rough, pitted and dissected by deep channels, but we still covered two hundred miles in two days.

It was nearly midnight when we reached the tiny settlement. Everyone was exhausted, but the usual routine had to be followed. First, tent hands marked out the area for the Big Top, then the trucks, caravans and wagons were parked in a wide circle around it.

Once the cages and caravans had been levelled, tired youngsters, including Johnny, were put to bed, lions had their last feed of the day, and horses were exercised before everyone settled down to sleep.

At dawn, we were all up again.

I had never been to a circus, not even as a child, and I was shocked to discover what a huge undertaking it was to put up a big top. Everyone, including all the tent hands, the performers, even the lion tamer, was needed. George and I joined the line with the rest, hauling up the billowing tent and hammering in tent pegs.

Once the canvas was up, the whole of the ground area inside the tent, except for the performing ring, was stacked with seating. Ropes hauled banks of lights up into place, and swings, trapezes, and platforms were installed.

Silvers Circus set up on a Sydney showground.

George was fascinated by the lighting plant. A fault had developed in it, due, no doubt, to bumping over the rough roads, but once he located the problem and put it right, the huge floodlights above the ring flared out. Everyone in the tent gave a cheer, and George looked immensely pleased with himself.

Mother and Father, too, seemed pleased to be in the middle of everything and to be accepted as part of the team. It was a long time since I had seen them so happy.

Hours before the show was due to start, the audience began arriving. They came in trucks of every shape and size, most of them ancient, noisy and covered in dust, but all crammed with families from babies to grandmothers.

Where they had come from, or how far they had travelled, I can't imagine, but they brought bags of food and lit campfires to boil their billycans and make tea while they waited.

They were a wonderful audience, loud and wildly appreciative of a great show. And it was a great show, so great that when it was over, the crowd was reluctant to accept it had come to the end.

Those with babies or young children in their arms, went back to their trucks, but many others stayed, listening to the music as it played on, and watched the pull-down of the circus as eagerly as they had watched the performance.

At last, the big top was down, folded carefully and packed back into its truck. The seating boards were neatly stacked. The banks of lights fitted into their travelling cases.

Everything was back to how it had been when we arrived, save for the band of tent hands gathering rubbish into sacks. The last of the audience came across and thanked the performers, then they, too, rattled off on their way.

A tent hand lit a campfire, and as the flames blazed, the cook brought out coffee and freshly made biscuits. Everyone gathered around and talked. There was a sense of excitement, coupled with relief. The overland trip was almost finished and normal life had resumed.

David touched my arm. "I have to check on Johnny," he said. "Would you like to come?"

I followed him to Johnny's truck, where a young tent hand was sitting on the floor. Johnny was asleep, his head resting on the lad's lap, his feet encased in red woollen bedsocks.

"Everything all right?" David whispered.

The lad smiled, and David nodded.

"Good. We'll be back soon with his milk."

Outside, we were heading back to the campfire when he stopped.

"Did you enjoy the show?"

"Yes, I loved it."

For a long moment, he was silent. I waited, but he stood, staring ahead, and I thought I must have offended him in some way.

"When you get to Adelaide, you're going back to England, aren't you?" he asked, still looking ahead.

"Yes."

"And you have a good job to go back to? A good life?"

"Not exactly. I'm a freelancer. I have a book to write, but apart from that, who knows?"

He was silent again, then, "I'll bet your family has a nice house with a lovely English garden."

"We used to..." I shrugged as I remembered. "But we'll have to start again. It's complicated."

This time, the silence seemed to go on forever. The darkness around us was broken only by the light from a nearby caravan and the flicker of the campfire.

At last, he turned to me.

"Look, I'd like to ask you something, but I don't want you to be angry. The last thing in the world I want to do is to upset you, but... How would you feel if I asked you to marry me?"

It was the greatest shock of my life.

He looked tense, but the sincerity in his face was unmistakable. I wanted to put my arms out and hug him.

But I didn't.

I barely knew him, and he knew nothing about me. Admittedly, I sensed a bond between us, and in time, it might have flourished into something wonderful. But we had no time. In a few days, I would be heading to the opposite side of the world.

I needed time to think.

My head pounded, but I tried to be logical. I had to consider my family. My life had always hinged on the needs and whims of others. From as far back as I could remember, I had been torn between what I dreamed of doing and what I felt was my duty. And my dreams had always lost.

Now, without warning, I had to make a decision that would shape the rest of my life.

Reaching out, I took David's hand.

"If you asked me, I would say, Yes, I would love to marry you."

I told him, as honestly as I could, about my parents. It wasn't easy, but he held my hand tightly as I explained. I told him they were my responsibility. They always had been and always would be. To my relief, he understood.

"We both have problems," he said, "but from now on we will share them."

It was as simple as that.

CHAPTER 48

I worried my parents would be upset by my news, that Mother would accuse me of being selfish, or complain I should have consulted her before making my decision, but their only reaction was amazement.

It seemed the arrival of the circus had transported them into a kind of fairyland where everything was wonderful and exciting. Mother went for days without arguing, and Father looked cheerful.

There was one sadness. Winkie died quietly in his sleep. We never knew how old he was, but it was a simple and peaceful end.

There was also a problem to overcome. David and I wanted a quiet wedding as soon as we reached Sydney, but his father had other ideas.

David's father was a prominent businessman and if his son was to be married, it must be a lavish affair. More than that, it must be well publicised. The romantic appeal of a stranded Fleet Street journalist being rescued from the

Nullabor by a showman nursing a baby elephant would be great exposure for Silvers Circus.

The fact his father insisted on footing the bill for the whole affair didn't make David any happier. Money had never meant much to him, he confessed to me. His father had always handled the finances from both the family canvas business, and later, from the circus. He promised that David, his brother and sister, would share everything when he died, and no-one had argued with him. He was not a man to be crossed.

I didn't know anyone in Sydney, and David was a quiet soul. We would happily have married in a registry office without any fuss, but I knew it would be seen as a snub.

I didn't want to cause trouble between father and son, or to start any arguments that might trigger another of David's headaches, so I persuaded him to give in to his father.

Mother was delighted at the idea of a lavish wedding and made sure an expensive dress for her, as the mother of the bride, was ordered at the same time as my wedding dress.

As I walked up the aisle, I carried a bouquet of apricot roses. It was a wonderful wedding, a wonderful reception and a wonderful honeymoon.

"Just like a fairytale," Mother said over and over again.

David and Diana on their wedding day.

Two months after we returned from our honeymoon, little Johnny died. Sadly, we knew it was inevitable. Without his mother's milk, his organs had not developed properly.

I had done my best to help. I wrote to zoos in Africa and Europe asking about diets and supplements, but no-one had any answers.

We took him out into the bush and buried him in the shade of a gum tree.

David said little. He was not given to big emotional displays, but by then I was close enough to him to understand how badly he felt.

A month later, the circus was back on the road, bright and shining from its annual overhaul. David drove the truck that towed the caravan we now shared. Seated beside him as we rattled along, I should have been happy.

I was loved by a wonderful man. The more I got to know David, the more I loved him. And the more I worried about him.

He was a perfectionist. Everything in the circus, every act, every costume, every piece of equipment, had to be flawless, even if he worked all day and night to achieve it. He never thought about his own well-being, and in the background, his headaches were always there, threatening. When they struck, they frightened me, especially when I overheard the performers whispering that one day he would work himself to death.

I persuaded him to see doctors, but it achieved nothing. They only shook their heads and told him he should rest.

I loved the circus too, but at times, when we trundled along lonely, dusty roads, I found myself remembering the old dreams. The little cottage George and I had planned, the endless green of an English countryside, woods carpeted by bluebells and hedgerows full of primroses.

But that was all in the past. Now, my life was with David. My parents were happy. George was planning a new lighting system for the show entrance. What more could I want?

We had been married for eighteen months when our son was born. We called him David. It was my choice, and no parents could have been more delighted with their son than we were.

Leila had become a close friend, and I knew I could confide my hopes and fears in her.

"The baby is just what he needs," she said confidently. "Now he'll have something else to think about besides work."

But it wasn't like that. David was a devoted father, but now, when he was more determined than ever to succeed, there were reasons to worry. Times were changing.

The show was wonderful and audiences loved it, but where once every night had been a sell-out, there were now empty seats. Like it or not, Australia was heading into a recession.

Things got worse, and the takings dropped as unemployment spread. Businesses closed and people couldn't afford luxuries like a night at the circus. David's father became disappointed, then angry, as profits turned into losses.

We cut back on tent hands and performers. We sold trucks and cut anything we could manage without. The recession would pass, we told ourselves, if only we could hold on.

We tried changing our routes, leaving the back country and showing in towns, but it was no better. Soon we were playing to half-full stands as the price of everything went up, petrol, animal feed, tyres, truck repairs, even light bulbs.

It was David's father who called a halt. The recession showed no sign of ending and he had no intention of spending any more money keeping a failure alive.

The circus closed. The performers packed their bags. The horses, lions and all the other animals were sold off. Those we couldn't sell, we gave away, and David's headaches got worse.

Mother was suffering too. She had been happy travelling with the show. There had been occasional lapses into depression, but they had passed quickly. Now everything changed. Fairyland was gone and harsh reality took its place.

David did his best. The family canvas factory was also struggling, and half of it stood empty. He persuaded his father to let a part of it to him, at a reduced rent, and he and George began repairing caravans. After years keeping the circus on the road, it was something he excelled at.

The repair work paid our bills, but David wanted more. He wanted to create a business that would support our family. He had a remarkable mind and an ability to invent. Some years before, he had designed a miniature refrigerator that could run on paraffin (or kerosene as it was called in Australia), and was small enough to be used in a caravan.

He was certain it would sell well as soon as the economy

picked up. Caravans were popular, and in a hot climate like Australia, a refrigerator was a sensible luxury.

Again, he worked day and night, stopping only when his headaches became too severe. His little son was growing up, and he barely saw him. I tried to persuade him to take life slower, to give himself some time to relax, but he was determined to succeed. He was certain the refrigerator business was a chance to build a new future for us all.

George was as enthusiastic as he was. Together they refitted the factory. They built all the equipment, installed spray painting booths, passed the tests needed to get government safety certificates, registered the designs with the patent office and persuaded stores to stock their new line.

Once everything was in place, David invited his father to see his dream for the future.

But it was too late. His father had been approached by a company who wanted to buy the entire factory. They had offered him a good price, considering the conditions in the country, and he had agreed to the sale.

A few days later, David collapsed. His face was grey and waxy, his skin cold, and this time I was frightened. I had a sickening feeling he had come to the end. The doctor looked grave as he referred him to a specialist.

When we arrived at the hospital, the specialist was direct. He told David he had driven himself too far. He needed to give in, to stop everything, and he needed a different climate. The heat of the Australian sun was too severe for him. He needed moderation. He needed peace. Above all, he needed to relax.

I left David in the hospital and thought long and hard before telling my family what the specialist had said. Since we married, I had relied completely on David. Now I had to take the reins myself. I knew it wasn't going to be easy, and I readied myself for objections, but they all listened and nodded. They, too, understood the seriousness of David's problems.

I waited for a few days until he had recovered. Then I sat beside him and took his hand in mine.

"David," I said, "we can't go on like this, can we? I've been talking to the specialist. He says you need a complete change of lifestyle and a change of climate or I shall lose you."

I waited, but he said nothing, so I went on.

"David, I want us to go to England."

I waited again, and this time he looked at me.

"For how long?"

"For always. I want us to start a new life there."

He was silent for a long time, then he nodded.

"If that's what you really want, love. There's nothing to keep me here now, is there? My life is with you and the little fellow, wherever you want us to go."

I squeezed his fingers, and he sighed.

"I've never been to England, but my mother was English. She died when I was young. She always said England was a beautiful place."

Four months later, we landed at Southampton. David and I and our little son, Mother, Father and George. They were still my responsibility. I couldn't leave them behind and David accepted that, so we brought them back to where we had started our crazy trip. Once again, we had to start afresh and put down new roots.

I could only pray life would work out for us. We didn't have much money, but I had a lot of faith. I knew we would build a life together, and we did.

I wrote my book, and it was published together with various magazine articles and George's photographs. I went on to write for numerous magazines, as well as radio plays and even a television play for the BBC.

And David and I had a beautiful little daughter called Diana.

~

David and I were married for over fifty years. It was a gloriously happy marriage to a wonderful man. In a way, it was a constant voyage of discovery. I found David was a natural artist, self-taught but lacking in confidence because he was partially colour blind. I arranged his palette in strict order and dared anyone to touch it, and soon he graduated from black and white sketches to vivid oil paintings of the beloved circus he never forgot.

Painting became a therapy for him. When he worked at his easel, he relaxed and the headaches became less severe. Mother loved watching him paint. She would sit in a corner of the room for hours and he was amazingly patient with her.

We brought very little from Australia with us, but we did bring a model that David had begun when he was only fifteen, a model of Silvers Circus, the show that, years later, he brought to life and lost.

He loved the model and over the years, helped by the family, he brought it to life, a replica of his real circus, perfect in every detail, complete with tiny moving figures.

~

As I said at the beginning, I was always a believer, even from my earliest childhood. I believed implicitly in fairies and elves and Father Christmas. I believed in God and the beautiful winged angels who kept watch over us mere mortals.

And I believed in miracles.

I still do.

My own miracle was that I finally came back to the country I had never wanted to leave. David and I walked in the green fields I had seen in picture books and among bluebells in shady woods. We watched the sun glint on tumbling streams, went to the seaside in summer, and laughed around a bonfire on Guy Fawkes Night. At Christmas, we played with snowballs and went to pantomimes.

David fell in love with England. He found peace and contentment here and I was able to enjoy all the things I had missed, not alone, but with the husband and children I loved.

To me, that was the most wonderful miracle of all.

Peace at last in Devon.

DID YOU ENJOY A DISAPPOINTING CHILD?

If so, will you help other readers to discover this book?

Ratings have a huge impact on the amount of exposure books are given online. Quite simply, the more reviews a book receives, the more often it is shown to people looking for their next read.

If you can spare a few moments to leave an honest rating or review on the platform where you purchased the book, it will be much appreciated.

Thank you!

REMEMBERING DIANA HARDIE

Diana with Custard

DAVID HARDIE - SON

Mum had a special companion who was very much like her, small, determined, and lovable.

Custard, a yellow Lucino parrot, was bought for me by my wife, but after my father died, he formed a close bond with Mum.

We all lived together in a rambling house near the sea in

Devon and whenever Mum came into our room, Custard would screech and protest until he was allowed out of his cage to sit on her shoulder and whisper into her ear.

He loved sitting with her in the evenings while she watched television and would protest bitterly when I took him back to our room.

Finally, I gave in to his protests and moved his cage in with Mum.

From then on, they were inseparable. Custard shared her treats and sat with her while she was writing. Every pen or pencil she used had a chewed end.

He loved to nuzzle into her neck and whisper to her or quietly chew holes around the collars of her blouses.

Unfortunately, Mum is gone now, but Custard is still with us, a small, cheeky and very vocal reminder of her.

CLAIRE RILEY - GRANDDAUGHTER

I remember my Grandma telling me that as you get older, you become more of the person you've always been, and that amuses me now because my fondest memory of her will always be at my hen party; we had a belly dancing class, and at the age of 92, far from sitting quietly at the side and watching, she was up there shaking it with the best of them!

All of my friends were impressed and she was embraced by the group, bringing a real sense of fun and enjoyment to the party. When she sadly passed away some years later, I received messages from friends who had only met her on that one occasion saying what a lovely lady she was and how they will always remember her for her spirit and her belly dancing!

That is also how I remember her, a woman who lived life to the fullest, with optimism and energy. She rejected the idea of ageing, choosing to get a year younger at each of her later birthdays instead of older, and taking every opportunity to enjoy time with her family, supporting and encouraging them to follow their dreams and to enjoy life.

MICHAEL HARDIE - GRANDSON

Whilst on Honeymoon at Tuggerah Lakes, New South Wales, my Grandma picked up a small sayings card. This token of her honeymoon, the kind that is so often discarded or lost, stayed with her all through her life. Below a picture of the Lakes, the saying reads:

LIFE'S A GAMBLE
God gave us two ends-
One to sit on
and the other
TO THINK WITH
Our success depends on
which end we use most:
HEADS WE WIN
TAILS WE LOSE

I can honestly say that my Grandma's life epitomises this saying. She was a lady who valued her intelligence and wit and paired them with a longing for adventure.

As a child, I remember seeing this worn, dog-eared piece of card propped on a ledge in her bedroom and fell in love with the saying. In a world where sayings and values are now printed on almost everything, I have never seen this one since.

If it would help to create more people with my Grandma's approach to life, maybe I should start a printing business…

Thank you for everything, Grandma.

ROBERT TOWNSEND – SON-IN-LAW

Although she was small and sometimes appeared frail in her later years, Diana had a strong constitution and survived several severe falls.

She once overheard me describing her as a 'tough old bird' - fortunately, she thought it was funny and took it as a compliment!

PHILIPPA HARDIE – DAUGHTER-IN-LAW

My mother-in-law, Diana, was a very kind lady who gave up so much of her time to her three grandchildren, helping them in her own unique way.

She did everything from helping them with their schoolwork to making costumes and cooking with them and she is missed by us all.

DIANA TOWNSEND - DAUGHTER

My mother was always my role model.

In the early 1960s when girls were told if they worked hard at school, they could become a secretary, a nurse, or if they were attractive enough, an air hostess, my mother was already living on her own terms.

She had travelled the world, survived a war, and was an equal partner in our family printing business.

She and my father were an indivisible unit, but Dad's health was poor, and it was Mum who prepared quotes, handled the company finances and made sure deliveries went out on schedule.

And when times were tough, it was Mum who sat up late into the night writing stories to sell to women's magazines to ensure we had enough in the bank to cover the household bills.

When she reached ninety-two, Mum told me she wanted to write an account of her life. She had stopped using her faithful Remington typewriter some years before, when she developed arthritis in her hands, so we bought her a new-fangled word-processor. They were considered 'cutting-edge technology' in 2010 and Mum was delighted.

I expected her to produce a slim volume, but over the following months, she typed every day and produced over one hundred thousand words.

"It was funny looking back," she said. "The world really was a different place. I thought I'd better put things down while I can still remember them."

It took me a day, a night and a box of tissues to finish the manuscript.

"You've read it, then," Mum said when she saw my face.

I nodded, still struggling to keep my emotions under control.

"What are you going to do with it?" I asked.

"Me? Nothing. It's for you and your brother. It needs tidying up a bit, but maybe someone else might like to read it one day."

I gave her a massive hug, and she laughed.

"It felt good to type again," she said. "I think I'll do some more. Maybe a novel about a ninety-two-year-old who goes off and has adventures. I haven't read one of those, have you?"

Mum lived with us until 11th March 2013 when she collapsed and never recovered consciousness.

The previous day was Mothering Sunday and we spend it repotting her house plants, chatting, and enjoying a leisurely cream tea with the rest of the family.

I will be forever grateful for that last day together.

It was a good way to finish.

Diana on her way to her granddaughter's hen night.

ABOUT THE AUTHOR

Diana Hardie's autobiography ends at the point when she and her husband, David, settled in England with their young son and daughter and started a silk-screen printing business.

However, their adventures were far from over.

Diana wrote regularly for several well-known magazines and had plays produced both on radio and television. She continued to write until shortly before her death in 2013.

David never forgot his beloved circus and spent much of

his spare time building an intricate, animated model of it. As they grew older, the children, also called David and Diana, became enthusiastic modellers too, and the family dreamed of exhibiting their miniature circus to the public.

Eventually, after a successful season displaying the model in Torquay, the family bought a derelict school set in fourteen acres of overgrown parkland with the intention of transforming it into a tourist attraction.

The family expected to face challenges, but they didn't expect them to include a demolition order, a deranged neighbour with a shotgun, a plague of rats and a resident ghost.

You can read the family's continuing adventures in a series of three books written by Diana Hardie's daughter, Diana Townsend.

DIANA TOWNSEND
Me,
My Family
and the
Poltergeist
How it all began...

Printed in Great Britain
by Amazon

25994568R00249